CLASS AND RACE FORMATION IN NORTH AMERICA

CLASS AND RACE FORMATION IN NORTH AMERICA

James W. Russell

UTP

University of Toronto Press

First edition published 1994 by Prentice Hall under the title *After the Fifth Sun: Class and Race in North America*.

LIBRARY AND ARCHIVES CANADA CATALOGUING IN PUBLICATION

Russell, James W.
  Class and race formation in North America / James W. Russell.

First ed. published 1994 under title: After the fifth sun.
Includes bibliographical references and indexes.
ISBN 978-0-8020-9678-4

  1. North America — Race relations — History. 2. Social classes — North America — History. 3. Equality — North America — History. 4. Race discrimination — North America — History. 5. Race relations — Cross-cultural studies. 6. Social classes — Cross-cultural studies. 7. Equality — Cross-cultural studies. 8. Race discrimination — Cross-cultural studies. I. Title.

E49.R87 2008   305.80097   C2008-905649-3

We welcome comments and suggestions regarding any aspect of our publications — please feel free to contact us at news@utphighereducation.com or visit our internet site at www.utphighereducation.com.

North America
5201 Dufferin Street
Toronto, Ontario, Canada, M3H 5T8

2250 Military Road
Tonawanda, New York, USA, 14150

ORDERS PHONE: 1-800-565-9523
ORDERS FAX: 1-800-221-9985
ORDERS EMAIL: utpbooks@utpress.utoronto.ca

UK, Ireland, and continental Europe
NBN International
Estover Road, Plymouth, PL6 7PY, UK
TEL: 44 (0) 1752 202301
FAX ORDER LINE: 44 (0) 1752 202333
enquiries@nbninternational.com

This book is printed on paper containing 100% post-consumer fibre.

Recycled
Supporting responsible use
of forest resources
FSC   www.fsc.org Cert no. SGS-COC-003153
© 1996 Forest Stewardship Council

The University of Toronto Press acknowledges the financial support for its publishing activities of the Government of Canada through the Book Publishing Industry Development Program (BPIDP).

Edited by Betsy Struthers.
Designed by Daiva Villa, Chris Rowat Design.

Printed in Canada

CONTENTS

NORTH AMERICA

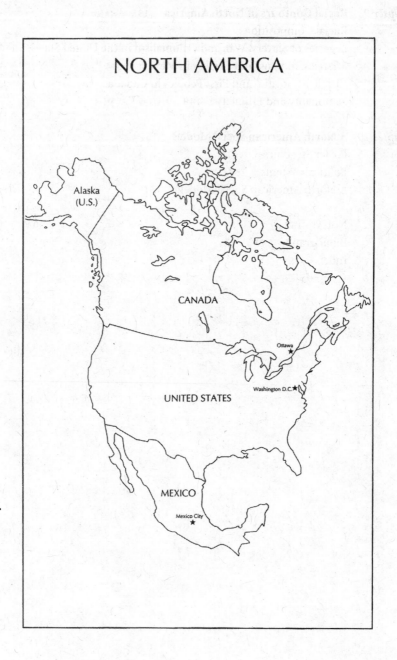

Alaska
(U.S.)

CANADA

Ottawa
★

Washington D.C.★

UNITED STATES

MEXICO

Mexico City
★

CANADA

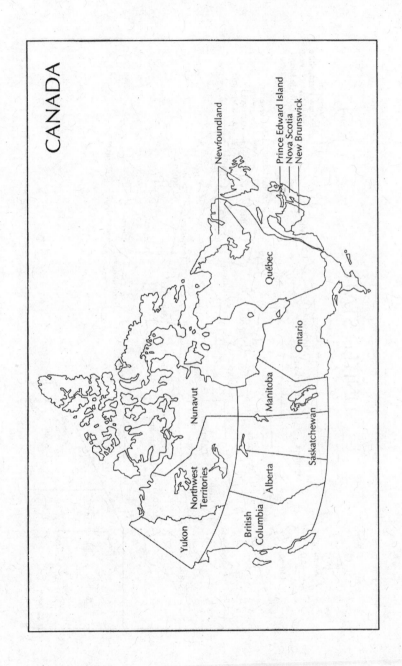

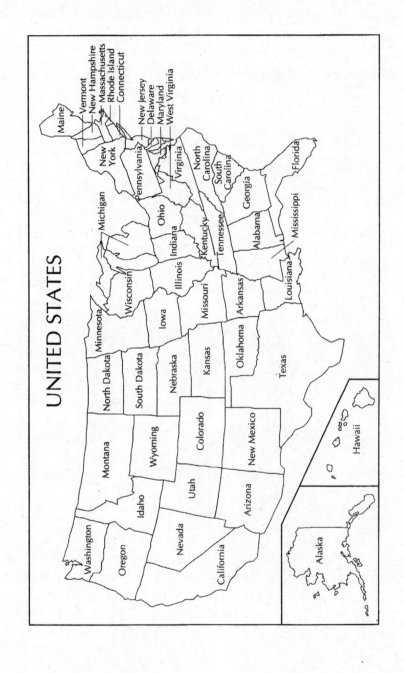

UNITED STATES

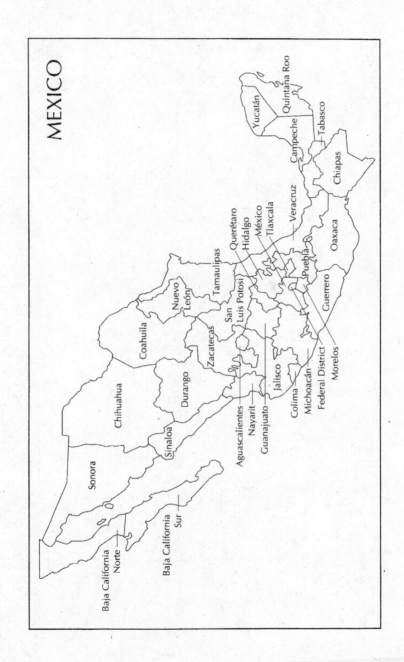

MEXICO

PREFACE

On August 13, 1521, the largest and most developed of North America's societies, the Aztec empire, fell to Spanish invaders. The conquest was a prophecy come true, for the Aztecs had believed that their era, which they called the Fifth Sun, was fated to end catastrophically, as it did. After the destruction of Aztec society, the Spanish and later European colonizers built new societies in which they occupied the dominant class positions and forced indigenous peoples, imported African slaves, and Asians into subordinate positions. As a result of the conquest, race became an issue in the class structuring of North America's societies, and it has been an issue ever since.

Class and racial relations thus developed in patterned ways in all parts of North America, but the patterns have had significant differences as well as similarities in the areas that became the United States, Mexico, and Canada. The development of these class and racial patterns over nearly 500 years of North American history since that fateful day in 1521 are the subjects of this book.

This project first began in the spring of 1990 during a Fulbright Fellowship at the Centro de Investigaciones sobre América del Norte of the Universidad Nacional Autónoma de México. At about the same time, the Mexican government announced that it was reversing its traditional economic policies and seeking dramatically closer economic ties with the colossus to its north. Specifically, it wished to follow the example of Canada, which two years earlier had signed a free trade agreement with the United States. It appeared to me that the trilateral Canada-United States-Mexico free trade agreement, which quickly came to be known as the North American Free Trade Agreement (NAFTA), was an event of overwhelming historical importance.

I still remember the day in 1992 when I went out from my apartment in Mexico City to buy a notebook. My Mexican-made notebooks had all come from DeTodo, a large store across the street. This time, though, the notebook selection was different — they were all made in the United States. It was a sign of what was to come with NAFTA. Eight years later, Wal-Mart would take over ownership of DeTodo. Several blocks up the street a large supermarket, part of the Aurrerá chain, was also sold to Wal-Mart. The millionaire owner of Aurrerá and other retail chain stores, Jerónimo Arango, became a billionaire after selling them all off to the American superstore.

At the time I knew that politicians and economists would be primarily involved in analyzing and commenting upon the advantages and disadvantages of NAFTA. Its proponents would argue that integration of North America's economies would bring about rationalization and efficiency and that this would be a logical development in the context of economic globalization. The United States, Mexico, and Canada would form a bloc to compete with European and Asian blocs. Critics of NAFTA would argue that integrating the First World economies of the United States and Canada with the Third World economy of Mexico would only advantage capital and not labor.

While these were obviously key issues, it appeared to me that there were other matters that did not quite fall within the strict considerations of politicians and economists. In particular, NAFTA would come about in societies that had different forms of social relations and therefore would force changes in at least some of those relations. That concern with the social consequences of NAFTA prompted me to embark on a study of the forms of social inequality in NAFTA's three member countries.

The initial result was *After the Fifth Sun: Class and Race in North America*, published by Prentice Hall in 1994. Since it was published as NAFTA was first going into effect, I could only predict some of the likely consequences of the treaty such as an increase in migration out of Mexico, contrary to the claims of NAFTA's official backers, and an increase in capital concentration. More than a decade later, we are in a position to analyze the actual consequences of NAFTA on a range of issues that have importance for class and racial relations. The opportunity to revisit, update, and rethink these issues with a completely new edition, including with a new title, was thus welcome.

NAFTA and its social consequences, though, are only part of what this book is about. Much more, it is about how class and race relations developed differently in the three countries of North America in the nearly half millennium since the sixteenth-century conquest. Even if NAFTA had never happened, it would still have been important to take a comparative account of the notable similarities and differences of class and racial relations that had formed in the three countries. Comparative analyses, by examining the different experiences of nearby countries, sharpen understanding of what makes each country unique and, at the same time, demonstrate the existing options in social thinking and policies.

In describing a particular country's class and race inequalities, I constantly found myself writing with the citizens of the other countries in mind. For example, a number of points that I have included about inequality in the United States will seem painfully obvious to people who have grown up there, although they may be less familiar to Canadians or Mexicans. People in the United States generally know that not all whites are literally Anglos, as they are often referred to in Mexico, but that fact is not as apparent south of the border. The same general approach was followed in deciding what to include about Mexico and Canada. People in Mexico are well aware of the country's indigenous background and character. Many people in the United

States, however, do not know that at least 70 per cent of North America's Indigenous peoples live in Mexico. Canadians know that they are culturally different from people in the United States, but Mexicans are less likely to appreciate those differences, and people in the United States are less likely to have thought about them. I have, therefore, written this book with an eye toward the curious in all three countries and have attempted to cover what is interesting as well as significant about the separate logics of social inequality.

This book is concerned with showing both how uneven economic development in North America has affected class and race inequalities in the three countries, how unique class and race dynamics in each of the countries have contributed to overall continental patterns, and how class and race inequalities have interrelated. Those are more modest and focused goals than producing an exhaustive and descriptive account of all class and race formation in North America, which this book is not. Nor is this book an account of all forms of North American social inequality. Most notably, it does not directly focus on gender inequality, as important as that is. Understanding how forms of gender inequality in the three countries have been interwoven with class and racial inequalities is a subject for further comparative research.

I have special debts of gratitude of a number of people from whom I secured leads and with whom I discussed ideas in e-mails and telephone calls and in offices and cafes. They include Alfredo Alvárez, David Barkin, Aviva Chomsky, Levon Chorbajian, John C. Cross, Teresa Gutierrez Haces, Thomas D. Hall, Elaine Levine, Silvia Núñez García, César Pérez Espinosa, Robert J.S. Ross, and Carlos Salas. Jerry Lembcke and Henry Veltmeyer gave exhaustive comments on the manuscript that were invaluable for sharpening the analysis. Anne Brackenbury and Betsy Struthers offered skilled and wise editorial guidance at every step. Thanks are also due to friends and colleagues at the Centro de Investigaciones sobre América del Norte at the Universidad Nacional Autónoma de México. It was with them that I first began thinking and writing about this subject in Mexico City, North America's largest city.

Chapter 1

INTRODUCTION

The visual evidence of social inequality between and within North American societies is glaring. Anyone who has traveled the length of North America knows of the vast gulf that divides the average standards of living of the United States and Canada from that of Mexico. The United States and Canada have all of the opulence of First World countries, while Mexico has all of the extensive poverty and misery of a Third World country. That Mexico and the United States share a common 1,945-mile border — a border that culturally separates Latin from Anglo America, as well as the two countries — makes the contrast all the more striking.

Unlike other areas of the world, where there is a continuum of gradual economic changes between bordering countries, between Mexico and the United States there are more jarring differences. The Rio Grande, as it is known on the U.S. side, or the Rio Bravo, as it is known on the Mexican side, is the world's only river that separates First and Third World societies. In all other parts of the world, the distances between First and Third World areas are much greater. But while tempting, it is misleading to see the First and Third World regions of North America as being entirely separated by that border, for Mexico contains First World-appearing neighborhoods, shopping malls, and work places while the United States and Canada contain Third-World-appearing pockets of poverty. Thus, North America's First and Third Worlds, while centered on opposite sides of the Rio Grande, interpenetrate each other.

The visual evidence of social inequality within each of North America's societies is everywhere. In the United States, homeless people wander downtown streets as private guards patrol the neighborhoods of the rich. In between are neighborhoods of modest working-class and more comfortable middle-class houses. Overlapping and cross cutting the urban geography of class is the geography of racial divisions. White and minority areas are immediately distinguishable, often divided by a clear physical barrier such as railroad tracks or a freeway. People in the United States prefer to keep at a distance as much as possible those whom they perceive to be social inferiors or whom they fear.

A tour through most large Mexican cities reveals other types of extremes. The

1

poor live nearly everywhere, but there are also neat middle-class houses and mansions, whose occupants are rich by anyone's standards. Unlike U.S. cities, where class and racial inequalities are compartmentalized or "rationalized" according to neighborhood and area, most large Mexican cities are more like helter-skelter mosaics of rich, poor, and in-between types of housing. Mexico City's rich, for example, move about between islands of privilege — mansions, expensive restaurants, clubs, exclusive stores — in what is otherwise a sea of poverty. They develop subjective blinders which allow them to see, but not see, the poor — to look through them as it were.

Monterrey, Mexico's third largest city and home to a substantial part of its business elite, is a bit different. There, the city's upper and middle classes, like their U.S. counterparts, have physically separated themselves over a hill from the poor into an area which architecturally looks like Phoenix and other climatically similar desert cities in the United States. Coming over the hill from the main part of Monterrey, one encounters U.S.-style lawns and suburban houses that sprout parabolic antennas from their roofs to capture U.S. television.

Monterrey, though, is an exception, as is Santa Fe, a new area for Mexico City's new rich that occupies a plateau above the city. In most Mexican cities, the upper and middle classes cannot put as much distance between their living quarters and those of the poor. Instead, they surround their houses with fortified walls, topped in many cases with barbed wire or jagged glass to discourage intruders. While railroad tracks and freeways separate classes and races in the United States, outside walls separate them in most parts of Mexico.

Three Faces of Capitalism and Democracy

The United States, Mexico, and Canada share, in addition to the North American continent, the same type of economic structure. All three are capitalist societies in which there is significant private ownership of businesses and the production and distribution of goods and services is according to market principles. Since each national class structure is based on that common capitalistic economic structure, it follows that the same types of economic classes exist in all three countries — owners of large businesses, employed managers and professionals, workers, and owners of small businesses.

At the same time as each national economy obeys capitalist principles, the economies themselves are continentally interrelated according to mainly capitalist principles. Trade, investments, labor migration, and financial relations significantly integrate the economic and class structures of the three countries. Owners of capital invest in each other's societies, and thousands of undocumented Mexican workers cross over to the United States in search of work.

Geographic location greatly influences the directions and volumes of these flows of capital and labor. The United States, as the country geographically in the middle, has extensive economic relations with each of its southern and northern neighbors, while the relations between those neighbors themselves are, for obvious reasons of physical distance, not as close. Canada and Mexico, while contiguous to and strongly influenced by economic relationships with their common neighbor, have a much less direct relationship with each other. This relative weakness exists despite it taking longer to fly from Vancouver to Ottawa than to fly from either city over the United States to Mexico City.

Though a capitalist economic structure exists in all three countries, there is no question that overall Mexico is a significantly poorer country than either the United States or Canada and, in some ways, a structurally different country. Many see the structural differences between the Latin and Anglo areas of North America as being between those of essentially First and Third World countries. Others define the differences vertically in terms of average levels of production and income within the world economy. The World Bank ranks the United States and Canada as upper income countries and Mexico as an upper-middle income country.[1] By other world standards Mexico is an average income country. Looking southward toward Guatemala and other Central American countries, its situation is enviable. But looking northward indicates a different reality.

Still others describe Mexico, variously as either an underdeveloped or developing country, and the others as developed countries. Developmentally, the United States and Canada are post-industrial societies in the sense that the largest fractions of their labor forces are no longer engaged in production of primary agricultural or secondary industrial goods. Mexico, however, until recently was still at the agricultural stage of technological development since the largest fraction of its labor force was still engaged in farming activities. But since the advent of the North American Free Trade Agreement in 1994, agricultural employment has declined significantly.

Politically, the United States is a two-party society. Republicans and Democrats almost completely monopolize electoral competitions and governmental offices with ideologies that range from conservative to liberal. In Mexico, one party, the Partido Revolucionario Institucional (PRI), held the presidency uninterruptedly for 70 years and virtually monopolized all other government offices for most of that time. The 1990s marked the end of this political monopolization as the PRI lost a number of local and state offices to rival parties and in 2000 lost the presidency. Today Mexico has three major political parties. In addition to the still-strong PRI, there is the left-wing Partido de la Revolución Democrática (PRD) and the right-wing Partido Acción Nacional (PAN). Canada also has three significant political parties — Conservatives, Liberals, and the social democratic New Democratic Party. These represent clearly defined and consistent ideological options.

The economic and social contrast between Mexico and her continental neighbors to the north has been statistically measured in a number of different ways. The gross domestic product (GDP) per capita of Canada in 2006 was $31,263; in the United States it was $39,676. These were from three to four times as high as Mexico's

$9,803.[2] The infant mortality rate—the number of children who die before their first birthdays per 1,000 live births—of the United States is seven and of Canada five, while that of Mexico is 23, from three to nearly five times higher. Put differently, every day 167 children under one year old die in Mexico, 116 more than if Mexico had the same infant mortality rate as the United States and 131 more than if it had the same rate as Canada.[3] As sharp as these inequalities are, they are not as sharp as they were in 1988, when the GDP per capita of Canada and the United States were between nine and eleven times as high as that of Mexico and the number of infant deaths from four to six times as high.[4]

Table 1.1: The North American Societies: Basic Indicators, 2004-2006

	UNITED STATES	MEXICO	CANADA	NORTH AMERICA
Population[1]	296	103	32	431
Area[2]	9,629	1,958	9,971	21,4558
Population density[3]	30	54	3	20
GDP per capita	$39,676	$9,803	$31,263	$32,117
Infant mortality[4]	7	23	5	13
Life expectancy	79	75	80	78
Human development[5]	8	53	6	—

Notes: [1]in millions; [2]thousands of square kilometers; [3]persons per square kilometer; [4]deaths in the first year per thousand live births; [5]ranking among world countries based on a composite index developed by the United Nations Development Programme of life expectancy, educational attainment, and income.

Sources: UNDP, *Human Development Report 2006,* 283, 315; UN Statistical Office, Table 3.

Cultural Metaphors

In overall cultural terms, there are clear differences between the three countries, though, once again, the cultures of Canada and the United States appear more similar than either does with that of Mexico. People in the United States see themselves as culturally different from Mexicans but rarely think much about their cultural differences from Canadians. Canadian intellectuals convincingly demonstrate that they have a different cultural identity than people in the United States, but they generally do not think too much about their relationship to Mexico. Mexicans find it difficult to distinguish the Anglos of the United States from those of Canada. In the same sense, most people in the United States and Canada have difficulty distinguishing the cultures of Mexico and other Latin American countries.

The cultural differences between Mexico and the two countries to its north are obvious, but those between the United States and Canada are also significant. The United States, as Seymour Martin Lipset has shown, is the society of revolutionary origins — as is Mexico — and rugged individualism, while Canada is a society of counterrevolutionary origins and order.[5] The national identity of the United States begins with the 1776 Declaration of Independence, which ignited the revolution; the national identity of what became Canada was influenced by the decision of the northern British colonies to not join the War of Independence. Much of the European settler population of Ontario, New Brunswick, and Nova Scotia was made up of the 50,000 or so Tory loyalists who moved north — voluntarily or involuntarily — after the War of Independence. Mexican visitors to Canada, who (like those from the United States) are steeped in the heritage of their war of independence, find it odd that many Canadians praise the colonial relationship that they had with Britain.

People in the United States tend to view Canada as a slightly calmer, perhaps more civilized society. Canadians view the United States as overly competitive and disorderly. Lipset cites the observation of Richard Lipsey as indicative: "I have stood on a street corner in Toronto with a single other pedestrian, and with not a car in sight, waiting for the light to turn green — behavior unimaginable in most U.S. cities."[6] The difference in Mexico City is that not only pedestrians but also motorists ignore street lights when they do not see any need to obey. In Mexico City I have observed cars quickly crossing over two lanes of traffic to make turns. Such traffic behavior would evoke a riot of horn blowing in the United States and, perhaps, stunned incomprehension in many parts of Canada. But in Mexico it rarely evokes anger or horns because other motorists are used to it. According to one apocryphal story, a travel writer recommended that U.S. tourists in Mexico City not rent cars unless their doctors have recommended that they need *more* stress.

Traffic patterns may reflect larger cultural patterns. Samuel Ramos, one of Mexico's most influential and provocative twentieth-century philosophers, could have been thinking about traffic when he went so far as to conclude that "Mexican society, without discipline or organization, is a chaos in which individuals fly about according to chance like disperse atoms."[7] But if traffic and society in general appear disorderly in Mexico, there is a cultural order within the disorder. While motorists in the United States and Canada drive like they play baseball — in straight lines — motorists in Mexico drive like they play soccer, darting for open spaces and opportunities regardless of nominal traffic rules.[8]

On the Language of Investigation

Before proceeding much further, some clarifications of terms are in order. A comparative exploration of this type that involves three countries and two major angles of analysis (class and race) presents a number of difficulties in geographical and social terminology. Mexico is variously considered to be a part of North or Central America. It is clearly on the North American continent, along with the United States and Canada. Yet, it is also a part of Latin America and shares many common cultural identities with its southern Central American neighbors. Mexicans, however, would be as little likely to refer to themselves as *Centroamericanos* as they would be to refer to themselves as *Norteamericanos*, a term they reserve for citizens of the United States. For our purposes, we will accept the geographical convention of considering Mexico to be a part of North America.

There are also terminological difficulties in how to name the people of the United States. There is no acceptable term comparable to "Mexicans" or "Canadians." The country term "United States" does not lend itself to suffixes (as in United States*ians*). People in the United States call themselves Americans. Many Mexicans and Canadians also refer to people in the United States as Americans, but that is an imperialistic appropriation of a term that logically applies to all of the peoples of the Americas, not just those of the United States. While Mexicans often call people in the United States *Norteamericanos*, that convention overlooks the Canadian claim to the label. It also is inconsistent with the reality that Mexicans are also North Americans in continental terms. The dilemma is more easily solved in Spanish than English, where it is grammatically proper to speak of *mexicanos, canadienses,* and *estadounidenses*. In the text that follows, I will refer to people in the United States in a variety of admittedly somewhat awkward ways, such as U.S. citizens, U.S. nationals, or people in the United States. This approach seems preferable to reproducing the national arrogance of exclusive appropriation of the terms "American" or "North American."

There is no complete consensus regarding the naming of people from non-European backgrounds within each of the North American countries. The most widely used term for the vast majority, but not all, indigenous peoples is "Indian." The obvious problem with the term is that it is a misnomer—the indigenous peoples of the Americas are not from India, as was thought by the early explorers. In the 1970s, as a result of movements among the indigenous peoples in the United States, the term "Native American" developed. Canadians distinguish the Inuit of the Arctic from indigenous peoples to their south, whom they refer to as Aboriginal peoples or First Nations. There is no one term that has won universal endorsement, nor one that appears to be considered universally as offensive. For that reason, in the text indigenous peoples and Indians will be used interchangeably when writing in general terms. Indians, though, do not have a common monolithic identity. Depending on the context, it will therefore be necessary to employ more particular tribal labels such as Sioux, Cree, and Yaqui.

In the case of African-origin people in North America, there has been a clear evolution in the use of naming terms. Up until the early 1960s, the terms "Negro" (from the Spanish for black), "colored people," and, to a lesser extent, "brown" were customarily used in the United States. The Black Power movement swept those terms away as offensive. It only took a couple of years, during the height of the black urban rebellions in United States, for whites to abandon use of the terms "Negro" and "colored." The terms "black," "Afro-American," and "African," in order of acceptance, took their places. In the early 1990s, Jesse Jackson proposed that "African-American" was the most desirable term. It paralleled the use of other hyphenated immigrant identities, such as Chinese-American, Polish-American, and Irish-American. Jackson's proposal gained acceptance. It remains to be seen how long it will prevail. For this text, the terms "black," "African-American," and "Afro-North American" will be used.

The naming of Latin American-origin people is a problem in the United States and Canada. There are a wide number of terms in use, some of which are considered objectionable by different people. The label "Hispanic" is the most widely used on the East Coast of the United States. It is also employed by the U.S. Census Bureau. Many people, though, object to it on two counts. First, it implies a complete Spanish background when the majority of Spanish-speaking people in the United States and Canada also have indigenous and African ancestors. Second, it implies that Spanish-speaking peoples have a unitary cultural identity when there are significant economic, social, political, and cultural differences between Mexicans, Puerto Ricans, Cubans, and Central Americans. The term "Hispanic" is not used south of the Rio Grande. It is only when Latin Americans come to the United States that they find themselves referred to as Hispanics rather than as their particular national identities— Mexicans, Puerto Ricans, Salvadorans, and so on.

On the West Coast, "Latino" is used more often than "Hispanic." It implies Latin American origin. But, like the name "Hispanic," it also suggests a common cultural identity when significant national differences exist. For this study, I will use "Latino" when speaking of all Latin American-origin people in the United States and the different national terms (Mexican, Puerto Rican, etc.) when speaking of the particular national communities. In a parallel sense, the Asian communities will be described in general terms as Asian-Americans and in particular terms according to nationality—Chinese, Japanese, Filipino, and so on.

The label "minority" itself is not without problems. Mexicans find that they become labeled as a minority when they enter the United States. Whites from the United States, however, rarely see themselves as a minority when they go to Mexico. Their domination, it seems, is portable, whereas that of Mexicans is not.

The very labeling of a group as a minority creates its own *sui generis* social reality. A group may accept its labeling as a minority but be very sensitive to the context in which it is used. In the course of the research for this book, I encountered a revealing incident of the linguistic politics of the "minority" label. I had just finished writing a review for a Mexico City newspaper of a book that dealt with minorities in Canada. I usually have other people review what I write for content, and since my written Spanish is far from perfect, I have it edited by native writers for grammar and style as well. The first Mexican person who read my review had grown up in Mexico but had spent a substantial part of her life in the United States, where a large part of her political consciousness had been formed through participation in the Chicano movement. She objected to my sentence "*Canada y sus minorías*" ("Canada and its minorities"), changing it to "*Canada y las minorías*" ("Canada and the minorities"). Her reason for the change was that *sus* as an article assumed that the minorities were objects belonging to Canada's white majority. The second person who looked over the review was also Mexican, but she had both grown up and had her political consciousness formed in Mexico. She changed *las* back to *sus* because it worked better stylistically. Having been a Mexican in Mexico all her life, she had never had the consciousness of being a minority imposed upon her and consequently never had to consider the political implications of *las* versus *sus*.

Related to the problem of how to name the peoples of North America is the problem of the meanings of the terms that will be used to analyze them—class and race, and, to some degree, nationality and ethnicity. The first issue to be resolved is the causal priority of the analytical concepts class and race. The origins of this dispute, at least in the United States, go back to the political debates between nationalists and Marxists—both activists and academics—that developed in the 1970s, as the most active phase of the civil rights movement was waning. Both sides agreed that minorities suffered from both racism and class exploitation, but they differed on which was causally more significant. The nationalist position held that blacks, Indians, and Latinos suffered discrimination and oppression in the United States mostly because the dominant group in the country was white and fundamentally racist. Nationalists further held that minority workers both experienced and felt more oppression because of the colors of their skin than positions in the workplace. The Marxist position countered that racial minorities suffered discrimination and oppression mostly because the capitalist system of the country had relegated them to an inferior class position.

Part of the debate became mired in a confusion between levels of analysis. In terms of perception, at least in the 1960s and 1970s, there was more of a racial than class struggle in the United States. The civil rights movement activated blacks and other minorities as racial groups struggling to reform the country so that there would be equality of opportunity among races. In this sense, the movement achieved its primary objective with the passage of the 1964 Civil Rights Act, which removed legal barriers to equality of opportunity for racial minorities. However, it had also set in motion large numbers of activists who knew very well that the passage of the act would not in itself produce substantive racial equality. In addition, once a reform movement has been historically set in motion, it often, at least for some of its members, moves beyond original issues to take up more general social issues such as the elimination of poverty. By the late 1960s in the United States, those who had been activated by the early 1960s civil rights movement were debating how to end a war in Southeast Asia and how to interpret spontaneous riots and rebellions that had ignited the country's largest black ghettos from Harlem, Newark, and the nation's capital on the East Coast through Chicago and Detroit in the interior to Watts on the West Coast. In one week in 1968 over 50,000 U.S. Army troops were deployed in black ghettos. It was clear that the country was experiencing more racial than class-based struggle and violence.

It is also clear that during determinant historical periods the bases of societal conflicts shift. In the 1930s most societal conflict in the United States concerned clear class questions. That was the period during which workers fought to establish unions in the nation's largest factories. During the 1960s the most salient societal conflict concerned racial inequality. However, by the end of the 1970s, as black and other minority movement mass activism declined, a number of writers began to argue that class was now a more salient issue than race per se for minorities in the United States.[9]

If we step back from the heat of given social movements and look at the intersections of class and race structurally, a different sense of causal priority emerges — one that does not shift according to historical periods or subjective perceptions. As described in the coming pages, indigenous peoples and blacks were first subjected to inequality on the North American continent when they were enslaved. That is, social inequality for them did not exist as an *a priori* racial condition but was imposed upon them because the European conquerors and colonizers of North America established a type of colonial class structure that contained an inferior position into which they were forcefully placed. There would not be and would not have been racial inequality in North America if there had not been a class structure that contained by definition unequal class positions. For that reason, on a theoretical and structural level, class is causally prior to race.

That conclusion, though, is not the same as arguing that racial inequality completely reduces to a question of class. For sure, a black or other minority worker who has the same type of job and receives the same income as a white worker suffers additional types of oppression. I argue that, in an exploration such as this of social inequality, the first thing to be established is the economic and class structures of the countries involved and from there to determine how racial minorities have been placed in inferior positions within them. For that reason, the theoretical premise of this study is that class inequality is causally prior to — but not an exclusive determinant of — racial inequality.

Despite the concept of class being central to social science, there is no consensus among social scientists as to what it means or how to use it: there is no one *correct* use of the concept. The best that can be hoped for is that each investigator who employs the concept explains what she or he means by it. Here, classes are defined as groups of people who share a common economic or social position within society. I then find it necessary to analyze economic and social class positions separately.

Economic classes share common roles within the work or labor forces of countries. In each of the contemporary North American countries, the following shared roles or economic classes exist: capitalists who are owners of large businesses, small business owners, the new middle class of professional and managerial employees, and wage and salary workers. In Mexico there has been an additional class of peasants, who are small farmers who produce more for their own subsistence needs than for market sale. The past of all three countries also contained slavery and the slave class.

By social classes are meant families and individuals who share common standards of living. The rich and the poor mark the polar upper and lower social class positions. In between exist working and middle social class positions.[10]

Employment of the concept of race is fraught with controversies and the pitfall of being potentially offensive. The concept arose in the seventeenth century from the belief that the human species was divided into distinct physical variations.[11] Since then there have been a number of attempts to determine the exact number of distinct human races. These attempts, however, produced no consensus. Estimates of the number of races have ranged from three to as many as 200.[12] Not only was the issue of determining the number of races a problem but so too was the criteria for distinguishing one race from another. Use of phenotype or skin color, for example, as the primary criterion presented problems because there are continuous rather than discrete differences in skin color shades from the darkest to the lightest, and there is no way to determine fixed racial boundaries. Because of these and other problems, by the middle of the twentieth century most physical anthropologists had abandoned use of race as a valid scientific concept for categorizing human beings. However, despite the decline of the scientific use of the concept of race, the popular and social uses of the term — as well as the beliefs and practices of racism — continue in vigor. It is in these latter senses that the concept is employed here.

What are socially perceived to be distinct races in North America are the descendants of Europeans, Africans, Asians, and the indigenous peoples of the Americas. These races, in the social meaning of that term, were the trunk lines from which the North American people have developed since the 1500s. Interrelations among them have produced a fifth synthesis race of individuals who combine ancestry from two or more of the originating races. The members of this fifth synthesis race make up the majority in one of the countries — Mexico — and in overall terms constitute the largest racial minority in the continent. In everyday experience and social perception, racial interaction in North America is, for the most part, between whites, blacks, indigenous peoples, Asians, and combined-race individuals, making these our main categories of analysis.

There are also linguistic, ethnic, nationality, and other differences within North American populations. Poles, Italians, and Irish, while all of white European descent, have felt the stings of discrimination and rejection from other whites in the United States and Canada. U.S. newspapers in the 1890s even referred to English-descent native-born citizens and Italian immigrants as separate races. Anglophone and francophone Canadians are far from homogeneous. Tarahumara and Xochimilca Indians in Mexico belong to distinct cultures. These types of differences will enter into our discussion when necessary, but the main focus of investigation will be social differences that are perceived to be class and racially based.

There is no necessary relationship between race and culture, national, or ethnic identity. I have observed a number of curious cases on university campuses where racial appearance was deceptive. Immigrant Latina students at the university where I teach in Connecticut puzzled over the identity of a secretary because she appeared but did not act Latina. During a brief teaching assignment in Monterrey, Mexico, I encountered students who appeared identical to the students I encounter in Connecticut. In both cases racially identical persons belonged to separate nations and hence cultures. The secretary had a mestizo French and Indian background, which produces the same range of physical appearances as mestizo Mexicans with Spanish and Indian backgrounds. Monterrey is in the north of Mexico, where the proportion of people of full European descent is the highest; people with names like Hernández and Gutierrez appear in physical terms to be identical to Connecticut students with names like Conrad and Jones.

When Caribbean blacks migrate or travel to the United States, they enter into a world in which their blackness becomes much more of a badge of identity than it was at home. A black college student from Puerto Rico states, "I am Puerto Rican, not black. I don't relate to blacks here. I relate to Latinos." For her, shared culture is the most important determinant of her self-identity and being. Whites and blacks in the United States, though, perceive her primarily as black and secondarily as Latina. Race and culture may overlap, as with domestic blacks in the United States, but it does not necessarily do so, as these examples have indicated.

Chapter 2

ORIGINS OF INEQUALITY
AND UNEVEN DEVELOPMENT

The modern history of class and race in North America begins with the violent imposition of European colonial rule over pre-existing indigenous societies. Never before or after has world history witnessed human devastation on this scale. Across all of the Americas as many as 150 million Indians succumbed within a century to the guns, forced labor, or diseases of their conquerors. During the same period, millions of Africans were kidnapped and brought to the Americas to work as slaves. It is impossible to understand the contemporary class inequality of Indians and African-Americans without first examining these historical antecedents.

It is further no accident that racism—the ideological belief that there are superior and inferior races—developed during this period of conquest and colonization. Europe had had only small-scale trading relationships with non-Europeans from Africa and Asia until colonization brought them into extensive contacts and exploitative class relationships with indigenous peoples. The colonization of the Americas represents the first time in world history that different races were combined in class structures on a large scale. It is in this context that Europeans developed the modern ideology of racism as a pseudoscientific attempt to rationalize and justify the social fact that they were forcing non-whites into the lowest economic and class positions.

Racist ideologists first questioned the degree to which indigenous peoples were human beings at all. In the decades following the conquest of the Aztec empire, there were actual debates in Europe over the question of whether Indians were fully human beings or beings lower on the scale of development. If they were lower beings, then Christian moral principles would not apply to them. Pope Paul III resolved the dispute in 1537, at least for the Church, when he issued a bull proclaiming Indians to be fully human beings.[1] That decree, of course, did not end white racist attitudes toward Indians.

The next targets of racist ideology were black slaves. Racists justified their enslavement on the grounds that they were inferior creatures to be treated not much differently than farm animals. New world slave masters agreed with the Roman distinction that an animal was an *instrumentum mutum* while the slave was an *instrumentum semi-vocale.*

The modern history of North American class and racial inequality thus begins with European conquest and colonization. The full history of North America, though, begins with the peoples who migrated from Asia across the Bering Strait and inhabited the continent for at least 22,000 years and perhaps as much as 50,000 years prior to European arrival.[2]

Indigenous Societies on the Eve of the Conquest

The earliest indigenous societies of North America were made up of nomadic hunters and gatherers. These types of societies continued for millennia. Among the most important were the Chichimecas in northern Mesoamerica—the area from about 100 miles north of present-day Mexico City to Panama—and the Apaches, Navajo, Plains Indians, Sioux, Iroquois, and Cree further to the north. They lived and moved together in small bands that rarely exceeded 50 persons.

There was an essential economic and social equality among these hunters and gatherers, making them, in social and economic terms, communal societies. There was no sense of ownership of land or any other type of means of production. There could be possession of tents and other articles, but because all possessions had to be moved from place to place as hunting territories shifted, these possessed articles were, of necessity, simple, and the opportunity to accumulate personal wealth was limited. The social differentiation that did exist was restricted to non-class status or prestige bases. The leader of a band enjoyed more prestige than the others but did not possess significantly more material wealth.

These were also stateless societies in the sense that there was no regular group of officials who lived off taxing the rest. Political decision-making certainly existed as adults within the bands met to deliberate over common problems such as when to move or how to confront enemies. However, because of the small band populations, it was possible and desirable for all members to participate. In this sense, communal societies were essentially democratic, not out of ideological conviction but because their small population bases made any other form of common decision-making unworkable.

Throughout Mesoamerica and in some regions to the north, beginning as long as 8,000 years ago—the dawn of the Neolithic revolution of the Americas[3]—groups of indigenous peoples achieved technological mastery of elementary farming. They lived within sedentary villages and cultivated the soil as their means of producing food, with supplements coming from hunting, fishing, and gathering. These village communities were the first locations of class differentiation in North America. Typically, as land became valuable as a means of production, households and families sought to obtain control over greater quantities of it and reserve for themselves the most fertile parcels. Land-rich families had the means to produce more for themselves and thus enjoyed greater levels of consumption and *social* class standards of living than land poor families.

Land-rich families at first relied on their own labor. Only later were they able to monopolize possession of enough land so that other community members became landless and forced into the subordinate *economic* class positions of being either renters or laborers. In this sense, social class differentiation preceded economic class differentiation in both world and North American history. Most of these village communities were within the Mesoamerican part of North America.

North of Mesoamerica, there were two important groups. Spanish colonizers originally applied the term "Pueblo" to describe all the Indians in their northern territories (centered mostly in present-day New Mexico) who lived within village communities. The Pueblos thus were not a culturally unified single tribe or nation but rather a heterogeneous grouping of village communities. At the time of first Spanish contact, there were between 130,000 and 248,000 Indians living within approximately 100 Pueblo village communities.[4] They practiced horticulture — use of hoes to cultivate small garden-sized plots of land — and there is evidence of elementary social class differentiation, with an elite having privileged access to consumption items.

The Iroquois, who lived across parts of what today is eastern Canada and the northeastern United States, were more developed than the Pueblos. They practiced horticulture, from which as much as 80 per cent of their food supplies came, the balance coming from hunting, fishing, and gathering.[5] Several families lived together within long houses, and a number of long houses were grouped together within village communities. At the end of the fifteenth century, well before permanent European settlement, five of the Iroquois tribes or nations, including the Mohawk, joined together in the Iroquois Confederation, the most complex indigenous political formation north of Mexico. The basic purposes of the confederation were to suppress internal warfare and join forces for an effective military alliance against other tribes.

State empires, which grouped together large numbers of village communities, were the largest in scale and the most complex societies of pre-Columbian North America. A number of these, of which the Aztec and Mayan are only the most well known, existed for some 2,000 years prior to the Conquest in the three main zones of Mesoamerica: the *altiplano* or central highlands spreading outward from the Valley of Mexico, where Mexico City is located today; the Gulf Coast, where the Mexican states of Veracruz and Tabasco are today; and the area that now contains the Mexican Yucatan peninsula, Belize, and Guatemala. The first state society of which there is evidence was the Olmec, centered in Veracruz beginning approximately in 1500 BC. The classic period of the Mayas was from 300 to 900 AD. In the central highlands the Aztec empire (1350-1522) was preceded by the Tula (856-1168) and Teotihuacán (200-650).

The state empires were class-based societies in which the dominant class exercised its domination by virtue of controlling the state, which in turn financed itself by collecting exploitative tribute payments from the village communities that it dominated. Roger Bartra, who systematically studied Aztec documents and generalized his findings to other similar types of pre-Columbian empires, concluded that "the exploitation took the form of a tribute imposed on the communities (paid in kind, work, or primitive forms of money) that was in reality a rent paid to the sovereign for the use of the land which, because of divine grace, he was the absolute owner."[6] Jared Diamond concluded that "the tribute received by the Aztecs each year from subject peoples included 7,000 tons of corn, 4,000 tons of beans, 4,000 tons of grain amaranth, 2,000,000 cotton cloaks, and huge quantities of cacao beans, war costumes, shields, feather headdresses, and amber."[7]

The Aztec empire was by far the largest and most developed of the state societies. It encompassed a territory the size of Italy and contained as many as 25 million people.[8] Its capital city, Tenochtitlán, where Mexico City lies today, had a population of between 250,000 and 500,000, making it one of the world's largest cities of its day — as Mexico City is today.

A fused ruling class of military, political, and religious leaders sat at the top. The economic role of this ruling class was to accumulate and direct the investment of tribute payments in products and labor. The leaders had their own tribute-collecting bureaucracy. Once collected, tributes were invested in — aside from consumption needs of the ruling class — military and infrastructure (roads, aqueducts, etc.) maintenance and expansion. At the base of Aztec society were peasants living in largely self-sufficient households and village communities. Most household food supplies came from horticulture, with supplements coming from hunting and gathering, fishing and herding. Surpluses — what was produced beyond household consumption needs — were destined to tribute payments and trade.

Village communities generally had at least sporadic market days when peasants would gather to exchange their surpluses. This gave rise to an economic class of merchants and craft workers who serviced the markets. The merchants specialized in buying and selling for a profit, and the craft workers sold their products and services. In addition to the economic classes of the ruling class, merchants, and peasants, there was also a small slave class drawn mainly from war captives, debtors, and criminals. Unlike the slavery of Ancient Greece and Rome or the slavery that would later come after the European conquest, this slavery was limited. The condition of slavery did not pass on to the children of slaves, and slave labor and products were not essential bases of the Aztec economy.

In terms of consumption levels — that is, social classes — Aztec society spread from the lower classes of poor peasants and slaves to the rich upper class, which was made up of the members of the ruling households. In between was a small middle class made up mainly of prosperous merchants in Tenochtitlán.

To this economic and social portrait of Aztec society must be added an account

of the Aztec worldview and profound religiosity, which both played important institutional roles in daily life and which became key factors that would influence the
course of the Conquest. The Aztecs deeply believed that they lived within a divine
order that governed every aspect of their lives—from the positioning of the stars to
their personal destinies. That was what made sense to them and what gave purpose
to their lives. Within this order, the god Huitzilopochtli, the incarnation of the sun,
continually had to fight against the forces of darkness and death. The sun had to
emerge victorious or life would be completely extinguished. Each darkening, from
sunsets to eclipses, marked the beginning of the sun's battle with the forces of darkness,
and each dawn indicated that the sun had emerged victorious and life would go on.

According to Aztec belief, the purpose of all activities—making war, harvesting,
and sacrificing victims—was to maintain this divine order. Any failure could disrupt
its functioning. If a drought came, that was a sign as well as punishment, indicating
that the Aztecs had not complied enough with their divine obligations. Sacrifices of
their own blood were necessary to put themselves back in place in the divine order.
This fatalistic worldview explains why the Aztecs went to the extremes of carrying
out human sacrifices. They both deeply believed that it was true and that they were
powerless to do anything but comply, otherwise the whole cosmological order
would collapse. That was their obligation if both they, not as individuals but as a
people, and the whole divine order were to survive. The Aztecs also believed that
their cosmological world—that of the Fifth Sun—had been preceded by four previous worlds, each one of which had ended in calamity. Their world also was destined
to end apocalyptically—as it did.

Europe on the Eve of the Conquest
Europe at the time of the conquest was at distinctly different levels of technological
and social development than the societies of North America. In contrast to North
America, where horticulture that relied on humans wielding hoes was the highest
level of technology achieved, Europe had known for more than a millennium more
sophisticated and productive agricultural technologies that employed animal-drawn
plows to cultivate fields. The Europeans would bring the animal-drawn plow with
them and introduce it to the Americas. In terms of social development, unlike North
America where the Aztec state society was the highest level of complexity, Europe in
the sixteenth century was passing from feudalism to capitalism.

European feudalism, as described most completely by Marc Bloch, was composed of essentially precommodity natural and self-sufficient manorial economies
in which landlords controlled use of the land, which they rented out to peasants.[9]
Peasants for the most part produced products for their own household consumption. Their surplus products were divided between those that were used for rent payments and those that were marketed.

Capitalism required a radical transformation of feudalism, necessitating the development of free markets in labor, the means of production (capital), and products. That meant that peasant labor had to be divorced from the land in order to be available for hire. Land—the principal feudal means of production—had to become available for sale. Products of labor were sold in markets rather than consumed directly by their producers. All three types of markets were already at various stages of development in Europe at the time of the Conquest to such an extent that it was possible to speak of the emergence of market-organized capitalist societies.

The Conquest

In North America the Spanish, British, French, and Dutch took control of different areas and the indigenous peoples within them. The largest scale and most spectacular of the conquests took place, logically, in what today is Mexico, where the indigenous population was the most numerous and developed. One of the great mysteries that has puzzled generations of historians was how it was possible for Hernán Cortés with just 500 soldiers to overthrow a warrior empire that controlled experienced armies with hundreds of thousands of men. The puzzle has generally been answered in three ways.

First, the Aztec empire did not offer unified resistance to the invaders. The Aztecs had enemies on their borders and discontented peoples within. As they continually sought to expand their boundaries and tributary areas, they met resistance from smaller state societies, such as Tlaxcala. Within the areas that they had conquered, there was resentment and discontent among many of the village communities and subject peoples. Cortés was able to take advantage of these fissures and enlist the Aztecs' enemies in his own armies. In other cases, he defeated smaller indigenous armies on the periphery of the Aztec empire and then added their ranks to his own. In part they combined with the conquistador cause as armies that have been thoroughly routed on the battlefield by overwhelming forces often do. In part Cortés obliged them to join his armies as a term of surrender. By the time he made his final assault on Tenochtitlán, his 500 men were backed up by over 100,000 indigenous soldiers.

There is a certain racial mythology surrounding these events. Because Cortés had substantial numbers of Indian allies, it is misleading to see the initial conquest as entirely a battle between Spanish and Indians. Cortés marched into a situation in which the indigenous peoples were not united. They belonged to different, and often warring, state empires (such as the Aztecs and Tlaxcalans); they were simple oppressed subjects of one or another empire; or they lived outside of the control of empires and only had localized identities. To believe that they could have developed a unity that overrode all of these divisions is to believe that common racial identity is (or should be) the moving force of history.

In this respect, Mexican nationalism and national identity have been largely formed out of a particular interpretation of the Conquest: they begin with the indigenous peoples long before the arrival of the Spanish who tragically ended their civilizations. The dominant interpretation views Cortés as an invader. For that reason there are no more than a handful of obscure statues of him today in the country. Even more disdained in Mexican history is Cortés's Indian interpreter and lover, Malintzin or *Doña* Marina, as the Spanish called her, whose advice significantly aided his victories. Referred to as *La Malinche*, a variation of her Indian name, she is seen as the great betrayer of pre-Hispanic Mexico. Today, many Mexicans denounce as *malinchistas* those compatriots whom they accuse of identifying more with foreigners than with their own country. The interpretation of the role of Malinche is also related to the cultural complex of *machista* ideas in which men see and fear all women as potential betrayers. The problem, as Roger Bartra has pointed out, is that there was no pre-Hispanic Mexican homeland to be betrayed. Mexico as a nation developed after, not before, the Conquest.[10] To see the indigenous peoples as having been a unitary nation not only ignores the realities of their divisions, it is to also, once again, to reduce national identity primarily to racial identity, that is, to Indianness.

The second factor instrumental in the defeat of the Aztecs was disease. When the Spanish arrived in the Americas, they unwittingly brought with them the germs of diseases that had spread earlier through Europe. The Spanish themselves over generations had built up relative resistances to these diseases, but the Americas had had no biological experience with them. Hence, when contact was made, diseases spread rapidly through the indigenous populations. Alfred M. Crosby, among others, has concluded that one of the reasons why the Aztecs could not put up stronger resistance to the conquistadores was that many of them were very sick or dying from European diseases during decisive battles.[11]

The third influencing factor was the Aztec worldview or belief system. As mentioned, the Aztecs deeply believed that sooner or later their world would end apocalyptically. It was within this context that the Aztec ruler Montezuma and most of his advisors initially believed that the Spanish conquistadores were gods and harbingers of a divinely ordered destruction of their world, against which there was nothing that could be done except to accept it fatalistically. This subjective factor weakened the Aztec defenses and allowed the conquistadores a relatively easy conquest. Even if the Aztecs were not completely sure that their doom had already been divinely ordained, there was enough of a generalized doubt throughout the ranks of their armies to vitiate resistance. The Aztecs had never seen guns or horses before. The deafening sounds and deadly fire spit out by the guns as well as the size and speed of the beasts that carried their bearers were terrifying. In addition, disfiguring diseases descended upon them. All these unsettling events confirmed their belief that the apocalyptic end was indeed near. Once conquered, the Aztecs were fatalistically predisposed, because of their deeply rooted belief system, to accept that the world of the Fifth Sun was no more and that a new world with a new god had taken its place.

Soon after conquering Tenochtitlán, the Spanish began their military push northward, provoking a series of wars with the fiercely independent Chichimeca peoples. Further north, in the areas that would become the Southwest of the United

States, the Spanish encountered further resistance, especially from the Apaches. As for the Pueblo village communities, the Spanish made peace with them at first. Then, in 1680, the Pueblos revolted and expelled the Spanish from New Mexico. Later the Spanish were able to return and coexist with the Pueblos, but they never were able to completely subdue the Apaches and other nomadic Indians, especially in western New Mexico, which is today Arizona.[12] The final submission of all of the indigenous bands came only with the U.S. military presence after the 1846-48 Mexican-American War.

The other conquests that took place on the North American continent were less epic than what took place in Mexico but were as consequential for the indigenous peoples. The first permanent British settlements on the east coast of what would become the United States, the Jamestown and Plymouth colonies, were not established until nearly a century after the Spanish conquest of Tenochtitlán. The British settlement differed from the Spanish in three ways. First, unlike the Spanish, who confronted relatively densely populated areas, the British encountered sparse populations. Secondly, again unlike the Spanish, who sought to take advantage of abundant Indian labor to construct their colonial cities and later farm their lands, the British from the beginning arrived with an enclave mentality. They built their cities like fortresses, always seeking to keep the Indians beyond the limits of where they lived. Finally, unlike the Spanish, who lived with, and who with increasing frequency interbred with, indigenous people, the British strictly segregated themselves. There was one similarity: as in Mexico, European diseases took a heavy toll among the indigenous people. For example, diseases reduced the population of Northwest Coast Indians from 180,000 to 40,000 within a century of contact.[13]

As more settlers arrived seeking choice land for planting, the colonies expanded at the expense of the Indians. In time, expansion provoked resistance and wars broke out. Around Plymouth in 1675, King Phillip's War, named after the English name for the Indian chief, broke out. After defeating and capturing the Indians, the settlers executed the chief and placed his head on a stake, where it remained for 25 years. His wife and children were shipped to the West Indies and sold into slavery.[14]

The first permanent European settlers of the area of New York were the Dutch who founded New Netherlands. They too expanded their holdings violently at the expense of the Indians. In 1641, Dutch soldiers massacred all of the occupants of two Indian villages on Staten Island, a part of present-day New York City, while they slept. They then burned the villages to the ground.[15]

French settlers founded Canada's first permanent European colony at Quebec in 1608, approximately the same time as the founding of the Jamestown colony. The French settlers pursued a different policy with the Indians than the British did. For the most part, instead of segregating themselves, they formed alliances with different Indian groups in various internecine Indian wars. The largest of these was between the Algonquians and the Iroquois; beginning in 1609, the French sided with the

Algonquians for a half century of fighting over control of the fur trade in the lower Great Lakes and St. Lawrence.

What sugar was to the Caribbean, fur was to New France. The French generally obtained furs, for which there was a growing world market subject to the dictates of fashion, from Indians, who often obtained them from other Indians further inland or collected them themselves. The French were thus the traders and the Indians the producers of furs. Unlike sugar, however, furs could not be produced under plantation conditions where a subjugated slave labor force could be concentrated. It had to be trapped over wide wooded areas. In 1649 the French decided to trap the furs themselves and dispense with the Indian middlemen, who were essentially "fur-collecting mercenary warriors."[16]

In most cases, the French attempted to work with Indian allies to defeat other Indians for the interests of France. The general policy of entering into alliances with one or another side of warring Indian tribes was not without exceptions, though. The first contact between the Beothuk people on Newfoundland and French fishers ended in confrontation, with the French attempting to hunt down and annihilate the entire Beothuk population.[17] As in all areas of North America, European diseases also took a heavy toll among the indigenous peoples in the north: in 1639, for example, a smallpox epidemic killed two-thirds of the 30,000 members of the Huron Confederacy.[18]

The indigenous societies of North America on the eve of the European conquests thus ranged, in developmental terms, from hunting and gathering bands of nomads to horticultural village communities to the state empires of Mesoamerica. Europe, by contrast, at that time was composed of agricultural societies in varying degrees of transformation from feudalism to capitalism. The conquest of North America started first in its most highly developed area, the Aztec Empire, and then over the next three centuries spread to remoter regions of the continent.

For the first time in North America class and race became correlates, with Indians being forced into the lower rungs of the colonial class systems as slaves, peasants, peons, and, certainly, the poor. There is a clear relationship between the Conquest and forced class subjugation of the indigenous populations and the continuing reality that today in the United States, Mexico, and Canada, they continue to suffer highly unequal standards of living.

Colonial Reconstruction

After the Conquest, capitalism as an economic system based on expanding markets and profit-oriented businesses grew and developed unevenly across the North American continent. That much is obvious from its contemporary features in the United States, Mexico, and Canada. This uneven development came in large part because the Spanish and British, as well as the Dutch and French, imported different varieties of it and did so under different conditions.

Capitalism as such had developed unevenly across Europe as it displaced feudalism.

Markets and workshops located in cities were its original centers, while the country remained mired in traditional feudal relationships. The economies of such countries as Britain and Holland became proportionately more capitalistic and less feudalistic at faster rates than countries like Spain and Portugal. Hence, the main colonizers of the areas of North America that would become the United States, Mexico, and Canada came from countries that represented significantly different hybrids of feudal and capitalist economic features.

In Spain, feudal features were proportionately more present then in Britain; thus, what the Spanish institutionally implanted in North America was proportionately more feudalistic than what the British implanted. In addition, the Spanish had to graft their economic practices on to those of the indigenous peoples who always greatly outnumbered them by ratios as great as 20 to 1. The British were not so encumbered by pre-existing indigenous practices since they quickly outnumbered the native population, which their colonists could push aside and economically marginalize. It followed that capitalism could and did develop much more rapidly in the British than Spanish areas.

The Spanish confronted large and complexly organized indigenous societies. They found it useful and relatively easy to absorb many of these indigenous state institutions into their own semifeudal forms of organization. The Aztec tribute payment, for example, was easily continued as a payment to the new Spanish authorities. This blending of two types of social organizations was possible because in many respects the prior indigenous state empires and the conquering feudal societies were similarly structured. In both, the ruling classes received payments of surplus products from subject classes, as tribute payments in the case of the indigenous state empires and as rent payments in the case of feudal societies. The main difference between the two was that the rule was centralized in the former and decentralized in the latter. But the form of domination, if not the source, was very similar.[19] Neither form of society, though, was compatible with capitalistic development. The noncapitalist aspects of Aztec and Spanish social and economic organization reinforced each other and acted as brakes on capitalism.

In contrast, in the British areas of North America, the indigenous peoples were from the beginning pushed away from the areas of colonization. Their forms of social and economic organization played no part in the social and economic organization of the colonies. In a double sense the conditions for capitalist development were much more favorable in the British than Spanish areas of North America. The British were more inclined to be capitalistic in the first place because their home country was experiencing rapid capitalist development. Second, North America represented a kind of institutional *tabula rasa* for them: they had a free hand to form the kinds of social and economic institutions that they wanted. They were not forced to absorb whole indigenous populations and take into account their pre-existing institutions, as were the Spanish colonizers.

To all of this must be added the different roles and consequences of religious institutions. The Spanish brought and deeply institutionalized a medieval Catholic creed that, as Max Weber powerfully argued, fettered capitalist development.[20] It held that the community had to devote a considerable amount of its labor and time to religious pursuits such as prayer and the construction of churches and viewed with suspicion labor directed at producing worldly wealth.

The Protestant theologies that reigned in British North America had a different view of economic activity. They found success in worldly pursuits to be positive signs of righteousness, and they were not so demanding of labor, time, and resources. The Protestant work ethic, the most important economic consequence of this worldview, resulted in generations of overproducers and underconsumers. Business owners reinvested their profits rather than spending them on luxury consumption items. Protestant workers were the answer to the capitalist dream: they worked hard without demanding high wages. Both classes of Protestants significantly accelerated the accumulation of capital. If the ornately constructed Catholic Church was the symbol of colonial culture in the Spanish-dominated areas, the no-nonsense simple New England church was the symbol of Puritan culture.

It followed that the Spanish and British areas developed unevenly at different speeds and with different features. Mexico inherited the institutional features of large haciendas, communal land holdings, significant natural economies, and a church that drained economic resources. The United States and Canada inherited an economic ethic more in tune with capitalist needs and an almost wide-open territory within which capitalism could develop, once it was cleared of the obstacles posed by the presence of its relatively few original inhabitants.

The indigenous populations were integrated into the social bases of the colonial class system in New Spain, composed of present-day Mexico and Central America, as slaves, laborers, peons, and peasants. The Spanish sought their labor. In the British areas, though, the dynamic was different. Indians were always outside of the evolving economic system. All that the new settlers wanted from them was their land.

If feudal and semifeudal institutions slowed the development of capitalism in part of North America, slavery, which existed in both the Spanish and southern British colonies, played a more supporting role. North American slavery, unlike peasant agriculture, was always related to capitalist development. The basic purpose of having a slave labor force was to produce products for which there was a market demand. Owners used slaves to mine silver and plant sugar, tobacco, and other crops for the world market. Slaves produced profits for their owners and significantly contributed to the overall accumulation of capital that launched international capitalism. It is yet to be determined whether more primary capital accumulation came out of the compulsive labor of the frugal Puritans or the overexploitation of slaves.[21]

In sum, the sixteenth-century varieties of capitalism that the Europeans brought with them were hybrids of feudal, slave, and capitalist formations. The three major varieties that developed were: a capitalism with significant feudal features in New Spain and New France; a slavery-based capitalism in the British southern colonies; and an elementary agrarian capitalism in the British northern colonies.

In one way or another, whites, Indians, and blacks confronted each other in the colonial projects and, inevitably, mixed-race offspring emerged. The language evolved to describe these mixed-raced persons differed in degree of elaborateness between the British colonies and those of Spain and France as we will see. This linguistic difference reflected the lack of integration of Indians in the development of the British colonies, in contrast to those of Spain and France. In the British colonies, Indians and mestizos were simply outside of—in both the physical and linguistic senses—the evolving colonial project; in the Spanish and French colonies they were an integrated, internal part of it, however much they were perceived as inferiors. In terms of psychological perception theory, the further an object is from a perceiver, the more it is perceived as an undifferentiated whole. Indians and mestizos, on the one hand, and slaves and the offspring of black-white relationships—commonly referred to as mulattoes—on the other hand, tended to be perceived as undifferentiated wholes in British colonial society because they were essentially outside of it, despite the fact that slaves were economically essential in the south. In the Spanish and French areas, such mixed-race peoples were perceived as being inside the colonial project, and, since they were closer, distinctions could be perceived among them.

Spanish Colonial Society

Colonial New Spain represented both a radical uprooting and restructuring of Aztec society and an adaptation to it. The Spanish took over as the new ruling class and razed Aztec cities and places of worship in order to construct a new society in their own image. One of the most graphic monuments to this policy is at Cholula in Puebla where the Spanish constructed a church precisely at the apex of the ruins of an indigenous pyramid. The visual symbolism of this act of cultural domination was paralleled later in the United States, when within a couple of decades of the final military conquest of the Sioux, the conquering power carved the faces of four of its presidents on the top of Mount Rushmore, a mountain sacred to the conquered. In both cases, conquerors through physical defacement of an indigenous shrine attempted to symbolize their power while simultaneously erasing the cultural pasts of the conquered.

The sheer size and cultural depth of the conquered indigenous population, though, forced the Spanish to include them within their institutions. They could not simply push Indians to frontier areas, as was done in the northern British colonies. Spanish feudal institutions were fairly easily transplanted and adapted to the new colonial conditions because, as mentioned above, the pre-existing Aztec state and the Spanish feudal economies shared a number of similar features. Peasant labor was the base of both types of economies, and, in both, peasants were accustomed to making tribute or rent payments to overlords. The Spanish, once they had lopped off the Aztec occupants of the ruling positions within the economic and social pyramids, simply took their places.

At the same time, after the fall of Tenochtitlán and even down to the present, as emphasized by Guillermo Bonfil Batalla, many Indians stayed on the periphery of the developing semifeudal and capitalist structures, ignoring the money economy as much as possible. They produce on small plots of land mainly for household consumption and reciprocally call on each other's labor as needed rather than resorting to hiring outsiders.[22] One of the obvious consequences of this is that, *ipso facto*, they have less money and higher rates of poverty. This poverty, in addition to being a result of social injustice, is therefore also, to an extent, self chosen, consciously or unconsciously, actively or passively, as an act of resistance to being completely absorbed by the imposed European capitalistic way of life.

The Spanish initially implanted the *encomienda* system. The Crown granted an individual, the *encomendero*, the right to collect tributes from the individuals, the *encomendados*, within an area. This was the first landlord-peasant economic class structure established by the Spanish in New Spain. The *encomienda* system represented not so much a break from as a continuation of the old pre-Hispanic state society forms of collecting tributes.[23] In that sense, it was an institutional form that functioned in both state and feudal modes of production, which, while distinct, contained many similarities.

Angel Palerm Vich argues that not only were there institutional continuities between the pre-Hispanic and Spanish colonial economic class structures but that there were also continuities of individuals. According to him, during this period substantial numbers of the old Indian upper class remained largely intact. The Spanish allowed them to keep some of their properties and political authority and to continue collecting tributes from the Indian masses. The Spanish did not totally displace them at first but rather moved in alongside them in the class structure. "The Spanish and the superior indigenous class," writes Palerm Vich, "lived over the mass of aboriginal agriculturalists from whom they wrested part of their product by means of tribute payments."[24] In time, though, the Indian component of the early colonial upper class was almost completely edged out, with the Spanish taking over virtually all opportunities for acquiring upper-class incomes.

The *encomienda* system did not last long. Instead of being content with collecting tributes from Indians who continued their economic activities as they always had, the Spanish sought to develop and exploit the land and other natural resources. Toward that end they built their own haciendas to control both agriculture and ranching; took over mining operations; and seized control of state administration, commerce, and some production in the cities. The major economic actors were the hacienda owners, whose labor force consisted mainly of indigenous peasants; the church, which was a large landowner in its own right and holder of credit capital;

and the colonial state, which controlled lucrative political and military positions.

Men could make their fortunes and insure their upper-class membership from the exploitation of peasant labor on the land they owned or from the exploitation of income opportunities afforded by controlling state posts. Although the church was a powerful economic actor, it did not so much generate upper-class members as receive them; that is, because of celibacy vows as well as the corporate organization of the institution, rich priests could not pass on fortunes to heirs. However, it was customary for at least one son of a rich family to become a priest who would quickly move into the upper echelons of the church. The church was thus a part of a colonial class society in which its priests along with landlords and state authorities ran the economic structure.

The colonial labor force was dualistic, as emphasized by Palerm Vich and others.[25] The core of the economy consisted of the hacienda, mining, and urban labor forces, but outside of that core existed subsistence-level villages and farms in which mainly Indians lived. These were in a double sense peripheral labor forces. First, they generated mostly subsistence products for household consumption. Such surplus products as they generated did not circulate beyond local markets. Second, they were outside of the control of the landlords and mine owners and thus outside of the main systems of exploitation.

A middle class—in both the economic and social senses—of professionals and merchants sputtered into existence in the cities by the late colonial period. Economically they were small business owners, and socially their businesses were prosperous enough to afford incomes above those received by the Indian and mestizo lower classes.

The New Spain colonial economy was feudal to the extent not only that a significant amount of peasant production was for self and household consumption rather than market sale but that the church's power as a large land controller and accumulator of capital acted as a brake on capitalist development. It was capitalist to the extent that increasing amounts of production were oriented to both domestic and international markets and that labor and capital markets were developing.

Slave labor was employed in households, plantation fields, sugar mills, and mines. It was legal and existed for the entire colonial period, but it was never practiced as extensively as in the southern areas of British North America. The first slaves were Indians. Some had been slaves before the Conquest and simply changed owners after it. Others were newly enslaved by the Spanish. Indian slavery legally ended in 1551 by order of the Spanish court. In practice, though, it continued in frontier areas of New Spain.

The burden of slave labor passed from Indians to Africans, as in the rest of Latin America, by the middle of the sixteenth century. During the colonial period, as many as 250,000 African slaves were imported through the ports of Veracruz and Acapulco into Mexico.[26] Some had already been slaves in the Spanish possessions within the Caribbean, while others were brought from Africa. There was also a much smaller trade in Asian slaves transported from the Philippines, also a colony of Spain, to the Pacific port of Acapulco. These were all referred to as "Chinos," though the majority were Filipinos.[27]

David M. Davidson calculated the distribution of Mexican slaves during the height of their use in the mid-seventeenth century. There were four main areas. The first was centered in the city of Veracruz, where about 5,000 slaves worked mostly as transporters and dock workers. Outside of Veracruz another 3,000 slaves worked on sugar plantations and ranches. The second area was north and west of Mexico City, where some 15,000 slaves worked in mines and as herders of cattle, sheep, and mules. The third area was in a belt from Puebla to the Pacific Coast, where some 3,000 to 5,000 slaves worked on sugar plantations, on ranches, and in mines. The fourth and largest area was in Mexico City itself, where between 20,000 and 50,000 slaves worked in urban occupations.[28]

Significant numbers of slaves rebelled and escaped during the colonial period. The fear of slave rebellion was always an undercurrent in colonial society. In 1537, as the African slave population of Mexico City was growing rapidly, rumors spread among the Spanish inhabitants that a rebellion was about to break out. They responded by publicly executing several dozen slaves through quartering.[29] That same year a number of escaped slaves—referred to collectively as *cimarrones* in New Spain—attacked a Spanish village.[30] Because New Spain contained many remote mountainous areas, *cimarrones* were able to establish themselves relatively easily and fend off attempts at recapture. Some of the mountain villages originally established by *cimarrones* in Veracruz, Oaxaca, and Guerrero continue today to be inhabited by their descendants.[31] The Spanish authorities attempted to deter escapes by establishing severely repressive punishments, including castration.[32]

There was a close correlation between race and social class position in New Spain. As Alexander von Humboldt, who traveled extensively through New Spain, famously noted, "The skin, more or less white, decides the rank that a man occupies in society."[33] The upper classes were completely white, but they were not without divisions. The top social class positions belonged to leading landlord, political, and military families, as well as the top echelons of the clergy, who were Spanish-born *peninsulares*. Below them in status, but still upper class, were wealthy landlords and merchants who were *criollos* (Spaniards born in New Spain). The small middle class was made up of moderately prosperous *criollo* merchants and landowners. The two lower classes were made up of the free poor (mixed race and Indians) and black slaves.

Throughout the colonial period the Spanish authorities attempted to categorize people racially, with people of mixed backgrounds being placed in what they called castes.[34] Europeans, Indians, and Africans constituted the three racial trunk lines and originating caste positions. Cross-racial unions produced three general mixed-race caste positions: *mestizos* (European-Indian), *mulattoes* (European-African), and *zumbaigos* or *mulattoes pardos* (Indian-African). The attempt to categorize the colonial population, though, did not stop with these six positions. Cross-caste unions among the different mixed-race castes produced still new combinations, which received their own labels. The offspring of whites and mulattoes were called *moriscos*. The offspring of a particular type of mixed union could also be labeled differently according to which parent had one of the particular racial backgrounds, such as whether it was the father or the mother who was the white in a white-Indian union. In time, as new types of combinations increased, the number of labels generated to describe their offspring multiplied to as many as 56 in the highly race-conscious discourse of colonial society.

Table 2.1: Population of New Spain, Various Years

	1570	1646	1742	1793	1810
Europeans	0.2	0.8	0.4	0.2	0.2
Africans	0.6	2.0	0.8	0.1	0.1
Indians	98.7	74.6	62.2	61.0	60.0
Euro-mestizos	0.3	9.8	15.8	17.8	17.9
Afro-mestizos	0.07	6.8	10.8	9.6	10.1
Indo-mestizos	0.07	6.0	10.0	11.2	11.5
Total	100.0	100.0	100.0	100.0	100.0
Total population (in thousands)	3,380	1,713	2,477	3,800	6,122

Source: Gonzalo Aguirre Beltrán, *La Población Negra de México* (1946; Mexico City: Secretaria de la Reforma Agraria, Centro de Estudios Históricos del Agrarismo en México, 1981) 234.

From the most positive point of view, the generation of an elaborate language of racial labels reflected a refined appreciation of how different combinations could produce an interesting mosaic of different physical types of people. Sor Juana Inés de la Cruz included mestizos and mulattoes in her seventeenth-century poetry, though most often as picturesque background characters. Racially mixed persons were the subjects of paintings, in some cases in their own right as interesting subjects, in others to aid church officials in classifying the members of their parishes. Art historians have recently collected and established these paintings as a focus of study.[35] Edward J. Sullivan notes that the paintings reflected the societal prejudices of the time: "Most of the depictions of the *castas* with the highest percentage of white blood show peaceful (even blissful) domestic scenes; some of those portraying people with predominantly black and Indian blood can be, from time to time, surprisingly violent."[36] The zoological origin of many of the names for castes—such as *mulato* (mule), *coyote*, and *lobo* (wolf)—reflected the deep prejudice with which the white colonial upper class viewed racially mixed persons.[37]

Catholic missionary work moved in tandem with the consolidation of Spanish economic and political power. The Indians' fatalistic receptivity to the rule of new gods facilitated the work of the church. Nevertheless, the conversion of millions of Indians to Catholicism was an extraordinary evangelical feat seldom if ever matched in world history, before or since. The depth of Catholic religiosity among the Mexican Indian population today, as evidenced by the huge crowds that turn out to see visiting popes, bears testimony to the success of the missionary effort.

A fortuitous and, in the eyes of some colonial critics, suspicious miracle greatly aided the conversion effort. In 1532, just 11 years after the final conquest of Teno-chtitlán, the Virgin Mary appeared in transfigured form as an Indian on a hill that today is within the limits of Mexico City. An Indian peasant, Juan Diego, witnessed her appearance. As evidence, she left her image on a piece of cloth. From that incident spread belief in the miracle of the Virgin of Guadalupe, which facilitated conversion of the indigenous population and which continues to be deeply embraced in Mexico, especially among the indigenous peoples.

In addition to allowing that divinity could take the form of an Indian, Spanish Catholicism had to adapt itself to some pre-existing Indigenous beliefs and practices while attempting to uproot those that were judged to be heathen. For instance, celebration of the indigenous Day of the Dead was incorporated into and became a part of the church's customary festivities, but adoration of idols had to end.

From the 1530s onward, the Spanish pushed northward, attempting to colonize frontier areas. The north was inhabited by a large variety of nomadic bands who spoke different languages. The Aztecs had pejoratively called them collectively *Chichimecas*—descended from dogs—and the Spanish adopted the term. Their hunting and gathering technology required large areas in which to search for sustenance, especially given the arid and semi-arid characteristics of the Mexican north. The Spanish sought to use that land in a different way for agriculture, ranching, and mining.

Two different uses of land thus competed. There is no question that the Spanish sought to use it more efficiently. A square hectare of land devoted to agriculture can support more people than can the same unit of land used for hunting and gathering. At the same time, because the nomadic bands required so much territory to survive, any intrusion by foreigners undercut their economic means of survival. The very presence of the Spanish created problems for the Indians.

Spanish colonization of the north followed a pattern. As haciendas, mines, and towns formed, the authorities established a presidio or fort near them for protection. The church in turn established a mission in its attempt to convert and pacify the nomads. As the frontier advanced and old towns disappeared, presidios moved, marking the progress of Spanish colonization.[38]

Spanish policy attempted to make the Indians sedentary and transform them from hunters and gatherers into a hacienda and mining labor force. None of these efforts proceeded peacefully. Almost continual warfare accompanied the Spanish colonization of its northern territories up through the nineteenth century. The sword and the cross were the primary Spanish instruments for overcoming nomadic Indian resistance and opening up the northern territories to agricultural, ranching, and mining exploitation.

Capitalism, Feudalism, and New France

Almost a century after New Spain was founded, Spain's neighbor, France, established its own colony in the northern reaches of the continent. Colonial New France was centered in Quebec and the St. Lawrence Valley. French explorers, traders, and military outposts extended its influence further west and south down through what is now the U.S. Midwest to Louisiana.

Since France, like Spain and unlike Britain, still had significant feudal economic vestiges slowing capitalist development in the sixteenth and seventeenth centuries, its North American colony was partially constructed according to feudal principles. An important part of agriculture in seventeenth-century New France, like that of New Spain, remained firmly embedded in feudal customs. The colonial authorities granted land as estates (*seigneuries*) to landlords (*seigneurs*) in the St. Lawrence Valley. The landlords inhabited the estates with French-origin peasants (*censitaires* or *habitants*). The estate economies followed almost completely French feudal precedent. The peasants owed rent (about 10 per cent of their yearly income, which was less severe than in France), military service, and, in some cases corvée labor, that is, compulsory work for the landlord. They were also required to work for the Crown a few days a year to maintain roads and bridges. Approximately half of the peasants produced only enough for subsistence and rent payments.[39]

At the same time, the fur trade was organized according to capitalist principles. French merchants bought pelts from Indian trappers that were then shipped for sale in France. The early fishing industry also was carried out on a profit-making basis, with the crews being paid wages.

New France, like New Spain, had a history of slavery on the margins of its economy, but it was even more marginal. No more than 4,000 persons were slaves in the entire history of the colony. The majority of these were Indians rather than blacks. There was even less of a basis for plantation slave systems in New France than there was in New Spain.[40]

Relations between whites and Indians developed in New France in a number of ways that paralleled those of New Spain. While there was no conquest comparable to that of Tenochtitlán, the early military history of New France saw French settlers aligning themselves with one or another Indian tribe against another. There was significant intermarriage among French and indigenous persons with the resulting off-spring sharing the same racial characteristics as Mexican mestizos. This was one of the roots of what would later become known as the Canadian *Métis* population.

Agrarian and Slave Capitalism in the British Colonies[41]

The British colonists who came to North America brought with them the attitudes of early capitalist development so that their colonies originated and developed much more in capitalistic conditions than did either the Spanish or French colonies. The Britain they left was in the late stages of its economic transition from medieval feudalism to capitalism. When they arrived, they encountered sparse populations of Indigenous peoples with communal modes of production that were distinctly different from either feudalism or capitalism. These peoples were mostly hunters and gatherers with no concept of private property. Two different economic and social ways of life thus confronted each other.

The colonists immediately sought land to develop into farms; to get it they had to, in one way or another, push the indigenous peoples back from the shore lands. This push immediately triggered resistance, touching off a series of coastal wars. By the eve of the War of Independence, Indian resistance in the 13 Colonies had been practically eliminated. But with more land-hungry settlers continually arriving and with the most fertile lands already claimed, pressure mounted for further expansion westward. The British colonial authorities, though, had negotiated a series of treaties with Indian tribes that limited such expansion. This was one of the grievances of the colonists that set off the War of Independence.

Indigenous peoples were always marginalized in the colonies. Unlike in colonial New Spain where the Spanish colonists encountered densely populated areas, the labor of whose people they sought to exploit, in the British colonies there was virtually no attempt to exploit indigenous labor. The only thing that the colonists wanted from the Indians was their land. The violent expropriation and appropriation of that land was the original condition for the economic development of what would become the United States.

From the beginning—also unlike in the Spanish or French areas—market production dominated colonial farming practices in the British colonies. Farmers produced for household consumption as well—mainly in remote areas, such as Appalachia, where peasant subsistence economic and cultural ways of life took hold—but that was never their primary goal. Market-oriented farming was the rule, a subsistence-oriented peasantry, as in New Spain, the exception.

Because of the increasing production of market-oriented agricultural surplus products, there was enough food to support immigration and population growth in colonial cities such as Boston, New York, Philadelphia, and Halifax. Within those and other cities, in turn, important industries such as shipbuilding and rum-distilling developed. These industries were both the seeds of the later development of industrial capitalism and sites of the original development of the urban economic classes of capitalists and workers.

The northern colonies thus developed predominantly — but not exclusively — with independent businesses and free labor. But not all labor was free. There were some black slaves. More significant economically, there were large numbers of indentured servants who were required to work for masters for seven years before becoming free labor. As much as half of the white population in the northern colonies came originally as indentured servants.

The use of indentured servants eventually died out for economic reasons. Investment in them was costly, considering that the owner would have to free them in seven years. Many escaped, causing immediate loss of investment. Finally, Britain ceased to encourage the indentured servant trade when it realized that it was having a harmful effect on its own domestic profits. Originally, British mercantile policy assumed that exporting the unemployed into the indentured servant trade would help insure social stability. However, this changed in the eighteenth century when it was realized that the maintenance of an unemployed population at home had a salutary effect on wages from the point of view of employers — that is, the greater the relative size of the unemployed population, the greater the downward pressure on the wages of the employed population due to the law of supply and demand.

The northern economic and class structure, although it rested for a long period on unfree indentured labor, always developed in the context of the primary capitalist goal of profitability and insuring growth through reinvestment of profits. If in New Spain spectacular amounts of wealth were made and squandered episodically, in British North America capital was accumulated methodically. However, it was no less accompanied by violence. The Massachusetts and Pennsylvania colonies established scalp bounties for Indians who stood in the way; and, as we will see, once the many small streams and rivulets of methodical accumulation joined together into an institutionalized national economy and self-evident national purpose, means of violence on a far larger scale would be accumulated to remove other obstacles.

The southern British colonies from 1660 to 1782 functioned within a world capitalist context. They employed slave labor to produce particular crops, such as sugar, tobacco, cotton, and indigo, for which there was a strong demand on the world market. In this sense, new world slavery was a necessary complement to the early development of capitalism. The trade in slaves themselves was exceptionally lucrative, with the profits generating capital formation; slave products were profitably sold on the world market; and, in many cases, slaves produced the raw materials that free labor in factories transformed into finished products.

In the New World as a whole, sugar was the most important slave-produced crop for the world market during the colonial period, but it was of minimal importance in the southern colonies because their climatic and soil conditions were not appropriate. For the entire colonial period, tobacco was the leading slave-produced crop. It was only after independence that the invention of the cotton gin facilitated the orientation of southern agriculture toward meeting the skyrocketing world demand for cotton. Because the demand for tobacco was considerably less than that for sugar, the southern colonies only counted a very small percentage of New World slaves. By 1700, they had imported no more than 30,000 African slaves, a small number compared to, for example, Brazil which had imported 500,000 to 600,000.[42] Nevertheless, the bases of the southern slave economy were established during the colonial period. These would allow the expansion of the system as world economic demands changed in the late eighteenth century.

The British followed the practice of systematically separating slaves from the same African linguistic groups so that they would not be sold together for work in the same area. This practice forced the slaves to learn the English language quickly. With no one to speak to in their native tongue, the languages eventually were lost. So too were African regional and tribal customs. British policy thus led to a rapid cutting of the slaves' African cultural heritage. As a result, black culture in the United States developed relatively autonomously unlike in the Caribbean and Brazil, where much more of a hybrid black culture with strong African influences in music, dance, religion, and language took root.

Chapter 3

A NEW EMPIRE

For 35 centuries different empires have formed, disappeared, and been in contention in North American history. The first empires, beginning with the Olmec on the Gulf Coast of what is now Mexico, formed among the indigenous populations. After the Spanish conquest of the Aztecs, the last and largest of a number of indigenous empires, European empires—including the French and British as well as Spanish—struggled over control of the continent. Wars of independence drove the Spanish and British empires out of the areas that would become Mexico and the United States. Canada evolved toward substantive independence through agreement and negotiation. As European empires left the content, the power of the United States began to grow, laying the basis for it to become a world power and empire by the twentieth century. If at the end of the sixteenth century Tenochtitlan was the capital city of North America's most powerful empire, four centuries later the new capital would be Washington, DC.

From the nineteenth century forward North America's three nations would all be affected by the growing continental and world power of the United States. In part because of that, capitalism would develop in the three countries in different ways that affected configurations of class and race.

Origins of Empire
In 1783, after an eight-year war of independence, the United States broke free from British colonial control. What had been subordinate capitalist development under colonial conditions was replaced by expansionary independent capitalist development.

In no other country did capitalism have a more favorable terrain on which to develop. Progressively land, labor, and products were turned into commodities. The wide open lands from the Atlantic to the Pacific became subdivided into individually owned properties for purchase and sale on real estate markets. A labor market of employees grew as it became less possible to gain livelihoods in any other way than to sell one's own labor to employers. Overall the economic culture shifted from producing one's own to buying needed goods and services.

As land, labor, and goods and services became commodified, capital accumulated and became more concentrated and centralized in fewer hands. Large businesses grew at the expense of smaller ones. By the end of the nineteenth century, what had been an economy of owners of small farms, stores, and workshops had been transformed into one in which large corporations dominated and would progressively squeeze out the smaller actors.

But as favorable as the terrain was in the United States for capitalist development, there were key obstacles in its path: not only did Indians and Mexico control needed lands but the southern political economy based on slavery, while important for early capitalist development, proved to be an obstacle to its further development. Elimination of those obstacles required the violent expropriation of Indian and Mexican lands and the northern victory in the 1861-65 Civil War, the most costly war in the nation's history.

Violent Expropriation of Indian Land

After the War of Independence, the new U.S. military was mainly preoccupied for the next eight decades, apart from the 1812 and Mexican wars, with pushing Indians westward in order to free up their lands for European settlement and market-oriented farming.

The British policy of limiting westward expansion of the colonies had won the support of most of the East Coast Indian tribes, who sided with the loyalist cause in the War of Independence.[1] The subsequent victory of the revolutionary army had disastrous consequences for them. The policy of the newly independent United States was to remove all barriers to further westward expansion. Because of having sided with the British in the War of Independence, the East Coast tribes could not expect favorable policies from the new U.S. government or treatment from its military.

It is significant that from the beginning of its existence, the U.S. military generally fought alone as an institution against various Indian enemies. Unlike the French and British, who formed military alliances with whole tribes, the U.S. military generally only fought with individual Indians, who had either betrayed their own tribes in time of war or were mercenaries.

In the first decade of the nineteenth century, Tecumseh, a Shawnee chief, formed the largest organized resistance to the policy of driving Indians westward. His confederacy of tribes carried out raids against the expanding white settlements, especially in the border areas of Ohio, Kentucky, and Tennessee. Many in the United States accused Britain of financially backing Tecumseh's campaigns. This, coupled with incidents caused by the British policy of boarding U.S. vessels in the high seas in search of deserters, led President James Madison, on July 1, 1812 to declare war on Britain.

The United States had two objectives in the War of 1812. The first was to eliminate Indian military resistance in the east, where most Indians continued to ally themselves with the British as they had during the War of Independence. The second was to drive Britain from the North American continent and take over its last holdings in the area that later became Canada. In pursuit of these objectives the U.S. military had to fight simultaneously against the British army, Indian armies, and Canadian civilian soldiers defending their border.

The United States was able to accomplish the first objective of eliminating Indian military resistance in the east. In 1813, Tecumseh was killed in battle, and subsequently his confederacy and Indian military resistance collapsed. The United States failed, however, to accomplish its second objective to expand its borders northward. U.S. leaders had counted on Canadians joining with them to overthrow British control, but that failed to materialize as most Canadians remained loyal to the Crown. They were not won over by U.S. arguments that being annexed to their southern neighbors would be good for them. William Hull, the U.S. commander at Detroit, sought the support of the Canadians, proclaiming, "You will be emancipated from tyranny and oppression and restored to the dignified station of freedom."[2] Hull's proclamation fell on deaf ears. No Canadians crossed over to his side, leading him to surrender without firing a shot to a superior British force significantly backed up by Indian allies. The successful defense of its territory in the War of 1812, significantly aided by Indian forces, was an important event in consolidating Canadian national identity.[3] It also led to Indians generally faring better, though not without serious problems, in Canada than in the United States.

With the last serious Indian resistance in the east quashed, the United States proceeded with its policy of pushing Indians westward. President Andrew Jackson's Indian Removal Act of 1830, which specified that all Indians should be moved west of the Mississippi River, consolidated the policy. Among the many atrocities it touched off was the forced march in 1838 of 14,000 Cherokees from Georgia to Oklahoma, during which 4,000 died.[4] After the Indian Removal Act several thousand Indians escaped to Canada and took up permanent residence.[5]

By the 1840s the location of Indian resistance and wars had thus shifted from the east to west of the Mississippi. The U.S. military took over from Mexico in 1848 the job of pacifying the southwestern Indians that had been initiated 300 years earlier by the Spanish and succeeded in less than four decades. It fought, at one time or another, against all of the major band societies — Apaches, Navajos, Comanches, and Utes.[6] Seasoned Mexican and Indian recruits joined in its campaigns, significantly contributing to its successes.[7] In 1886, Geronimo, the last of the Apaches' warrior chieftains, was captured and, along with his followers, imprisoned, ending the Indian wars in the United States. The last of the imprisoned Apaches was not released from Fort Sill, near Lawton, Oklahoma, until 1912. A number of other Apaches, who escaped imprisonment, took to the hills, made their way to Sonora, and integrated themselves into the Yaquis — the origin of Apache names among a number of Yaquis today.

Although 1886 marked the end the Indian wars per se, it was not end of military repression. In the northern plains the Sioux had resisted white encroachment on their lands up through the 1870s, culminating in the 1876 Battle of Big Horn, in which they defeated General George Custer's army. After that, their warriors dispersed into smaller bands, which the army systematically tracked down and defeated. In December 1890, a cavalry division of the U.S. Army entered the Pine Ridge, South Dakota reservation and massacred 300 Sioux men, women, and children at Wounded Knee Creek. This marked the final military defeat of Indians in the United States.

Once Indians were no longer a military threat, various attempts were made to integrate them into the evolving social structure of the country. Policies shifted back and forth between treating Indians as peoples and placing them on reservations, and treating them purely as individuals to be integrated as individuals into U.S. society.

Among the most ambitious and disastrous of the integrationist policies was the Dawes Allotment Act of 1887, which sought to turn Indians into family farmers by subdividing reservation lands, a policy similar, as we will see to what had just occurred in Mexico with Indian communal lands. Some 150 million acres of reservation land were subdivided and turned into the private property of individual Indian families. However, most of the families, who came from hunting and gathering backgrounds, were ill-prepared or unwilling to become farmers. Many quickly fell into debt and were forced to sell their land in order to raise funds for repayment. Other land, which had not been distributed to Indian families, was declared to be surplus and distributed to whites. By 1934, when the Dawes Allotment Act ended, Indians had lost 90 million of the original 150 million acres of reservation land.[8]

Violent Expropriation of Mexican Land
By the third decade of the nineteenth century, Indian resistance had been largely eliminated east of the Mississippi. To the west lay a vast, though sparsely populated and lightly defended, territory belonging to Mexico. Increasingly in the 1820s and 1830s southern planters eyed Texas for expansion of the slave system. East Texas was geographically identical to Louisiana and thus suitable for growing cotton, the South's major cash crop. Increasing world demand for cotton, associated with the growing textile industries in Britain and the North, as well as soil exhaustion of some plantation lands already in production, stimulated the need to find new fields.

Shortly after Mexico achieved its independence from Spain in 1821 the first Anglo settlers, with permission from the new Mexican authorities, began moving into Texas. Most of them came from the contiguous slave South. The Mexican authorities granted permission for them to settle because they saw in them a stabilizing force against Indians. From 1821 to 1836, some 35,000 U.S. citizens entered Texas and quickly outnumbered Mexicans ten to one.[9] They brought their slaves with them and established plantations. By the fall of 1825, there were 443 slaves and 1,800 whites in the first U.S. immigrant colony, which was established by Stephen Austin, the namesake of Texas's capital city today.[10]

The pace of immigration, much of it illegal, from the United States accelerated to the point that by end of the decade there were more Anglos than Mexicans in Texas. In 1827, authorities in Mexico City, concerned that they were losing control over their northern border area, sent General Manuel de Mier y Terán to investigate. In his reports the general confirmed that the growing Anglo presence threatened continued control of the area.[11] In one of history's many ironies, over a century and a half later there would be similar fears about illegal immigrants threatening control of the border—but this time coming from the other direction.

On September 15, 1829, Mexican President Vicente Guerrero decreed an end to slavery, causing panic among the Anglo slaveholders in Texas. Stephen Austin immediately traveled to Mexico City and petitioned for an exemption from abolition for Texas, which was granted reluctantly. Despite the exemption, though, the future legality of slavery in Texas remained in doubt and a worry to slaveholders.

With a majority Anglo population and a frustrated slave economy, the pressures for separation from Mexico grew in the early 1830s. The predictable Texas War of Independence broke out in 1835 and the Anglos, 75 per cent of whom were from the U.S. South,[12] with help from other Anglos who streamed in mainly from the southern states, were quickly victorious. Mexico, wracked with civil wars and other internal disputes, was unable to hold onto its northern territory.

One of the first acts of the new Republic of Texas government was to legalize slavery. Between 1836, the year of independence, and 1840 the slave population doubled; it doubled again by 1845; and it doubled still again by 1850. In 1836 there was one black for every six whites; by 1847 it was one black for every three whites— 38,753 slaves and 102,961 whites.[13] Mexican control had been a dam holding back the development of slavery. Once the dam was removed, slavery expanded greatly in size and density. It is thus no accident that today the overwhelming majority of Texas's black population lives in the eastern portion of the state, where in the 1820s to 1850s a slave economy was established on lands geographically contiguous and climatically similar to the original slave South.

Mexican authorities did not accept the loss of Texas as permanent and made several unsuccessful attempts to recover it. From 1837 to 1839 Mexican agents were active in fomenting rebellions by Mexicans, Indians, and escaped slaves living in Texas. In 1842 the Mexican Army twice occupied San Antonio.

The border of the new republic remained in dispute. During the Spanish and Mexican periods, Texas was a part of the larger state of Coahuila y Tejas. The Texas part of the state began at the Nueces River, 150 miles north of the Rio Grande. The Republic of Texas extended its claim to the Rio Grande while Mexico continued to consider the Nueces to be the border. Between the two rivers lay one of the potentially most agriculturally productive river valleys in North America. Though the future value of what today is called the Valley in Texas was unclear, whether its future produce would flow northward or southward depended on which country controlled it.

The Republic of Texas lasted until 1845 when it was annexed, with the agreement of the Texas authorities, by the United States, which then claimed the Rio Grande as the border and sent troops to make good the claim. The U.S. troops marched across the Valley, fought a series of minor skirmishes, and made it to the Rio Grande, where Brownsville, Texas is today, by early 1846. There they fought their first major battle with Mexican troops and were successful. They pushed southward and within months occupied Mexico City. They remained in Mexico City until 1848, when in return for their withdrawal, Mexico was obliged to sell for a token sum the rest of what today is the Southwest of the United States. The land taken from Mexico amounted to some 814,145 square miles and now encompasses all of New Mexico, California, Nevada, Utah, Arizona, most of Texas, half of Colorado, and small portions of Oklahoma, Kansas, and Wyoming.[14] It represented more than half of Mexico's previously existing territory.

Among the historical consequences of these events was the transformation of Mexicans living in the Southwest into the first Latino minority living in the United States. The problematic nature of their new status in the eyes of their dominators was indicated by Stephen Austin, the early leader of the colonists, who explained the Texas War of Independence as having been "a war of barbarism and of despotic principles, waged by the mongrel Spanish-Indian and Negro race, against civilization and the Anglo-American race."[15] The subsequent decades would see considerable violence between Anglos and Mexicans in the Southwest as the former moved into dominating positions and took over the land of the latter in New Mexico, California, and other territories and states.

How instrumental was and is the Southwest to the economy of the United States? In 2004 approximately 35 per cent of the mining and 26 per cent of the total GDP of the United States were produced there.[16] If those products were a part of the Mexican rather than U.S. economy, the economic differences between the two countries would be considerably less. The objection can be made that even if the Southwest had remained with Mexico, Mexico would not have been in the position to develop it to the degree that the United States did. Nevertheless, even if that had been the case, the United States still would not have been able to develop the economic power that it has today, and its average standard of living would not have been so much higher than that of Mexico. U.S. economic development would not have been the same without Texas oil, New Mexico and Arizona copper, the southwestern cattle industry, and California gold and agriculture.

The Civil War

The United States in the 1850s now controlled the land on which 48 of its 50 states existed or would be formed. Its external borders were essentially in place. However, the internal contradiction between a growing industrial capitalism based on free wage labor in the North and plantation capitalism based on slave labor in the South was coming to a head. The issue was not so much the morality of slavery—though moral concerns fired the ire of the northern abolitionist movement—as it was the purely economic interests of the two different systems. Slave and wage labor capitalism had complemented each other during the early decades of the nineteenth century. Slaves toiled in southern fields to produce cotton that was spun and woven into textiles in British and northern factories. Northern and southern elites had joined together to wrest independence from the British.

By the 1850s the interests of the two elites were diverging. The North was expanding the infrastructure for the marketing of its products and wanted to use the federal government to finance construction of a railroad to the west coast. It wanted preferential access to southern raw materials and tariffs to protect its resulting products from foreign, especially British, competition. The South had little interest in financing a railroad to California since its raw materials went mostly east to be shipped to Britain and secondarily northward. The South with no industries to protect did not favor tariffs, which would only make its imports more costly. The South seceded when it lost control over the direction of federal policy. Because the North saw the southern territory as being an integral part of the country's economic destiny, loss of it would severely weaken its own developmental prospects.

The nation's most costly war in lives broke out in 1861. The northern victory settled the issue, and the United States embarked upon its most ambitious period of industrialization with the active support of the federal government. The Civil War removed the final obstacle, the slavocracy, in the path of the full industrial development of the United States. After the war, the United States was able to rapidly industrialize and move into being a world power by the next century.

Abolition of slavery was a byproduct of the Civil War, which was fought primarily over the issue of the secession of the Confederacy. The Emancipation Proclamation, which President Lincoln signed on January 1, 1863, was designed to create a fifth column in the South. The Proclamation specifically did not abolish slavery in those areas that had remained loyal to the North. Nevertheless, it was soon followed up by other measures culminating in the Thirteenth Amendment to the Constitution, ratified in 1865, which completely abolished slavery.

It had taken two nineteenth-century acts of force parallel to the expropriation of Indian land to prepare the terrain for the emergence of the United States as a world industrial power—one directed against Mexico and the other against the southern slavocracy. In sum, the acquisitions through conquest of Indian and Mexican lands removed two key spatial obstacles to the development of the U.S. economy, and the northern victory in the Civil War removed the agrarian slave system that had been an organizational obstacle to corporate-led industrialization.

The northern victory in the U.S. Civil War insured the end of slavery, but many questions still remained about the future political and economic fate of blacks. There was considerable disagreement among the victors over the exact political and legal status of ex-slaves or freedmen as they came to be called. There was resistance even in the North to granting them the same legal status as whites or allowing them to vote. By 1870, though, the resistance had been overcome and the states had ratified the Fourteenth and Fifteenth Amendments to the Constitution, which guaranteed respectively black legal equality and the right to vote.

Reconstruction (1863-77)

Reconstruction is the period during which the northern victors militarily occupied the South and attempted to restructure its political life and economy. The period began in 1863, before the end of the war, in those areas of the South already under Northern military control and ended with the withdrawal of northern troops in 1877.

Generations of historians have offered sharply different appraisals of Reconstruction. For decades southern and many northern historians interpreted it as a period in which misguided northern policies resulted in great harm and tragedy. This interpretation prevailed largely unchallenged until the 1930s, when W.E.B. Du Bois published a massive defense of Reconstruction's progressive features. Du Bois had been asked earlier by the editors of the *Encyclopaedia Britannica* to submit an article on the history of the American Negro for its fourteenth edition. The editors accepted the article but cut out all his references to the progressive features of Reconstruction since they contradicted the then orthodox view. Du Bois refused to allow publication.[17] In the 1930s a number of historians associated with the Communist Party in the United States also argued that Reconstruction had been an important period of progressive and democratic change.[18]

The northern occupying armies insured that blacks could vote as mandated by the Fifteenth Amendment. As a result, in areas where the former slaves were a majority, they were able to elect mayors, governors, congresspersons, and senators. On the state level they elected more than 600 legislators and 18 major officials, including one governor and six lieutenant governors. On the federal level they elected 16 members of Congress and one senator. The Forty-third Congress (1873-75) alone counted seven black members.[19] During Reconstruction there was more black democratic political participation than in any period before, obviously, or after until the gains of the civil rights movement restored democratic participation for blacks in the South, some 90 years after the end of Reconstruction.

During Reconstruction blacks and a number of white northern allies sought to match democratic political gains with economic gains, advocating breaking up the plantations and distributing the land to the former slaves under the slogan of "Forty acres and a mule." Had such a radical land reform been carried out, the subsequent history of blacks and the South would have been substantially different,[20] but the northern elites never embraced land reform as a solution to the problems of ex-slaves. During the Civil War, large amounts of planter land had been seized by the occupying northern armies. In a number of cases, after the white owners fled, the land was turned over to blacks, with its ownership status remaining ambiguous as they worked it. The issue was settled at the end of the war, in September 1865, when President Johnson, who had succeeded the assassinated President Lincoln, ordered that land be restored to all pardoned owners in the South. Blacks living on that land were then required to either work for wages or leave. From 1865 to 1867 the northern occupying army evicted thousands of blacks from land restored to its former owners.

The reluctance of northern elites to push through a radical land reform for ex-slaves was in part based on what they feared blacks would do. In Haiti and the British Caribbean after the abolition of slavery in 1791 and the 1830s respectively, the ex-slave populations gained their own land and retreated into subsistence rather than market production. Consequently, sugar production plummeted. The same tendency to retreat into subsistence farming occurred in the South during and after the war in those areas where blacks were able to control land. They were more interested in becoming independent peasants than agricultural wage laborers, to the consternation of white elites in both the North and the South.

Many blacks saw the end of slavery as giving them more autonomous control if not over land then at least over time for personal development. As a result, a shortage of black labor developed, according to Eric Foner, "largely because all former slaves were determined to work fewer hours than under slavery, and many women and children withdrew altogether from the fields." Black families were determined "to use the rights resulting from emancipation to establish the conditions, rhythms, and compensation of their work, and to create time to pursue ... personal and community goals."[21] The black quest for increased autonomy clashed with the planters' need for a disciplined labor force, and, through one means or another, white owners sought to drive blacks back "into their places."

White violence against the black population broke out immediately after the war in 1865 with many beatings and murders. In 1866 the Ku Klux Klan, the largest and most violent of the terrorist organizations that sought to restore white domination, formed in Tennessee and quickly spread to other areas of the South. Plantation owners and their supporters made it violently clear that, although now legally free, blacks were still subjected to their rule and domination. Those blacks who thought emancipation meant equality were publicly repressed to teach others a lesson. Thus, at the same time that blacks were making enormous political gains during Reconstruction, a white counterrevolution was gathering steam.

Reconstruction and northern military occupation of the South ended as a result of the Hays-Tilden Compromise of 1876. Rutherford B. Hays was the presidential candidate of the Republican Party, and Samuel Tilden was the Democratic Party candidate. The election was fiercely contested with many acts of violence. Tilden undoubtedly held the lead in the popular vote, but Hays most likely had the decisive Electoral College vote lead. There were large numbers of disputed returns, with rival vote counts being sent to Washington to be decided in the House of Representatives. There was even talk of a new civil war.

The crisis was resolved through political maneuvering and compromises that ultimately ended Reconstruction. First, an electoral commission was established to rule on the disputed elections. The Republicans outmaneuvered the Democrats in the establishment of the commission, which then awarded all of the disputed elections to Hayes, giving him enough electoral votes for the presidency. The Democrats threatened to filibuster in the House of Representatives to block the tally of the electoral vote. It was at this point that Hayes's supporters negotiated an agreement with key southern Democrats: as president, Hayes would recognize the right of the southern states to govern themselves without northern interference in return for the southern Democrats ceasing to obstruct the count of the electoral vote. One Republican commented, as noted by Foner, "the policy of the new administration will be to conciliate the white men of the South ... and niggers take care of yourselves."[22] After assuming office, President Hayes quickly began to withdraw most of the northern troops that were still occupying the South. With that, Reconstruction ended, and the fate of the ex-slaves was sealed for the next 90 years of U.S. history.

What would have happened if the North had pushed Reconstruction to a more radical restructuring of the South rather than allowing the white counterrevolution to succeed? A more radical restructuring would have meant confiscating the property of the planter class and redistributing it to poor blacks and whites alike. If that had happened, then the old southern ruling class would not have been able to re-establish domination as it did. Poor whites would have had common cause with poor blacks, setting a basis for an interracial political alliance. Certainly the North would have had to continue military occupation for decades, and there would have been constant resistance from large numbers of whites. But if Northern elites had been willing to completely restructure the Southern political economy, they could have avoided much of the racial tension that later plagued and continues to plague the United States. But they did not, choosing the easier course of allowing the old southern ruling class to resume control. Rather than struggle at all costs to establish the basis for interracial harmony, they tacitly allowed segregation of the races to be institutionally consolidated.

Segregation

Northern elites had forged a new tacit agreement with their southern counterparts. In return for their national loyalty, the legal edifice of segregation was consolidated. Instead of backing reforms that would have enabled the ex-slaves to compete with some modicum of equality in the postwar South, the northern elites abandoned the initial aims of Reconstruction and gave tacit approval to allowing the old plantation owners to reassert control and re-subordinate blacks in the class structure.

With the northern troops withdrawn, the ex-slaves were left defenseless as the white counterrevolution triumphed, dismantled the institutions of Reconstruction, and restored white supremacy. All ex-slave claims to the land became moot. Whites rapidly re-established control over local and state governments and disenfranchised blacks. They instituted segregation of the races in education, eating establishments, hotels, and public transportation as a legal principle. White vigilante groups, such as the Ku Klux Klan, employed terrorist means, including lynchings, to enforce white control.

The terrorism had a number of classic sociological elements. It took place mostly in small rural towns whose traditional code of class and racial relations was being threatened. It was employed by a ruling class to intimidate and drive back into a subordinate position a rural lower class that had sought and temporarily enjoyed limited upward mobility. It was employed in an exemplary fashion in the sense that lynchings were carried out publicly with the victims left hanging as examples to other blacks of what could happen to them if they too stepped out of line. Most often local law officials took part unofficially in white vigilante actions.[23]

The legal basis of segregation in education was confirmed by the 1896 *Plessy v. Ferguson* decision, which established that education could be separate for the races as long as it was equal. A type of domestic apartheid thus existed from the end of Reconstruction in 1877 until the 1950s and 1960s when this legal structure was dismantled. It would be a mistake to believe that segregation existed only in the South. Northern establishments generally followed the southern lead. In the 1920s in New York City it was common for fashionable midtown restaurants to refuse service to blacks. The U.S. military fought in World Wars I and II with separate white and black companies. The principle of segregation even applied to blood, with blood drawn from blacks and whites being kept in separate banks.

Orderly Expropriation in Canada

What is striking about Canadian economic history is its relative absence of obstacles to capitalist development. There were problems to be overcome, but none as formidable as those that confronted the United States. It required no war of independence to allow a domestic bourgeoisie to accumulate capital. Canada was after all created by the colonial subjects of British America who did not go along with the War of Independence that created the United States, and its population was significantly increased by loyalists who fled north after the war. Even today Canada retains some colonial, albeit essentially symbolic, ties to Britain.

Once the British Crown, through its victory in the French and Indian War, secured control of all of the areas that would become Canada, its policies dictated how Indian issues were to be handled. As indicated earlier, the most important of those policies was the Royal Proclamation of October 7, 1763, which established the principle that governed all future expropriations of Indian lands: they would be open for settlement after treaty negotiations and Crown purchase *before* European settlers could establish farms on them.[24] The lands could not simply be taken as they would be later in the United States, and settlement proceeded peacefully. At the same time, the treaties divided off non-alienable lands or reserves on which the Indians could continue their traditional hunting and gathering. That principle was continued by Canadian authorities after the British North America Act established home rule in 1867. Thus, as Canada expanded from east to west in the nineteenth century, its new territories were occupied relatively peacefully. Unlike in the United States, Canada fought no large-scale wars against Indians. For that reason and general cultural reasons the Canadian frontier experience was significantly less violent than that of the United States.[25]

Between 1871 and 1910 the Canadian government, continuing the principle of the Royal Proclamation of 1763, opened up the country to westward expansion by negotiating ten major treaties with Indians in what were to become the prairie provinces of Manitoba, Saskatchewan, and Alberta. The Indians relinquished rights to certain areas in return for being guaranteed rights to reserves. According to Brown and Maguire, all of the treaties had provisions for "reserve lands; monetary payments, and occasionally medals and flags, at the treaty signing; suits of clothing every three years to chiefs and headmen; yearly ammunition and twine payments; and some allowance for schooling."[26] The experience in British Columbia was slightly different. There, in 1861, three years after it had become a Crown colony, the governor simply identified Indian lands to be held in trust by the Crown as reserves. Unlike in the prairie provinces, no treaty negotiations were involved.[27]

As Canadians moved westward and the government bought land from Indians for orderly settlement, the North West Mounted Police, formed in 1873, set up operations to keep order, enforcing Indian as well as settler rights in the relinquished territories. In sociologist Seymour Martin Lipset's formulation, the law arrived before individuals on the Canadian frontier, while individuals, embracing a strong cultural preference for individualism, arrived before the law on the U.S. frontier. The lynch mobs, vigilantism, and Indian massacres that were so much a part of the U.S. frontier experience were virtually absent during the settling of the Canadian frontier. In the United States the military was almost always on the side of the settler. In Canada, the state militia, in the form of the North West Mounted Police, was much more neutral in enforcing law and order.

Indians knew the difference between the two countries. The Sioux, for example, took refuge in Canada during their wars with the U.S. cavalry. This is not to argue that there were no problems between whites and Indians on the Canadian frontier or that the Canadian frontier was inhabited by European-background peoples without severe injustices being done to the indigenous peoples.[28] In all three countries, the indigenous peoples have suffered severe injustices, but they have suffered the least in Canadian history.

The long-term goal of British and Canadian policy was to transform Indians so that they could be assimilated into the dominant society. Toward that end, they pressured Indians to take up farming and abandon their hunting and gathering economies. In time, large numbers of boarding schools for Indian children were established. Many of the schools were entrusted to religious groups that were more interested in teaching the dominant society's language, values, and religious beliefs than the skills necessary to compete in the labor force. The assimilationist emphasis of early twentieth-century Canadian policy was similar to that of the United States, where boarding schools were also used to break adherence to Indian languages and cultural values.

Marginal Slavery

Canada required no civil war for industrial capitalism to supplant slave capitalism because the latter, while it existed, was never significant. The first blacks were brought in as slaves in the 1600s, with slavery lasting for over 200 years until 1834, when by imperial act the British Parliament abolished it in all of the colonies. Slavery was never practiced on a large scale because the country was unsuitable for plantation agriculture. The slave population most likely never exceeded 5,000 at any one time.

The War of Independence in the United States and the War of 1812 led to an increase in both the free and unfree black populations. During the War of Independence, the British promised freedom and land to slaves who deserted their rebel masters. Following the war, a number of loyalist slave owners fled to Canada with about 2,000 of their slaves.[29] During the War of 1812, the British repeated the policy of offering freedom and land to escaping slaves, resulting in an addition 2,000 blacks entering the country.[30]

By 1834, the year of abolition, there were perhaps 20,000 blacks in British North America. Of these, no more than 50 were slaves.[31] Although Canada allowed slavery to exist until 1834, it considered runaway slaves from the United States to be free as soon as they touched Canadian soil. As a result, at least 10,000 southern slave runaways traveled the Underground Railroad to freedom in Canada.

Estimates of the size of the Canadian black population at the time of the U.S. Civil War range between 20,000 and 75,000.[32] Robin W. Winks considers 62,000 to be the most reasonable estimate, with about two-thirds of these having arrived as either fugitives or free migrants from the United States.[33] Many fugitive slaves only stayed in Canada temporarily, returning to the United States after the abolition of slavery. As a result, Canada's black population went into a century-long period of demographic decline, with the 1961 Census reporting only 32,127 blacks in the country, probably barely half the number in 1861.

Several thousand blacks from Caribbean British Commonwealth countries entered the country before 1961. About half came to work as domestics,[34] but their numbers were not enough to significantly offset the demographic decline of the black population overall.

Tandem Development

Though no civil war was necessary to unleash industrialization as in the United States, in large part capitalist development in Canada proceeded in tandem with that of its southern neighbor, one step behind perhaps, but close enough to travel together into the ranks of the First World by the twentieth century. This tandem development was a result of the extremely close integration of the two economies historically. The vast majority of Canadians have always lived within a short distance of the border. As a result, much Canadian economic activity is oriented toward the United States, with the cities of Boston, New York, Buffalo, Detroit, Chicago, Minneapolis-St. Paul, Seattle, and Portland acting as economic and metropolitan hubs.

Friedrich Engels visited Canada in 1888 and was struck by how alike it was to the United States. He viewed the border between the two countries as artificial and "ridiculous," even assuming that it would soon vanish because Canadians would want to be annexed by their more economically vigorous southern neighbor.[35] Though annexation did not occur, Canada's economic development was inevitably pulled along by events to the south. In this sense Canadian capitalist development directly benefited from the nineteenth-century removal of obstacles to capitalist development in the United States.

Frustrated Capitalism in Mexico

Mexico achieved independence in 1821 after an 11-year war. Its colonial period had started 100 years earlier than that of the United States and ended 48 years later. Its colonial stage was thus more formative, and Spanish colonial semi-feudal institutions significantly slowed capitalist development as did the country's demographic reality. Unlike the United States or the area that would become Canada, Mexico continued to contain a large population of Indians who had their own non-capitalist economic institutions.

Indians

Because of their numbers, Indians in Mexico could not be shoved aside quite to the degree that they were in the United States and Canada to make way for white European settlers to take over and develop the land. As late as 1810, at the beginning of Mexico's independence revolution, Indians still made up 60 per cent of the population[36] and had to be incorporated into the base of the post-independence labor force. However, as in the colonial period, not all Indians were willing to accept a subaltern role in the criollo nation-building project.

The vast majority of Mexico's Indian population has lived in the center and south of the country since pre-Hispanic times. Large numbers of Indian farming villages, surrounded by communal lands, dotted that part of the country. Throughout the nineteenth century, as large criollo-owned haciendas grew, they encroached upon these lands and touched off sporadic Indian uprisings, the most serious in Guerrero,

Hidalgo, Morelos, Oaxaca, Veracruz, and Yucatán.[37] Clashes were more frequent in the north, though, despite the area being much more sparsely populated by indigenous peoples. These, since pre-Hispanic times, were nomadic warrior hunters and gatherers, unlike the sedentary horticulturalists of the center and south. Thus, the fighting in the north was not over encroachments on communal lands being used for farming but was triggered by the resistance of nomadic bands to the habitation of their hunting lands by outsiders moving up from the center and south. The Indian problem of the northern frontier dogged the Spanish for the entire colonial period. For example, they were never able to develop stable colonies in western Nuevo México, which then contained Arizona, because the Indians kept wiping them out.

The intensity of Indian resistance on the northern frontier led the colonial authorities to carefully restrict gun trading in the area. By the end of the eighteenth century, the Spanish had achieved a delicate peace, but that broke down in the early decades of the next century. Following independence in 1821, Indian fighting increased in Sinaloa, Sonora, Chihuahua, and Nuevo México with Utes, Apaches, Comanches, Navajos, Mayos, Yaquis, and Arapahos.[38]

The westward advance of the United States contributed to the increase in fighting. In 1821, the same year that Mexico gained independence, the Santa Fe Trail opened between Independence, Missouri and Santa Fe, then in the Mexican north. Increased trade stimulated non-Indian immigration from both the south of Mexico and the east of the United States to take advantage of new economic opportunities. As more people entered the area, they competed with the nomadic Indians for use of the land, and frictions grew. Adding to the problem was the practice of newly arrived U.S. citizens of trading guns for property that Indians had stolen from Mexicans. The effect was both to encourage the Indians to resume raiding and to give them the means to do so. In 1826 the Mexican government formally complained to the U.S. government that the trading practices of its citizens were instigating Indian violence in the frontier areas.[39]

The newly independent Mexican government was ill-prepared to insure order in its northern territories as fighting intensified between Indians and the increasing population of non-Indians. It reacted by developing extreme policies, including offering bounties in Chihuahua and Sonora for Apache scalps.[40] From the 1820s to the end of the Mexican-American War in 1848, some of the sharpest fighting took place in northern Sonora, including the areas that would become southern Arizona around Tucson, as the Mexican Army sought to protect beleaguered outposts of Mexican settlement from Apache raids.[41]

The Apaches were divided into a large number of small bands. Some lived in the Mexican settlements and sided with the Mexican Army in defending them from other Apaches. The Spanish and Mexicans referred to these as *mansos* (tame ones). Most though — the *broncos* (wild ones) — were outside of the settlements, living in nomadic bands that practiced hunting, gathering, and herding. In earlier times they had practiced horticulture, but this was abandoned of necessity as fighting developed with the Comanches in the 1700s.[42] Raiding developed as an important adjunct to the Apache economy. Livestock raided from Mexican ranches could be used for their own purposes or sold to U.S. citizens.

After the 1836 Texas War of Independence and the 1846-48 war with the United States, Mexico no longer had to deal with pacifying the warring Indian peoples within the ceded territories. However, particular nomadic bands, such as the Apaches and Comanches, did not let the new border detain them from raiding on both sides. For that reason, in the Treaty of Guadalupe Hidalgo, which ended the Mexican-American War, Article XI specifically dealt with trying to control Indians who crossed and raided on both sides of the border.

The Indian wars in Mexico continued into the beginning of the twentieth century. Apache raids through the 1880s delayed the development of mining in Northern Sonora. The most sustained resistance in that state, though, was waged by the Yaquis, who staged major uprisings in 1885 and 1895.[43] Unlike the Apaches and Comanches, they were a mainly farming people. As late as 1905 some 500 Yaqui guerrillas staged raids on Hermosillo, Ures, and Guaymas.[44] Even in the 1920s there was still fighting between Yaquis and government troops.

To the criollo leaders of nineteenth-century Mexico, the Indian was not only a real or potential military problem but also a social problem. Most of Mexico's Spanish-descent upper class saw the Indian as backward and an obstacle to their plans for national development. In order to overcome this, they developed a series of cultural, demographic, and economic policies. They were greatly influenced by European, especially French, cultural and liberal ideas and sought to model Mexico's constitutions and other institutions after those of modern European countries. However, the majority of Mexicans were Indians, not Europeans, with different cultural traditions and institutions. Samuel Ramos advanced the hypothesis that the country suffered so much political instability in the decades following independence precisely because its Indian reality was always at variance with the European-inspired constitutions; thus, the reality was always illegal.[45] The policy of Europeanizing the Indian failed to transform the millennia-old culture of most of the population, which continued to frustrate upper-class goals.

If Indians could not be transformed into dark-skinned Europeans, then the next logical solution was to alter the country's racial mixture demographically by encouraging immigration of enough whites so that eventually the Indians would be outnumbered, as they were in the United States and Canada. This policy also failed, however, as most migrants from Europe preferred to go to the United States, where they perceived economic opportunities to be more promising.

From independence in 1821 to Juárez's liberal constitution of 1867, Mexico's landowning upper classes also sought to transform the nature of Indian land tenure. During the colonial period, the Spanish Crown had protected the legal existence of

Indian communal lands, which remained non-alienable properties of Indian villages. That is, they were neither owned by individuals nor could they be sold like private properties, remaining outside of the market and capitalist development in general. The landowning upper classes, therefore, sought to transform them into individually owned properties and the Indians into family farmers as was the intention of the Dawes Act in the United States. Various states between the 1820s and 1860s began the encroachment on the legal existence of the communal lands, and the liberal 1867 constitution completed the process. However, Indians were turned not into middle-class family farmers but into landless peasants. The main beneficiaries were large hacienda owners, who quickly were able to buy up the communal lands. The liberal and well-intentioned expropriation of Indian communal lands helped to set the stage for the 1910 Revolution, one of whose outcomes was to legally reinstate most of them, which in turn created a new obstacle to the capitalist development of rural Mexico.

Landlords and the Church

The hybrid formation of capitalist and feudal features that the colonizers implanted created further problems for future capitalist development. Commodities were produced for, as well as bought on, domestic and world markets. But a significant part of the colonial economy was devoted to non-commodity production (rents, tithes to the church, and goods for household consumption) that was outside of the capitalist market and performed under at least semi-feudalistic conditions. The rural economy was dominated by large landed estates in which landlords collected rents from otherwise largely self-sufficient peasants. Much of agricultural production, therefore, was oriented toward the landlord's traditional household needs or supporting peasant households. There was little incentive to produce agricultural commodities for sale on open markets.

The church was an important pillar of the semi-feudal structure, becoming the largest single institutional holder of land and an important source of credit. It thus controlled enormous economic assets, but it did not manage those assets according to strictly capitalist principles. It was more interested in using them to advance its spiritual mission. The church had the power to orient work and economic activities in general away from the narrow ends of profit-making and capital accumulation.

The visual evidence of the church's enormous economic power during the colonial period is, as mentioned, the large number of aesthetically and architecturally impressive buildings that remain from that time. As in medieval Europe, a small village devoted an enormous amount of voluntary labor in constructing its cathedral. Quite clearly this work was diverted from the accumulation of capital; in other words, the accumulation of churches took priority over the accumulation of capital. Nothing on that scale existed in the British areas, where most Protestant churches were quickly built only to serve their strictly functional purposes of being places to meet and worship; they were not meant to be monuments to the Almighty.

Finally, as in feudal Europe, the colonial church mandated a large number of holy days when economic activities were suspended. There were comparatively fewer of these in the British areas.

The church's economic power was recognized as an obstacle to capitalist development and economic progress in general after independence in 1821. In 1856 the Mexican government took the most important step in curtailing its power, issuing the Ley Lerdo, which prohibited churches from owning properties not used directly in their religious activities. The struggle, however, did not end until the separation of church and state was consolidated in the 1910-17 Revolution. The 1917 Constitution forbade not only church ownership of land and interference in politics but also the wearing of religious clothing by priests and nuns on public streets.

The final blow to church power was delivered in the Cristeros Rebellion (1926-29), in which thousands of Catholics, under the cry of "Viva el Cristo Rey," rose up against the Calles government (1926-29) and its radical anti-religious policies. The Mexican Army defeated the Cristeros in a cruel war. The crushing of the Cristeros rebellion can be interpreted as necessary to end church-imposed obstacles to economic development in the same sense that the Civil War in the United States was necessary to remove the slave system as an obstacle to industrial development. But that would be overstating the parallel. The church's economic power had already been broken long before the war broke out. What it still exercised was political power, and that was what Calles sought to and did break. After the defeat of the Cristeros, the church retreated completely from Mexican politics.

If the logic of capitalist development always won in U.S. history and moved forward without major impediments in Canadian history, in Mexican history it always had to accommodate itself to pre-Hispanic forms of organization and Spanish semi-feudalism. In addition, Mexico's future economic development was further severely constrained when it lost its northern territories, which proved to be the most valuable, to the United States.

The Third Root

Slave capitalism existed in Mexico, but, as in Canada, it was marginal. Only 0.1 per cent of New Spain's population in 1810, at the beginning of the War of Independence, was made up of fully African-origin people, but a much larger and more significant 10.1 per cent was made up of mixed-race persons with at least some African descent.[46] Because slavery was practiced to greater and lesser extents in all of the areas of New Spain, it follows that the African ancestry population exists to greater and smaller degrees in all parts of Mexico today. It is, after Indian and Spanish descent, the third root of Mexican racial identity.

The greatest number of slaves was concentrated in and around Mexico City. Most of their descendants in time interbred with the large Indian, mestizo, and white population that surrounded them. The proportion of slaves to the total population was higher in the tropical flat lands near Veracruz on the Gulf of Mexico coast, where sugar plantations were established. For that reason, there are today more people who appear as blacks in Veracruz than any other part of the country. The second-largest concentrations of black-appearing people are in the mountainous coastal areas of Guerrero and Oaxaca on the Pacific Coast. These are mostly the mixed-race descendants of escaped slaves who made their way to remote areas of these mountains and managed to resist capture. Within 50 years of the conquest, the Guerrero mountains were known as a refuge of escaped slaves. The seriousness of the problem for owners was indicated by the 1579 Spanish policy of mutilating the genitals of recaptured slaves as punishment.[47]

In 1948, Mexican anthropologist Gonzalo Aguirre Beltrán studied the town of Cuajinicuilapa, which is located on the mountainous coast between Guerrero and Oaxaca. Cuijla, as the town was called for short, had been established by escaped slaves in the late 1500s. They had chosen the location because it was isolated and could be easily defended. Over the next 200 years the inhabitants of Cuijla had pushed the indigenous population out of the area and resisted all attempts to recapture them. They were thus on hostile terms with both the Spanish authorities and the surrounding indigenous population. At the same time, over the centuries they progressively interbred with the indigenous population. When Aguirre Beltrán conducted his study, the African origins of most of the mixed-race inhabitants were clearly visible not only in negroid somatic features but also in cultural practices that were clearly different from those of the indigenous peoples of the region. The Spanish spoken by the town's inhabitants contained African-origin terms. Women went bare-breasted in public and carried jugs on their heads. The town and surrounding area contained African-origin round huts with conical roofs.[48]

Another root of Mexico's black population came from slaves escaping from the United States. It was a destination for them from 1829, when Mexico abolished slavery, to the end of the U.S. Civil War. While much more is known about the Underground Railroad traveled north by runaway slaves to Canada, there was also an Underground Railroad traveled south and west to freedom in Mexico.[49]

There was a strong anti-slavery sentiment and considerable sympathy for the plight of escaped slaves in Mexico. During the 36-year period from 1829 to 1865, this was one of the major problems in the relations between the two countries. Texas was the key link on the escape route. Before 1822, when the first Texas colony of Anglos was established by Stephen Austin, a number of runaway slaves crossed from Louisiana into the area and established themselves as free persons. After the migration of mainly southern whites into Texas, the area became not so much a destination as a transition point for escaped slaves. During the 1836 Texas War of Independence, a number of slaves fled to the Mexican armies combating the Texans, where they were immediately freed and sent further south in Mexico for their safety. The proximity of Mexico to the slave South was a consistent problem for owners. A runaway slave simply had to make it to the border, and then she or he was free. Even the Texas Republic's first president, Sam Houston, suffered the misfortune of having two of his personal slaves escape to Matamoros, which was just across the Rio Grande.[50]

The seriousness of the problem prompted the slave owners to pressure the federal government to seek a treaty with the Mexican government for the return of runaway slaves. From 1826 to the late 1850s, the U.S. government unsuccessfully attempted to get Mexico to sign a treaty with a provision for the return of fugitive slaves. Because most Mexican politicians and the balance of public opinion favored the abolitionist cause, the government never agreed. To the contrary, the Mexican government, by its antislavery attitude, encouraged an increase in runaway slaves to the country. During the 1850s it granted land in Veracruz and Coahuila to runaways who wanted to establish themselves.[51] In 1858 a slave ship destined for the United States ran aground off the Gulf coast Mexican town of Cabo Rojo. The captain was obliged to unload his human cargo as he sought repairs. The authorities seized and formally freed the slaves under a provision of the constitution that all persons who step on Mexican soil are free.[52]

Estimates of the total number of fugitive slaves who escaped to Mexico during this period vary widely from several hundred to hundreds of thousands. Rosalie Schwartz, who has done the most extensive research on the subject, believes that there were probably several thousand.[53] Some undoubtedly returned after the Civil War and emancipation in the United States. The majority remained. Their descendants are to be found today in the states of Tamaulipas and Coahuila, which border Texas, and Veracruz, which borders Tamaulipas to the south.

Chapter 4

IMMIGRATION

Because Britain, Spain, and France were the major colonizers of North America, they accounted for the original white immigrant stock and cultural practices. For that reason, today, English, Spanish, and French are the predominant languages of the continent, being spoken respectively by approximately 62, 29, and 2 per cent of its occupants.[1] The largest proportions of North America's European-origin or white population continue to be British Isle, Spanish, and French descendents.

Different combinations of these nationalities produced different cultural patterns in the three countries. British immigrants were significant in the United States and Canada but not in Mexico. Spanish immigrants were significant in Mexico, but not in the other two countries. French immigrants were significant in Canada but not as much in the United States and not in Mexico — though French influence, if not immigrants, was great there in the nineteenth century and the country even had a French emperor for a short time.[2] The three resulting countries of the United States, Mexico, and Canada experienced postcolonial immigration differently in the formation of their respective white populations.

European Immigration in the United States

At the end of the War of Independence, more than 90 per cent of the white population in the United States had British origins, and up to 1840 most immigrants continued to be from Britain. Smaller minorities came from Germany and the Netherlands. Thus, from the beginning of the colonial period to 1840, it was a specifically British-origin cultural identity that forged the predominant national identity of the United States. Subsequently, non-British immigrants had to conform to that identity and often felt oppressed by it.

Historians divide non-British European immigration to the United States into two periods. The first, from 1830 through 1882, brought northern and western Europeans — Irish (the most numerous), Germans, French, and Scandinavians. Most of the Irish were unskilled workers and peasants who left their homeland because of the potato famine, which by 1847 resulted in over half a million deaths by starvation.[3] The immigrants arrived in the United States to occupy the lowest rungs of the newly forming industrial working class. The traditional cultural and religious cultural tensions between English and Irish were reproduced in the new country with native-born British-origin whites occupying privileged economic and social positions compared to the Irish immigrants.

The first wave of Irish immigration coincided with the 1845-48 Mexican-American War, and the tensions between the British-origin population and the Irish immigrants played a role in the war. At the onset, a number of unemployed Irish immigrants joined the U.S. Army that invaded Mexico. They entered an army plagued by desertions, which at a rate of 8 per cent was the highest of any war in U.S. history. Among those were at least 200 men, about 40 per cent of whom were Irish immigrants, who, in addition to abandoning their units, changed sides and formed a special unit in the Mexican Army, the Saint Patrick's Battalion. It is the only case of desertion and switching sides in U.S. military history.

On August 20, 1847, the U.S. Army secured control of Mexico City by defeating the Mexican Army, which included the Saint Patrick's Battalion, at the battle of Churubusco. Thirty-five members of the battalion were killed, 85 taken prisoners, and close to 90 escaped. Of the prisoners, 68 were sentenced to be hanged and two to be shot, with 18 of the sentences being later reduced. On September 10 and 12, the U.S. Army hanged 50 of the Saint Patrick's prisoners as deserters and traitors. The members of the battalion who had escaped capture continued to fight with the Mexican Army until the end of the war, with the battalion increasing its size as new deserters joined its ranks.

The example of the Saint Patrick's Battalion, while largely forgotten in the United States or, if remembered, remembered only as a negative example of wartime betrayal, remains firmly embedded as a positive act in the Mexican national consciousness, which views these soldiers as oppressed Catholics in an army commanded by Protestants and who changed sides after seeing the invasion as an injustice. A special public plaque honoring 71 of the *San Patricios* was placed in the Mexico City *colonia* of San Angel in September 1959, near the site of the hangings, containing in Spanish the words, "With the gratitude of Mexico, 112 years after your sacrifice." Each year on the anniversary of the hangings and on Saint Patrick's Day there are public commemorations of the Saint Patrick's Battalion there. There is also a public elementary school in Mexico City named Battalón de San Patricio.[4]

In 1848, while U.S. troops were still occupying Mexico, revolutions and civil wars swept across France, Germany, and other European countries. The German revolution was initially successful but then lost momentum. Repressive authority was restored. This provoked many Germans to leave for the United States where they formed the nuclei of German-American communities in Milwaukee and other cities. The communities attempted to preserve their separate cultural and language identities by educating their children in private schools where German was the lan-

guage of instruction. The schools lasted until World War I, when anti-German sentiment caused their closing.

During the second large period of immigration (1882-1930) the source countries
shifted from northern and western to southern and eastern Europe, including Poles,
Czechs, Italians, Russians, and others. By 1920, a full 13.2 per cent of the U.S. population was composed of foreign-born individuals.[5] As these non-British-origin
immigrants entered the country, they encountered prejudice and intolerance for
their different languages, religions, and customs. They were the butt of jokes and
suffered from derogatory nicknames. Not only were they considered to be culturally
different, up until the late 1890s, they were often considered to be *racially* different.

Both as a result of being outcasts and in order to preserve their own cultural
identities, Irish, Italian, Polish, and other non-British European minorities developed ethnic neighborhoods in eastern and midwestern cities in which ethnic and
class identity largely overlapped. Since ethnic minorities — the Irish and southern
and eastern Europeans — made up a majority of the late nineteenth- and early-twen-
tieth-century factory working class, ethnic neighborhoods were thus, for the most
part, also working-class neighborhoods.

The Polish immigrant experience was typical. By 1914, there were about 3 million Poles in the United States, virtually all living in the East and Midwest. Chicago
in that year was the third-largest Polish center in the world. Polish immigrants saw
themselves first and foremost as a subculture rather than individuals to be assimilated into the dominant culture. Most had come from conservative peasant villages
with the intention of returning home after making enough money in the United
States. The most important institution around which many oriented their social
lives was the Polish-American Catholic parish, where Polish could be freely spoken.
When a large number of Poles settled in a city, the church established a parish in an
inexpensive working-class neighborhood. The parish then drew more Poles, other
nationalities left, and the area then became solidly Polish.[6]

The growing multi-ethnic, not to mention multiracial, nature of the working
class became a source of division that frustrated attempts of organizers to promote
class solidarity in the face of capital. Frederick Engels, who visited the United States
in 1888, was immediately impressed by the immigrant character and consequent
internal ethnic diversity of the working class, which he saw as an obstacle to the
development of class solidarity. First, there was the division between native-born
workers, who mainly were Protestants with British-origin ancestors and cultural values, and immigrant workers, who were mainly Catholics — and to a much lesser
extent Jews — from Ireland and continental Europe. That gave rise to the famous
identification of "real Americans" with White Anglo-Saxon Protestants: WASPs for
short. Second, among the immigrant working class were internal nationality and
ethnic differences.[7] Being culturally Irish or continental European, no matter how
hyphenated with American, or being Catholic or Jewish, no matter how white,

marked one with a foreign identity. To be "100 per cent American" one had to be a native-born WASP: that is, someone with British descent

Throughout the nineteenth and the first part of the twentieth centuries, cultural hegemony in the United States revolved around the values and identity of so-called WASP citizens. Ethnic minorities had to conform to WASP values and images if they wished to be successfully transformed into "100 percent Americans." To look and speak "like an American" meant looking and speaking like a WASP. Hence, within two generations Italians, Czechs, Poles, and other immigrants from other non-English-speaking countries learned to speak English without an accent and correspondingly lost the ability to speak their original languages.

The predominance of WASP norms was so strong that no Catholic was elected president until John F. Kennedy in 1960. Yet, as more Catholics and Jews from Ireland and continental Europe entered, the proportion of WASPs among the white population steadily declined. Today, less than one-quarter of U.S. native-born whites in the United States are WASPs.

The distinction between WASPs and non-WASPs among whites in the United States is most often not apparent to Mexicans, just as the distinctions between whites, mestizos, and Indians among Mexicans are unclear to whites in the United States. In the southwest of the United States, the preferred term used by Mexican-descent residents for their white neighbors is Anglo, which, at this point in history, is a misnomer in terms of nationality, if not culture, for the majority of U.S. whites. In Mexico itself there is also a strong tendency to assume that all whites coming from the United States are WASPs.

In sum, the white population of the United States was drawn from a number of European ethnic and national sources. This cultural multiplicity created an initial barrier to the forging of a unitary national identity. Social scientists and others often evoke the image of a melting pot to indicate how the immigrant ethnic groups were assimilated into the national identity of the country. If we follow the image, the different immigrant groups had their initial ethnic and national characteristics melted down and then they were all blended together to create what today is the national identity, at least of whites, in the United States.

The analogy accurately evokes the pressure that immigrant groups experienced to shed their original cultural identities if they wanted to be perceived as unhyphenated citizens, but it conveys the misleading impression that all national identities were equally subjected to this process of nation-building. On the contrary, those with British ancestry were largely spared the ordeal. The process of assimilation and nation-building in the United States was much more of a process of conformity to the dominant WASP culture than of an egalitarian melting pot.

Anglophones, Francophones, and Multiculturalism
Unlike the United States and Mexico, Canada has maintained and reproduced the

two roots of its original white population and cultural institutions. The rivalry of France and Britain for control over the area that would become Canada produced the original French- and British-origin inhabitants. These never fully combined over the generations to form an integrated identity.

The great importance of the French and Indian Wars for Canada's future is reflected in references to it among Canadian writers as the Conquest with a capital "C." It was a founding formative event that was comparable—if not in scale, then in its cultural implications—to the Conquest, also always written with a capital "C," for Mexico's history. In contrast, there are no capital "C" conquest conceptualizations in U.S. historiography, although there have been conquered peoples.

That Canada was a bicultural country has been assumed throughout most of its history, only recently being supplanted by its current multicultural identity. In 1867, at the time of Confederation, 92 per cent of the population had either British or French backgrounds. The British North America Act recognized the country's bicultural nature by allowing French as well as English to be used in courts and Parliament. French speakers today make up 23 per cent of the population.

While French-descent citizens are a minority in the country as a whole, they make up 81 per cent of Quebec's population, with almost all of them continuing to speak French in the home.[8] The possibility that Quebec might secede from Canada and form its own country has always been at least a latent issue in politics. In 1995 a Quebec referendum on separation lost by the extremely narrow margin of 50.58 to 49.42 per cent of votes.[9]

John Porter, in his study of ethnicity and class in Canada, argued that in Quebec, "because British and French live as largely separate social groups there are two class systems, each bearing the stamp of its own culture. Both French and British have their old aristocratic families as well as their lower classes." Porter was careful to point out that "these two class systems while operating side by side are also firmly interlocked in the economic system."[10] In other words, Quebec contains one overall economic class system but two separate social class systems.

The francophone population in Quebec clearly meets the objective test of being a nationality as opposed to an ethnicity: they occupy a definable territory and continue to speak their own unique language. They practice a unique culture that is different from that of the rest of Canada. They have even established their own separate social class system. As a result, there is a significant political movement that seeks to establish Quebec as a separate country.

French Canadians on average have traditionally occupied lower positions in the labor force and earned lower median incomes than English Canadians: for instance, in 2000 their per capita income was 12.1 per cent lower.[11] The economic differences between the anglophone population in Canada as a whole and francophone population in Quebec have been sufficient to provoke severe resentment among the latter, which at various times has led to violence.

There are two main explanations for the history of this economic inequality. The first is that France's defeat in the French and Indian War meant that British citizens gained privileged access to economic opportunities in the colony. Even if France had become the colonial power, another cultural factor might have affected the extent to which the roles could have been reversed: English Canadians are mostly Protestants, while French Canadians are usually Catholics. Max Weber, in his study of the different roles of Protestants and Catholics in the development of capitalism in Europe, demonstrated that Catholic education prepared students more for humanistic than industrial occupations; for that reason, among others, Catholics were underrepresented among industrial owners and managers.[12] The same observations, as John Porter noted, can be made of Quebec.[13] Even if English Canadians had not had privileged colonial access to economic opportunities, they may have been more culturally predisposed than French Canadians to pursue acquisitive capitalistic occupations.

Carey McWilliams, in his path-breaking history of Mexicans in the Southwest United States, compared their condition to that of the French in Quebec. Both were oppressed minority language and cultural communities within the contexts of their respective countries.[14] The analogy is limited, however, because there is an important demographic difference between the two: the French quickly outnumbered the indigenous population in Quebec and have maintained that majority position to the present. The Spanish and Mexicans, on the other hand, were never the majority in the Southwest—before 1848, they were outnumbered by Indians two to one. After that date, waves of Anglos swept into the newly conquered territories and quickly became the demographic majority.

Largely as a result of this significant demographic difference, Canada and the United States pursued different policies with these respective minorities. In Canada, the French-origin community could easily reproduce its language because it was the majority within a large territory and the issue of possible political separation was real. In the southwest United States, the Spanish-speaking community faced increasing difficulty in reproducing its language due to its minority position and the penetration of roads and television. This has only been partially offset by family ties to Mexico and new immigrants from there. Despite some fledgling attempts during the height of the Chicano Movement in the 1970s to project a separate national identity, there has never been a serious prospect of Mexican-origin people in the Southwest forming a politically separate entity.

Not all of Canada's white population, however, has either directly English or French backgrounds; it has also been significantly increased by migrants from the United States. In 1910 there were 304,000 U.S.-born persons living in Canada, and between 1910 and 1988 a total of 1,601,665 U.S.-born persons took up residence. However, for every one of these immigrants, at least two Canadians left for the United States. There have always been more Canadian-born persons in the United States than U.S.-born persons in Canada.[15]

The other, and more important, non-British or French source of the Canadian white population has been immigrants from Germany, Italy, Russia, Poland, and other European countries. They came in three waves. The first, mainly East European peasants, came between 1896 and 1914; by 1911, they made up 40 per cent of the population of Saskatchewan and one-third of the populations of Manitoba and Alberta. The second wave came in the 1920s; by 1931 the percentage of immigrants in the population rose to 18 per cent. The third wave came in the late 1940s and 1950s. By 1961, it accounted for 26 per cent of all Canadians.[16] Today, approximately 32 per cent of all Canadians and 41 per cent of Canadian whites have non-British or French backgrounds.[17]

The Fathers of Confederation in 1867 recognized the different needs of the English- and French-speaking communities, but they did not contemplate the cultural rights of other immigrants. European immigrants from countries other than France or Britain faced considerable pressure, as in the United States, to assimilate into the dominant Anglo-defined Canadian culture. Thus, according to Palmer, it is a myth that Canada has always adopted a mosaic approach to minorities in contrast to the U.S. melting pot: "Perhaps immigrant groups did not 'melt' as much in Canada as in the United States, but this is not because Anglo-Canadians were more anxious to encourage the cultural survival of ethnic minorities." Quite the contrary, he argues, "There has been a long history of racism and discrimination against ethnic minorities in English-speaking Canada, along with strong pressures for conformity to Anglo-Canadian ways." The same derogatory ethnic slurs that were used in the United States — such as dagos, wops, and Polacks — were also common in Canada, and the Ku Klux Klan, as in the United States, actively opposed new immigrants in the 1920s.[18]

An informal Anglo-conformity expectation thus prevailed up through World War II. The majority of native-born Canadians expected non-English-speaking immigrants to assimilate into an Anglo-defined Canadian culture and shed their original languages and cultural practices. But this view lost favor in the public mind and was replaced by a more even-handed expectation that Canadian national identity would be forged from the merged identities of its constituent groups.

In October 1971 Prime Minister Pierre Trudeau proclaimed Canada to be a *multicultural* country.[19] *Multiculturalism* itself arose in reaction to the assertion of *biculturalism* (English and French only). Canada's policy now is to encourage retention of minority languages and cultural practices in the context of an overall multicultural society. The Canadian public remains, though, yet to be completely convinced of the desirability of multiculturalism.[20] At the same time, as immigration from countries other than France or Britain has increased, there are increasing numbers of Anglophones who see themselves simply as Canadians rather than English Canadians.[21]

A Dearth of Immigrants in Mexico

What stands out about immigration to Mexico is that it was and continues to be so small. The percentage of the foreign-born in the population reached its height in 1930 at 1 per cent.[22] By way of contrast, in that same year, 12 per cent of the U.S. population was foreign-born.[23] Today only 0.5 per cent of the Mexican population is foreign-born, compared to 11.1 per cent in the United States and 18.2 per cent in Canada.[24] On the other hand, Mexico led the world in total number of emigrants between 1970 and 1995.[25] If the United States and Canada are among the world's greatest migrant-receiving countries, Mexico is among its greatest migrant-sending countries.

During the nineteenth century, especially during the Porfiriato (the 35-year reign of Porfirio Díaz, which began in 1877), the Mexican government defined the country as underpopulated and actively attempted to encourage immigration. Many in the white upper classes held the additional hope and racist belief that immigration of European whites would alter the country racially by diluting the proportion of Indians and mestizos in the population. These efforts failed; relatively few immigrants came, and many of those who did migrated later to the United States or returned home.

The New Crossing

The first Asian migrants came to North America, it is important to remember, some 30,000 years ago across the Bering Strait. The facial features of many contemporary indigenous peoples in North America as well as genetic testing confirm that they are Asian descendents. In the nineteenth century a new Asian migration began, this time crossing the Pacific Ocean.

Chinese-North Americans

Chinese laborers first entered North America in the mid-nineteenth century through Pacific Coast ports in California, British Columbia, and Baja California. In all three countries they faced similar economic conditions and social experiences, working originally in mining, railroad construction, and agriculture and then later moving on to service employment as owners of small restaurants, laundries, stores, and the like. In all three countries, they encountered racism and discrimination.

The first wave of immigrants came to California, beginning in 1849, just after the area had been taken by the United States from Mexico. By 1852 at least 20,000 had arrived. Warfare, poverty, and natural disasters pushed them out of China, and the gold rush lured them to California. Most were too poor to pay for their passage. Some obtained tickets on credit, agreeing to pay off the loan on the California side. Once there, it usually took five years of labor to accumulate enough to retire the debt. Others voluntarily entered into contract labor arrangements — a form of indentured servitude — signing contracts to work for a specified number of years in return for the passage. These contracts were then sold to employers, mainly gold-mining companies, in California.

Throughout the 1850s mining absorbed the largest number of Chinese contract laborers in California, but by the end of the decade the mines had been played out. Simultaneously gold was discovered in 1858 in British Columbia and that drew a number of laborers northward, producing the origins of Canada's Chinese population. Later emigrants left directly from China for British Columbia. With white labor in short supply, employers sought Chinese labor both because it was cheap and because it was available. As in the United States, significant numbers of the Chinese originally came as contract laborers, having to pay off the cost of their passage before they were able to keep the full amount of their wages.

In California by the late 1860s, after the mines were depleted, the Central Pacific Railroad became the largest employer of Chinese labor. At one point 90 per cent of Central Pacific workers were Chinese.[26] Canadian employers similarly used Chinese labor to construct the Canadian Pacific Railroad from 1881 to 1885, as Mexican employers in later decades used them to construct their country's railroad infrastructure.

In the early 1860s a small number of Chinese laborers found their way to the Baja California peninsula of Mexico. Most came from Chinese communities already established in California. Many made livings fishing for abalone, which they sent to San Francisco for export back to China.

In October 1871, Cuba expelled a small number of formerly indentured Chinese workers who then entered Mexico through Veracruz, touching off a national debate often couched in racial stereotypes over the desirability of Chinese immigration. From the time of independence Mexico's leaders sought immigrants — but only European immigrants — to populate and bring progress to the country. They did not have Asian immigrants in mind.

In the 1870s in California, after the completion of the railroads, Chinese labor was employed in land reclamation. In that decade they made up 75 per cent of seasonal farm workers in California and 14 per cent of the state's overall labor force.[27] McWilliams noted that it was the availability of cheap Chinese labor that made the development of California fruit production possible.[28] In British Columbia, Chinese laborers were significantly employed in salmon canneries and vegetable cultivation.

By the end of the 1870s with mining in decline, railroad construction over, and land reclamation finished, Chinese labor left the countryside for the Chinatowns of San Francisco and other cities. There it would reform around small businesses — laundries, restaurants, shops, and the like. At the same time, because of the completion of the primary infrastructure of agriculture and railroads, whose construction had sustained high labor demand, massive unemployment descended upon the California economy. California's whites, themselves immigrants, saw the Chinese as outsiders who threatened their economic interests. They felt entitled to the state by virtue of their victory over Mexico, and they were willing to make good their claim with acts of violence against Chinese immigrants as well as the original Indian and Mexican inhabitants. In 1862 alone, 88 Chinese were murdered in the state.[29] In the

1870s, with unemployment on the rise, the Chinese immigrant worker became the scapegoat for the ills of the economy and anti-Chinese agitation accelerated. In 1882 the U.S. government responded to the anti-Chinese sentiment in California by passing the Chinese Exclusion Act, which barred laborers, but not merchants, from entering the country.

One of the outstanding demographic features of the original Chinese communities in all three countries was that males heavily outnumbered females. In 1911, for example, there were 28 Chinese males for every Chinese female in Canada.[30] Mainly single men migrated, and the costs and other difficulties of the long trip from China discouraged married men from bringing family members. Many in this generation assumed that they would make money in North America and then return home to China to start or rejoin their families, an assumption that generally did not work out. The lack of a family unit for most of the early Chinese males encouraged the growth of gambling, drug use, and prostitution in the early Chinatowns of North America. In all three countries a common theme of anti-Chinese sentiment was the association of the population with vice.

The Chinese Exclusion Act sealed the gender imbalance by blocking the entry of family members to join males who had already established themselves in the United States. Anti-miscegenation laws in the United States and Mexico further restricted the possibilities for male Chinese to establish families. As a result, the rates of natural increase of the North American Chinese populations were much lower than average.

Because of the Chinese Exclusion Act, Chinese emigrants now entered Mexico for the first time in significant numbers. Some used Mexico as a point of entry into North America and later crossed the U.S. border illegally to rejoin family and other contacts who had established themselves earlier in California.[31] The majority, however, stayed in Mexico, with many moving on from Baja California to Sonora, Chihuahua, Mexico City, Chiapas, and the Yucatán. They worked at first in fishing; coffee, cotton, and henequen farming; mining; and the building of the railroads. Later they opened laundries and specialized in the production and sale of ice cream. They entered for the most part during the 30-year rule of President Porfirio Díaz, who had a policy of encouraging immigration. Díaz preferred European immigrants in order to increase the white population, but he was willing to accept Chinese.

By the 1880s enough white laborers had arrived in British Columbia to significantly decrease the area's labor shortage. The labor market advantage then passed to employers, and laborers had to compete among themselves for existing jobs. It was in those conditions, as in California, that anti-Chinese sentiment and racism began to build among whites. In 1875, Chinese were specifically banned from voting in British Columbia. By 1885, Canada passed its first specifically anti-Chinese federal legislation, requiring that all Chinese—but not Europeans—entering the country pay a $50 tax.

The balance of Mexican public opinion found the Chinese to be undesirable immigrants. Most Mexicans viewed them, in addition to being non-Christian, as depraved, plagued with sicknesses, and addicted to innumerable vices. In addition, they considered Chinese culture to be completely foreign and unadaptable to their own. They especially viewed with alarm and horror the prospect of intermarriage between Chinese and Mexicans, which they thought would surely produce racial degeneration.[32] Nevertheless, contracting Chinese immigrants solved the problems of employers who needed labor that they considered to be cheap and docile. Thus, the Chinese kept arriving, never in large numbers—by 1895 there were only 1,026 Chinese in all of Mexico—but enough to be noticed.

Immigration increased significantly in the next 15 years. Estimates of the 1910 Chinese population in Mexico range widely between 13,000 and 40,000 out of a total Mexican population of 15,160,369. About one-third of these resided in the northern border state of Sonora, which would become the center of anti-Chinese sentiment.[33]

The 1910-17 Mexican revolution awakened a deep nationalism, which was directed against all foreigners, including the Chinese. This was in large part because the Porfirio Díaz government, against which the revolution was initially fought, had given favored treatment to foreign capital and foreigners, especially those from the United States, for whom the best jobs were reserved in the areas of the economy, such as the railroads, that they controlled. The belief that foreigners were benefiting economically at the expense of Mexicans was one of the indignities that fired the ire of revolutionaries.

Much of this nationalistic anti-foreigner resentment, which was mostly targeted at U.S. citizens, spilled over onto the Chinese who had been modestly successful in their commercial enterprises. Women were often at the forefront of the anti-Chinese campaign during the revolution because they viewed the Chinese as taking away their traditional source of income from washing clothes, sewing, and cooking.[34]

During the revolution, there were outbreaks across northern Mexico, usually by local revolutionary forces, against Chinese residents. The worst incident took place in Torreón, where the Chinese community numbered some 700 persons and contained laundries, shoe repair stores, restaurants, hotels, farms, and a bank. On May 15, 1911, revolutionary troops, led by Emilio Madero, brother of Francisco, the future president, took Torreón. A detachment surrounded a Chinese-owned bank. When two of the bank's employees tried to keep the troops at bay by firing arms into the air, the troops opened fire. The two defenders were immediately killed, and the troops then went on a rampage against the whole Chinese community. By the end of the massacre 303 Chinese and five Japanese lay dead.[35]

In Sonora the anti-Chinese movement was the most pronounced. There, the Nationalist AntiChinese League was founded; by 1916, under Governor Plutarco Elías Calles, further Chinese immigration into the state was prohibited, and two laws were passed to require Chinese already living there to stay in segregated residential districts. By then 100 Chinese had already lost their lives as a result of anti-Chinese violence.[36] In 1919 the mayor of Cananea, Sonora, ordered that all Chinese businesses close and that all Chinese residents, about 1,000 of them, leave the town. The president of the country, Venustiano Carranza, countermanded the order on the grounds that it would harm diplomatic relations with China. Plutarco Elías Calles and Adolfo de la Huerta, both future presidents of Mexico, supported the anti-Chinese campaign in Sonora.

The decade of the 1920s saw a consolidation of anti-Chinese legal measures in all three countries. Canada banned further immigration of Chinese in 1923 and required all Chinese living in the country to register with the government. The next year the United States passed the Immigration Act of 1924, which banned all Chinese from entry as immigrants. In the 1920s every Mexican city with any significant Chinese population also had an anti-Chinese organization. Anti-Chinese committees were especially active in Sonora, Sinaloa, Baja California Norte, Chihuahua, Coahuila, Veracruz, Chiapas, and Yucatán.

The legislature of Sonora in 1923 approved laws that required Chinese in the state to live in segregated districts, prohibited them from having businesses outside of those districts, and prohibited marriages between Chinese and Mexicans. In 1930 the Sonora government prohibited anyone from sleeping on the premises of a business, a measure aimed specifically at Chinese owners who kept their operating costs to a frugal minimum by living above or behind their place of business. Throughout this period Chinese government leaders, including Sun Yet-sen, repeatedly protested through diplomatic channels to the Mexican government about the treatment of its emigrants.

In 1929 the leaders of post-revolutionary Mexico founded the Partido Nacional Revolucionario (PNR), the precursor of the long-ruling Partido Revolucionario Institucional (PRI). The PNR participated in the anti-Chinese movement, including being actively involved in creating an anti-Chinese committee in the House of Deputies.[37]

In 1931 the government of Sonora enacted a series of measures to close down Chinese businesses. Vigilante groups, called *verdes guardias* (green guards) stationed themselves outside of Chinese stores to keep customers out. That same year a number of towns in Sonora, including Hermosillo, Guaymas, and Nogales, began to physically expel Chinese residents, some to neighboring states and others to the United States. On August 2, 1932 police in the border city of Nogales took 58 Chinese to a hole in the fence that marked the frontier with the United States and ordered them to cross to the other side or be shot. The U.S. government then deported them to China.[38] In November 1932 the U.S. government formally requested that Mexico stop forcibly expelling Chinese into Arizona, and the practice ceased. One of the consequences of the expulsions was that a number of Chinese males returned to China with their Mexican wives and children. As a result, according to Hu-DeHart, there continue to be definable Mexican barrios in certain south China villages.[39]

By the end of the 1920s the Directorate of the Nationalist Anti-Chinese Campaign in Mexico claimed that it had 215 affiliated organizations that counted 2 million members.[40] The claim was undoubtedly exaggerated, but it nonetheless indicated that anti-Chinese sentiment was both widespread and organized. However, the campaign never achieved its main goal of having federal anti-Chinese legislation enacted. It did, though, influence considerable anti-Chinese legislation on the local and state levels, and the virulent anti-Chinese campaign succeeded in driving three out of every four Chinese out of Mexico. The 1927 Census found 24,218 Chinese-born residents in the country; the 1940 Census found only 5,848, less than one-quarter, remaining.

During and after World War II the legal situation of Chinese in the United States and Canada improved considerably. The United States in 1943 repealed its Chinese Exclusion Act and in 1945 allowed Chinese to become naturalized citizens for the first time. After the war Asian anti-miscegenation laws were repealed by the states. In Canada, Parliament in 1947 repealed the Immigration Act of 1923. By the 1950s, British Columbia and other provinces repealed legislation that had banned Chinese from voting. On June 22, 2006 Prime Minister Stephen Harper formally apologized for the head tax and issued symbolic payments to living head tax payers and their spouses along with funding of community projects.[41]

Japanese-North Americans

Japanese immigrants first started arriving in California in small numbers, about 1,000 a year, in the 1890s. Hawaii had had a large Japanese-descent population for years. At the time of its annexation by the United States in 1898, some 40 per cent of its residents were of Japanese descent. Most of Canada's early Japanese immigrants only used the country as a jumping-off point for getting to the United States, because if they were subsequently deported from the United States, they would be returned to Canada rather than Japan.[42] The same dynamic occurred among Mexico's early Japanese immigrants. Some 14,000 migrated to Mexico during the first part of the twentieth century. Of these, though, nearly 10,000 stayed in Mexico only briefly and then went on to the United States.

In California, the Japanese took laboring positions, mainly in agriculture; in 1909 they made up 41.9 per cent of the labor force.[43] They encountered the same hostility from whites as had Chinese immigrants. E.A. Ross, a prominent sociologist, argued that the Japanese were unassimilable, worked for lower wages, had a lower standard of life, and were not prepared for democratic values. In 1900 the San Francisco Labor Council sponsored a meeting which urged that the 1882 Chinese Exclusion Act be extended to the Japanese as well.[44] Anti-Japanese riots broke out in San Francisco in 1906. That was the same year that the San Francisco School Board attempted to segregate Japanese with Chinese students in Chinatown. There was tension not only between whites and Japanese in California but also between the

United States and Japan. The Japanese government protested the school board's decision. President Theodore Roosevelt, fearing that the incident was serious enough that it could lead to war, convinced the school board to reverse its decision in return for halting some immigration.[45]

Tensions also grew between permanent Japanese and white settlers in Vancouver. In 1895, British Columbia extended its disenfranchisement of Chinese to Japanese residents. Because of the tensions, Japanese immigrants were one of the targets of an anti-Asian riot in 1907.[46]

In the United States, Japanese immigrants quickly moved out of laboring positions and into small business ownership, excelling at making marginal enterprises in agriculture and commerce prosper. They were especially good at making small farms thrive in large part because they brought with them from Japan knowledge of intensive cultivation, fertilizers, land reclamation, and drainage. They were also able to succeed by running their businesses in exceptionally thrifty manners. Shopkeepers kept living costs down by living on the premises and labor costs down by using the labor of family members, as did Chinese immigrants.[47] By 1941, the Japanese controlled 42 per cent of commercial truck crops in California and produced between 50 and 90 per cent of such crops as celery, strawberries, cucumbers, artichokes, cauliflower, spinach, peppers, and tomatoes. They were the original developers of West Coast berry production.[48]

As in the United States, the Japanese-Canadian community gradually developed unusually successful small businesses in fishing and farming by the 1930s despite continually having to overcome discriminatory laws. Canadian whites viewed the Japanese as threatening their economic interests up through the beginning of World War II. In Mexico also by the 1930s the Japanese immigrants who remained in the country generally established successful businesses in farming and the professions.

Following the December 7, 1941 Japanese attack on Pearl Harbor, all three North American governments interned their Japanese-descent residents, ostensibly for security reasons. On February 13, 1942, President Franklin Delano Roosevelt signed Executive Order 9066, which required that anyone of one-eighth or more Japanese descent be removed from the West Coast to a relocation center. In all, some 113,000 Japanese-descent residents on the West Coast, two-thirds of whom were U.S. citizens, were then gathered at assembly centers for transport to relocation centers in California, Arizona, Idaho, Wyoming, Colorado, and Arkansas. The authorities gave the future internees little time to arrange their affairs before being relocated. Many saw little alternative than to liquidate their small businesses at bargain basement prices. A total of 120,000 Japanese-descent residents served time in these centers.[49] Public opinion largely supported the internment because of identification of the Japanese-descent residents with a wartime enemy, decades of racist hostility, and resentment over the success of Japanese-owned small businesses.

The U.S. government called the camps relocation centers. Their harshest critics called them concentration camps. The connotation of a relocation center is that it is a place to which people are moved after a natural disaster such as a flood or hurricane. The connotation of a concentration camp is that it is a place where prisoners are kept under the most repressive of conditions, as in the Nazi camps for Jews. The camps where the Japanese were interned were neither. To classify them as relocation centers obscures the fact that their residents came involuntarily. To call them concentration camps is an exaggeration. The camp residents were there involuntarily, but they were not routinely abused or harshly treated as were the Jews in the Nazi concentration camps. Essentially, these were internment camps — places where Japanese-descent individuals were interned involuntarily and unjustly for the duration of the war.

German and Italian-descent residents and citizens were interned as well in Canada and Mexico but not in the United States, where only slight surveillance measures were taken against recent immigrants from those countries. Recent German immigrants, for example, could be required to not leave their city of residence for the duration of the war. Schaefer suggests that the Japanese were interned in camps whereas German and Italian-descent residents were not because many of the people involved in designing the internment policy had German and Italian ancestors.[50] The difference between the treatment of Asian- and European-descent residents, who both originated in countries with whom the United States was at war, has often been taken as proof of a fundamental racism, paralleling, in this respect, the U.S. decision in 1945 to drop the atomic bomb on an Asian but not a European enemy.

After the attack on Pearl Harbor, the Canadian government immediately took action against its Japanese-descent citizens and residents. It impounded some 1,200 Japanese fishing boats, closed down Japanese language newspapers and schools, and initiated removal of Japanese living on the Pacific Coast to the interior. The removal process began in the spring of 1942, and altogether some 21,000 Japanese Canadians were removed to towns, internment camps, farms, and work projects, most of which were in British Columbia. The government took over custody of the properties, including land, that the internees had to leave behind. Later, it disposed of them in a compulsory sale.[51]

On December 11, 1941, four days after the Japanese attack on Pearl Harbor, the Mexican government ordered the removal of Japanese residents from its northern border and coastal areas and their internment in the center of the country. The internment order was issued by the Secretary of the Interior, later President, Miguel Alemán, after a meeting with U.S. Undersecretary of State Sumner Welles, who expressed fears that Japan would invade Baja California.[52]

Some 800 families, including Mexican citizens, were interned at centers and camps within cities, such as Mexico City and Guadalajara, and in rural areas in the center of the country. These locations were guarded, though the inmates could leave with permission for short periods of time. Though the Japanese-Mexicans were involuntarily kept in internment camps, their conditions of incarceration was not as severe as those in the United States. The same fate was shared by German and Italian nationals in the country. Mexico thus differed in this respect from the United States.

Once the war ended, in all three countries the ex-internees found that the lands and businesses that had cost them so much intensive labor to develop had been taken over by others. In the United States many who had worked and developed rented lands found that the lands had been rented to whites. Because of their age, they were not able to redevelop farming operations on different marginal lands. In Canada, when the internees were released after the war, many returned to find that their lands had been sold to others and they were unable to restart their businesses. In 1947 a special commission was established by the Canadian government to settle claims resulting from these property losses. Property disputes continued in the Canadian courts until the late 1960s. In Mexico, after the war ended, the internees' rights were restored, and they were allowed to return to the northern areas. Many, however, found that their lands had been taken over by others or that irrigation arrangements for them had been diverted.[53]

Following the war, many of the children of the ex-internees entered universities in all three countries, presaging a postwar shift in the distribution of the Japanese labor force away from agricultural employment toward urban-based professional and managerial occupations. In the 1980s ex-internees in the United States and Canada successfully completed long legal struggles to receive reparations for their unjust treatment during the war. In 1988 both the U.S. and Canadian governments announced that they would pay reparations to surviving internees.

In Mexico, however, there has been no attempt on the part of the Japanese community to petition for reparations. The lack of a similar reparations movement is due partly to the lack of a tradition and basis in Mexican civil law for victims of injustices to receive financial compensation. More importantly, it reflects the cultural reality that Mexico generally does not recognize non-Indian ethnic minorities as having identifiable rights. Members of these minorities rarely confront their society as pluralist pressure groups seeking redress for harms suffered.

What is striking about Chinese and Japanese history in North America is how similar and interconnected the experiences were in all three countries. The Chinese began coming immediately after the United States took California from Mexico and began developing its mining, railroads, and agriculture. In the nineteenth century Chinese entered North America's Pacific ports from Baja California to British Columbia. In all three countries they met antagonism on the part of native-born citizens and suffered decades of discrimination. Japanese immigrants began entering about a half century after the Chinese. In all three countries they moved successively through laboring, small-business, and professional positions in the labor forces, eventually achieving relative economic success. The Japanese suffered uniquely, though, the experience of being involuntarily interned in all three countries during World War II as security risks and consequently lost much of their pre-war gains.

Filipino-North Americans

The first Filipino immigrants to North America may have arrived in Mexico as slaves through the port of Acapulco in the 1600 as mentioned earlier.[54] Since both Mexico and the Philippines were Spanish colonial possessions with regular shipping contact between them, inevitably there was some Filipino voluntary and involuntary migration. The numbers, however, were so slight as to have left no noticeable Filipino presence in Mexico.

Filipino immigration to the United States began in 1903, shortly after the United States took the Philippines from Spain. Up until 1935 some 150,000 migrants arrived. From 1906 to the 1920s most went to Hawaii. Sugar and plantation owners there sent recruiters to the Philippines in search of cheap labor, for which they were willing to pay transportation costs. Most of the early Filipino migrants, therefore, were poor peasants, who were recruited for their agricultural labor abilities and who were willing to leave their homeland because of crushing poverty.

In 1925, after the 1924 Immigration Act banned other Asians from entry, some 45,000 Filipinos moved to California and other western states to fill the consequent agricultural labor shortage.[55] Filipino migration thus moved eastward, as had Chinese and Japanese labor before it, to California, whose growers needed large supplies of cheap labor. McWilliams concluded in summary form that "the history of farm labor in California has revolved around the cleverly manipulated exploitations, by the large growers, of a number of suppressed racial minority groups which were imported to work in the fields." In particular, "the growers, at an early, date, began to look Eastward, to the Orient, and south, to Mexico, for coolie and peon labor."[56]

As with Chinese immigrant laborers, males heavily outnumbered females, 14 to 1, among these Filipino laborers. By 1930 there were 20,000 Filipino West Coast farmworkers, 11,000 service workers in hotels and restaurants, and 4,200 workers in Alaska salmon canneries.[57] There were also a number of kitchen workers in the merchant marines and on U.S. Navy ships. By the 1960s California replaced Hawaii as the state with the most Filipino residents.

The early Filipino population faced the same discrimination as other Asian immigrants. There were anti-Filipino riots in California farm areas in the 1920s and 1930s. In 1937, Oregon enacted a law that specifically forbade marriages between whites and Filipinos.[58]

This first generation of Filipinos continued to play a significant role in agricultural labor force of California into the 1960s alongside Mexican migrant laborers, especially in the formation of Cesar Chavez's United Farm Workers Association. In the 1960s a small number of the children of this first wave of Filipino immigrants entered universities. There were then no specifically Filipino student organizations in existence, but because of a sense of common identity that came from being the offspring of farm worker families, many participated in and socialized with Chicano student organizations.

During World War II a number of Filipinos served in the U.S. Army. In return they were granted citizenship, benefits for ex-soldiers (through the GI Bill) and the right to migrate to the United States. Between 1946 and 1956, some 30,000 Filipinos entered the United States in this fashion to augment the original Filipino-American community.

Filipino migration to Canada did not begin in significant numbers until the 1960s. Economic problems and two decades of the Ferdinand Marcos government's martial law stimulated emigration out of the country. Most of those who entered Canada were relatively highly educated. That and their ability to speak English, the language of the former colonial controller, the United States, enabled them to fare well with Canada's eligibility criteria for immigrants. By the turn of the century approximately 300,000 had settled in the country. Since the 1990s Filipina women have been the major entrants into Canada under a government program to redress a shortage of domestic workers for care giving.[59]

Chapter 5

RACE MIXTURE

The four races—Indians, Europeans, Africans, Asians—that have co-inhabited the North American continent for the last half millennium have inevitably produced mixed descendants, the pioneers of a new synthesis fifth race in world history. These mixed-race individuals now make up one-quarter of the contemporary population of North America. They have become the second-largest racial category and, in a continental sense, the largest racial minority.

Contact between European conquerors and indigenous peoples produced the first mestizos, North America's largest type of mixed-race individuals. Contact between whites—slave owners and indentured servants—and African slaves produced another type of mixed-race persons.[1] Contacts between Asians and whites[2] as well as between blacks and indigenous peoples[3] have produced numerically smaller types of race mixture.

México Mestizo

The origins of race mixture in Mexico go back to the epoch of the Conquest when Spanish males heavily outnumbered Spanish females ten to one. For most Spanish males to be able to fulfill their sexual instincts as well as reproduce they had little choice but to find mates, willing or otherwise, in the Indian population. At first, the mixed-race products of these unions were accepted on equal terms in New Spain. Prejudice and discrimination by the Spanish colonial population against them began to develop only when the number of Spanish female immigrants began to equal the number of Spanish males.[4] Male black slaves faced the same sexual imbalance in the early colonial period. They outnumbered female slaves at least three to one.[5] This demographic situation led them to find mates among the indigenous population and resulted in the birth of mixed African and indigenous children.

Early colonial society generally accepted legitimate offspring of Spanish-Indian matings as occupying the same social status as *criollos*, that is, American-born Spaniards. Illegitimate offspring of Spanish-Indian sexual relations and encounters occupied a distinctly lower status. The term "mestizo" in large part became a synonym for these latter mixed-race individuals and, at least during a substantial period of colonial society, was used as a pejorative. The stigma disappeared only after the 1910 Revolution.[6] Mörner argues that although colonial society developed an elaborate list of categories to represent the infinite fractional possibilities of race mixture, in practice it separated people into five groups: whites, mestizos, mulattoes, blacks, and Indians.[7]

Colonial policy tolerated marriages much more between Spaniards, criollos, mestizos, and Indians than it did between any one of those groups and Africans or mulattoes. Quite clearly, the Crown considered African-descent people to be inferior to Europeans and Indians in this respect and went to some lengths to discourage intermarriage between them. One reason for this was that owners wanted to avoid depleting the slave stock, since the products of such unions would not be born in bondage as would the products of unions among slaves. At various times such mixed-race marriages required special permission from the authorities, whereas mixed-race marriages involving Europeans, mestizos, and Indians did not.[8]

In the nineteenth century many, mainly white Mexican intellectuals viewed the country's growing *mestizaje* — race mixing — both in nationalist and racist terms. They believed that the country was divided between whites and Indians and that this division prevented the development of a unitary national identity. For them, the *mestizaje* represented the merging of the two races into a unique hybrid race that would underpin the country's national identity. At the same time it would serve to eliminate Indian cultures, which they saw as holding back progress. The ideal mestizo, in their view, imbued European cultural values. To further insure the country's cultural and racial Europeanization, as mentioned earlier, they advocated large-scale European immigration. Not only did they hope that what they perceived to be Indian cultural backwardness would be eliminated, one intellectual, Francisco Pimentel, went so far as to predict that "the mixed race would be a transitional race; after a little time everyone would become white."[9]

During the Porfiriato (1876-1911) various estimates placed the mestizo proportion of the population at 44 per cent.[10] By the 1921 census, 60 per cent of the population was identifying itself as mestizo.

Throughout the twentieth century, a number of Mexican intellectuals continued to link *mestizaje* to the country's national identity, though the interpretations of *mestizaje* as an antidote to Indian cultural backwardness or as a strategy for whitening the country disappeared. Instead, intellectuals in the post-revolutionary era of the 1920s and 1930s saw *mestizaje* in positive terms as a source of national strength and pride. José Vasconcelos (1882-1959) is the best known of these Mexican intellectuals.[11]

Vasconcelos wrote *La Raza Cósmica* (The Cosmic Race) originally as an essay in 1925. For most of world history, he argued, the four races — whites, blacks, Asians, and Indians — developed separately because they lived in geographic isolation from each other. The colonization of the Americas brought them together, and they began to combine through *mestizaje*. In Vasconcelos's words, the Americas were predestined in world history to "construct the nest of a fifth race founded from all of the peoples to replace the four that in isolation have been forging history." In even more Hegelian-like prose he maintained that "the hidden (ulterior) end of history is to achieve the fusion of all peoples and cultures."[12]

Vasconcelos, a critic of the cultural values of Anglo-America, noted acerbically that Anglo-Saxons in the Americas had been the reactionaries in this inevitable development by abhorring *mestizaje* and seeking to preserve the so-called purity of their race.[13] Latin Americans, on the other hand, had been in the world historical vanguard by embracing *mestizaje*. It was no accident therefore that Vasconcelos as rector of the Universidad Nacional Autónoma de México inaugurated the slogan that continues to appear on all official documents today: "*Por mi raza hablará el espiritu*" ("Through my race the spirit will speak").

Nevertheless, during the same period that Vasconcelos was promoting race mixture and Mexican revolutionary nationalists were celebrating *mestizaje*, the rampant anti-Chinese sentiment mentioned in the previous chapter incited pressure to ban marriages between Mexicans and Chinese. After the state legislature of Sonora outlawed such intermarriage in 1923, a Chinese man who was found with a Mexican woman was jailed; in 1926 a Chinese man was prohibited from marrying a Mexican woman; and in 1928 the authorities, citing the 1923 law, annulled the six-year marriage of a Chinese man and Mexican woman. The town council of Fronteras, Sonora, lamented that "it is positively distressing to see walking though the streets children with yellow skin and oval eyes, products of marriages of Mexican women with Asians. These children appear in a sickly state, an evident demonstration of the degeneracy of the race."[14]

The horror with which some Mexicans viewed *mestizaje* with Asians notwithstanding, the particular form of *mestizaje* between Spanish and Indians is the reality by which the country identifies itself. But not everyone has seen it, like Vasconcelos, as necessarily being a source of strength, racial or otherwise. Other Mexican intellectuals have seen it as contributing to a sense of inferiority, divided psychological complex, and self-denigration, with mestizos feeling ashamed of the Indian part of their identity. According to Ramos, the birth of Mexico was a traumatic encounter—the Conquest—in which a small minority of Spaniards set out without success to Europeanize a much larger indigenous population. By continually holding the unachievable goal of Europeanizing Mexico, they insured that they would always feel a sense of failure and inferiority for three reasons: first, the Spaniards were racially absorbed through *mestizaje*; secondly, they lost their identity as Spaniards; and thirdly, they destroyed the value of the indigenous cultures. The result was to create a national character that could never be satisfied with what it was. Ramos thus implied that the exaltation of European and depreciation of indigenous cultures created, in individuals who biologically incorporated genes from both, a sense of inferiority and self-denigration that was based on *autoracism*, that is, racism turned inward.[15]

Octavio Paz, in his exceptionally influential *The Labyrinth of Solitude*, argued that a deep-seated conflict related to *mestizaje* rested at the base of the Mexican national character. In the minds of most Mexicans, the original *mestizaje* resulted from Spanish conquerors raping indigenous women. Mexico's *mestizaje* thus descended from an act of violence about which mestizos have mixed feelings.

Hernán Cortés and Doña Marina, La Malinche, represent the symbolic father and mother of Mexico. Their son, Martín Cortés, was the first mestizo. If Hernán Cortés represents strength, *el machismo*, and violent imposition, La Malinche, in contrast, represents the victim and, more importantly, betrayal, since she aided the Spanish in the Conquest. Neither the symbolic father nor the mother is a positive figure, since the one represents foreign domination and the other betrayal. To their symbolic descendants, according to Paz, the two "are symbols of a secret conflict that we have still not resolved." That conflict is that "the Mexican does not want to be either an Indian or a Spaniard. Nor does he want to be descended from them. He denies them. And he does not affirm himself as a mixture.... "[16]

Whatever the truth of Paz's interpretation as a characterization of all or even most Mexicans—an interpretation which Bartra and others dispute[17]—it is widely believed to be true and hence forms a part of the national culture. That Paz's account may have contributed to the formation of the stereotypes of the Mexican male as having a *macho* exterior that masks an inferiority complex and of the Mexican female as being long-suffering does not mean that it is necessarily invalid. For it to be so widely accepted, as it has been, indicates that it struck a truth. Stereotypes, as suggested by Emile Durkheim, are by definition exaggerations and falsifications, but they are nonetheless real if they enter into the collective consciousness of a people as social facts.[18]

Mestizaje continues to be the driving force of Mexico's racial identity. At one point all Mexican third graders read in the social sciences textbook provided by the Department of Public Education that during the colonial period, "indigenous people and Spaniards interrelated and from them mestizos were born, from whom we Mexicans are descendants today."[19]

The Canadian Métis

The roots of Métis identity go back to the period of French rule and the frontier fur trade. French men took Indian wives or were otherwise involved in sexual relationships. By 1760, when French rule ended, the mixed-race offspring of these encounters were numerous enough to have established noticeable communities in the Upper Great Lakes region. By the end of the eighteenth century, there were other large Métis communities in what are now Manitoba and Saskatchewan on the western prairies.

Canadian Métis thus are virtually identical racially to Mexican mestizos. Both populations are the products of encounters between Europeans and Indians, and the

European origins of the entire Mexican mestizo and the majority of the Canadian Métis populations were the contiguous Latin countries of Spain and France.

There are, though, sharp cultural differences between these populations despite their common racial background. In Mexico mestizos are the majority; in Canada they are a small minority. In Mexico, this majority position resulted from Spanish settlers entering the region of North America that was the most densely populated by indigenous peoples. Spanish settlers and their criollo descendants would never gain numerical superiority over the indigenous population. In time, sexual encounters between the Spanish and Indians developed, resulting in a certain percentage of mestizo offspring. In time, mestizos became the majority.

The same process occurred in Canada but in different demographic conditions and with different results. French and British settlers entered areas that were sparsely populated by indigenous peoples. Sexual encounters and mixed offspring resulted, but French and British migrants quickly outnumbered them. The European-origin population was eventually so much larger than the indigenous population that it had enough of a base to maintain its separate racial identity throughout succeeding generations. Unlike in Mexico, the mixed population became marginalized as a minority and much more subjected to cultural racist-tinged oppression. Although "Métis" is the most acceptable term for this population today, until the early twentieth century it was common for the majority British-origin population and the Métis themselves to use the terms "half-breeds," as in the frontier United States, and "half-castes."

In the nineteenth century, particularly in the Red River colony, where Winnipeg, Manitoba is now, the Métis first began to see themselves as a people with a distinct national identity. Because that identity was formed first from the mixed-race offspring of French and Indian encounters, it had a strong French component, but later it embraced the mixed-race offspring of British and Indian encounters as well.[20] The Métis dominated the buffalo hunt, were fur trappers, transported goods, and acted as interpreters between whites and Indians on the western Canadian prairies. On different occasions they fought against Sioux and Canadian government troops, proving that they truly occupied a separate position from either one.

Métis identity as a separate racial and cultural group reached its zenith in the last half of the nineteenth century with an attempt at national secession. Increasing white settlement, the end of the buffalo hunt, and the development of railroad links to the east were undermining the Métis economy. Métis leaders, most importantly Louis Riel, concluded that the wealth produced by them in their area was being expropriated by eastern Canada and Britain. To end the expropriation, Riel advocated overthrowing the territory's colonial powers and establishing an independent republic that would be able to maintain control over its economy.

There were two Métis rebellions. In 1869 the British government arranged for the Hudson Bay Company, which controlled the Red River colony, to sell out its rights and transfer control of the area to the new Dominion government of Canada. This was done without consulting the Métis. Under the leadership of Riel, the Métis organized and demanded representation in the transfer of power. In October 1869 they set up barricades and successfully blocked the entry of the designated governor into the territory, forcing him to withdraw into U.S. territory. The Dominion government chose to negotiate with the National Métis Committee. As a result, Riel and the Métis insured redress for their grievances in the Manitoba Act of 1870, which created Manitoba as a province in the Confederation. The Dominion government also set aside a 1,400,000 acre land grant for the Métis in which each family was allotted 160 acres.[21]

In the 1880s, conflict between the Métis and the Canadian government emerged again, this time to the west in the North-West Territories, where Saskatchewan is today. Many Métis had moved there from Manitoba. A number had sold their interests in the land grant to retire debts and were landless. Others simply sought to escape the advance of eastern settlers. Declining economic conditions, which they blamed on increasing non-Métis settlement and competition to their freight business from the railroad, had squeezed their living conditions. They enlisted the aid of Riel, who returned from Montana, where he had been living. He believed that the solution to their problems lay in self-determination, which could only be achieved through secession from Canada. Riel's program of national independence attracted some Indian and white as well as Métis support.

In order to secure independence, which the Dominion government was not willing to grant, Riel and Gabriel Dumont formed a Métis military force. The newly formed North West Mounted Police, in conjunction with a contingent of Canadian soldiers, put down the rebellion after several battles. Riel was captured, tried, convicted of treason, and hanged in 1885.

The thorough defeat of the 1884 rebellion sent the surviving Métis scattering throughout western Canada, never again to pose a serious threat to national authority. In historical retrospect, the rebellion represented the last obstacle to Canada's expansion to the Pacific as a unified national territory and was disastrous for any further development of Métis national self-determination and autonomy.

By the 1950s over 80 per cent of Métis descendants had fully integrated into white Canadian society.[22] A smaller group maintains a separate identity and some have assimilated into Indian bands and live in their reserves.

Racially Mixed and Socially Black in the United States

The history of biracial blacks and whites in the United States begins with the seventeenth-century founding of the Chesapeake colonies, Virginia and Maryland. The first mixed-race offspring came probably from encounters between black slaves and white indentured servants, who initially outnumbered slaves in the colonies three to one.[23] Soon after, the more known pattern of relations between slave owners and slaves developed.

The physical structure of the plantation economy encouraged close daily contact between slave owners, their sons, and slave women. In such conditions, chance and long-term cross-racial sexual relations developed. In addition, the patriarchal structure of plantation households additionally favored such relationships. The owner almost always had a white legal wife who bore legitimate heirs to the property. But if that relationship was not sufficient to satisfy his sexual or emotional needs, there was little to stop him from also maintaining a compensatory relationship with a female slave. A substantial number of cross-racial sexual encounters also occurred between poor whites and slaves, but as Joel Williamson concluded, "by far the most dramatic and the most significant portion [of miscegenation] was between upper-class white men of the slave holding class and mulatto slave women engaged in domestic service."[24]

The plantation household was similar in this respect to the feudal landlord households of medieval Europe and parts of Latin America. In each it was assumed that the owner and his sons had as a right of property sexual access to the dependent population, be it serfs or slaves. In Mexico, the landlord had the "right of the first night." When peasants on his estate married, he, rather than the husband, had the right to sleep with the bride for the first night. For that reason, in many cases the first child of the peasant couple was often the offspring of the landlord. In the South, there was no traditional recognition of a "right of the first night" but a kind of right of any night. The result was the same, with many of the children of slave couples being the offspring of owners.

Cross-racial sexual encounters and offspring also occurred in the British, Spanish, and French Caribbean colonies, but they were viewed differently. There, during the early stages of the development of plantation economies, both white males and imported female slaves heavily outnumbered white females. For that demographic reason, white plantation owners frequently engaged in cross-racial sexual relations and encounters that led to the birth to mixed-race children. From the beginning the practice and its result thus became an accepted pattern of Caribbean society as it was for planters to recognize, free, and provide for the education of their mixed-race offspring.

The situation was different in the U.S. South, where this marked imbalance between while males and females in the planter class did not exist. Cross-racial sexual encounters between plantation owners and slave women certainly occurred, but their existence was frowned upon from the beginning. Thus, in the Caribbean race-mixing occurred openly, but in the South it was always an underground phenomenon. No cultural pattern developed for plantation owners to accept responsibility for their mixed-race illegitimate children, who were considered to be undifferentiated members of the slave class.[25] White males from the southern planter class could, more easily than those from the Caribbean planter classes, take an irresponsible attitude that they were simply spreading wild oats among the slave class.[26] By the end of the seventeenth century, a substantial biracial population had developed in a number of areas of the South. The majority were slaves. In a minority of cases plantation owners manumitted their biracial offspring; these manumissions provided most of the populations of the early freed-slave communities.

In 1860, on the eve of the Civil War, the U.S. Census found that over three-quarters of free persons who had been or were descended from slaves were mixed race. At the same time, though, 88 per cent of the people that the census takers thought had visible evidence of being mixed race were still slaves.[27] Thus, throughout the period of Southern slavery, although mixed-race persons were more likely to be free, the vast majority were still enslaved. For the most part mixed-race persons who were free viewed themselves as having an identity that was neither black nor white. It was only later in U.S. history that their identity was merged with that of blacks. Separate mixed-race identities developed the most in those areas that had been more related culturally to the Caribbean and Latin America than to the rest of the South.

South Carolina was settled by planters from the British West Indies who brought with them their cultural values regarding race mixing. In 1850 about one-quarter of the population of South Carolina's capital, Charleston, was composed of mixed-race persons that included a small elite of educated, rich slave owners. Whites in South Carolina tended to view mixed-race society more as a kind of shadow of their own society than as being attached to slave society. They accepted mixed-race persons as having an in-between status closer to their own than that of black slaves. Mixed-race persons thus occupied a position that was dramatically better than that of black slaves and almost as privileged as that of whites. It is not surprising that they were, in general, allies of whites rather than blacks.

Louisiana before becoming a part of the United States in 1807 had been a possession alternately of Spain and France. The proof that a separate legal identity for mixed-race persons existed in Louisiana was that in 1808 its Civil Code prohibited "free people of color" — that is, biracial persons — from marrying either whites or blacks.[28] There were 14,083 free biracial persons in Louisiana in 1850. A small number of these were slave owners themselves, with some owning as many as 100 slaves. The New Orleans biracial community operated its own schools and churches. Biracial persons participated significantly in the building trades and the cigar industry and as barbers and tailors.[29]

In addition to being culturally linked to the Caribbean and Latin America, South Carolina and Louisiana were also located in the black belt South where the slave population was densest. In those demographic conditions, the development of an in-between identity for free mixed-race persons, known as "mulattoes," as a buffer group between whites and blacks, helped to protect the slave system. In the 1820s a legislative committee that had investigated the Denmark Vessey insurrection in South Carolina concluded that mulattoes were "a barrier between our own color and that of the black — and, in cases of insurrection, are most likely to enlist themselves under the banners of the whites."[30]

Thus at first mulattoes had a unique social identity that was different from those of either whites or blacks — the term "mulattoe" appears in many writings in the United States up through the nineteenth century. But by the end of that century, they were considered to be undifferentiated members of the black population. Part of the reason for the shift was the erasing of the distinction between free and slave biracial persons. The separate biracial in-between position had been most pronounced among the small minority of persons who had lived in free conditions before abolition. The end of the slave system ended their special position as well.

Part of the shift in perception, though, arose in the 1850s before the Civil War from a more directly economic reason. In the early nineteenth century, the importance of slavery to the southern economy grew with the Industrial Revolution and its need for cotton as a raw material. Mills in Britain and the North, employing free workers, spun the cotton planted and picked by slaves in the South. The Industrial Revolution enabled textiles to become a mass industry, thereby dramatically increasing the demand for southern cotton. The southern slave economy thus rode on the crest of the Industrial Revolution with an increasing need for slaves. At the same time, slavery spread westward into Texas, which had been seized from Mexico. The increasing demand for slaves, who could no longer be legally imported after 1808, drove many plantation owners to blur the distinction between mixed-race and black persons. If mixed-race persons were no different than blacks, then there was no legal, moral, or other reason for them to be freed. They could, without qualms, be considered as undifferentiated members of the slave labor force whose economic importance grew with the demand for cotton.

The mixed-race elites in Charleston and New Orleans maintained their alliances with whites at the beginning of the war, even to the point of offering to serve in the Confederate Army and raising funds for the families of its active soldiers, but by the end of the war, all had shifted their allegiances to the Union cause.[31] Other free mixed-race people had moved to the North and served in its army during the war. At the end of the war, many of these decided to return to the South either to pursue economic opportunities or for more altruistic motives to give professional aid to the ex-slave population as teachers, ministers, doctors, and the like. This movement from the North to the South obeyed the same altruistic motives of the earlier abolitionist and later civil rights movements. In both an ethic of anti-racist idealism moved large numbers of young people to attempt to rectify through their actions the horrendous treatment that blacks have received in U.S. history. The same attitude prevailed among the educated elite of Southern-based mixed-race persons.

During Reconstruction mixed-race persons, largely out of disgust with white racist attitudes, fused their identities with the black population. Williamson argues that they provided much of the leadership of the ex-slave movement during this period: "It was precisely where Negro numbers were high [South Carolina, Louisiana, and Florida] and mulatto leadership most concentrated and aggressive that Reconstruction had its longest and most significant life."[32] The inauguration of segregation following Reconstruction added additional pressure to dissolve the in-between social identity of mixed-race persons. During slavery, whether a particular mixed-race or black person was free or a slave could be easily determined because the condition was legally registered. The goal of segregation legislation, though, was to maintain the supposed purity of the white race by socially separating it from all people of color, biracial, mixed-race, or black. Segregation thus established the Manichean definition that people were either black or white with no space left for in-between possibilities.

In pursuit of their primary goal of protecting the purity of the white race, the southern states, building on prewar precedents, carefully demarcated whites from mixed-race and black persons according to what came to be known as the one-drop rule: a person was black who had any amount, no matter how slight, of African blood. For different reasons the one-drop rule became increasingly accepted by mixed-race and black persons. By the early decades of the twentieth century, biracial persons had all but completely dissolved their separate identities and merged with the larger black community, and after 1920 the U.S. Census stopped distinguishing mulattoes from blacks.

However, mixed-race persons did not merge as undifferentiated members of that community. Instead, a distinct tendency for them to move into the top economic, social, and political positions of the black community was already evident during Reconstruction. In class terms they tended to merge upward. As segregation set in, the upper rungs of the black community became increasingly occupied by lighter-skinned individuals and families. In this sense, skin color corresponded to class position to some extent within the black community,[33] paralleling the same phenomenon among Mexican mestizos.

In the eyes of many in the early part of the twentieth century, the merger of mixed-race and black identities produced a new synthesis identity that was neither black nor biracial. Thus, in the 1930s and 1940s, many of the products of this new identity called themselves brown Americans. Joe Louis, the boxer, for example, was known as "the Brown Bomber." "Brown" indicated that they were neither black nor white since race mixing had produced a new type.[34] It was only in the 1960s as a consequence of the black nationalist and power movements that "black" definitively replaced "brown" as the color adjective. There is, though, no reason to assume that "black" or the more recent "African-American" will remain as permanent labels because, as post-Civil War history as shown, the self-identity of that community evolves and shifts according to a number of internal and external conditions.

There is also no reason to assume that the children of black and white parents will necessarily always be identified as members of the black community. Since 1967, when the Supreme Court ruled all anti-miscegenation laws to be discriminatory and therefore unconstitutional, the number of black-white married couples has increased greatly. With the number of first-generation cross-racial persons increasing, there could well be a questioning of the cultural legacy of the one-drop rule, which is unique in the hemisphere.

Today, at least three-quarters of the population in the United States that is socially perceived to be black is in reality composed of mixed-race persons of European as well as African descent. Some academics, such as Davis, estimate that the proportion of mixed-race blacks may be as high as 90 per cent.[35] The vast majority of all African-Americans thus have at least one white somewhere in their family trees and therefore carry at least some caucasoid as well as negroid genes. Another implication of this biological reality is that a substantial number of whites, perhaps the majority, in the United States are distantly related to blacks. Since most cross-racial encounters took place in the slave South, it follows that most southern Ku Klux Klan members today share common ancestors with, and are technically cousins to, southern blacks. In a similar sense, many of the black belt South's most racist politicians fathered black children. It was revealed in 2003, for example, that Strom Thurmond, the conservative South Carolina senator until his death that year and presidential candidate for the segregationalist Dixiecrat States' Rights Party in 1948, had fathered a child with a black maid.

Chapter 6

ACCUMULATION OF CAPITAL AND DEPENDENT DEVELOPMENT

In his discussion of Canadian economic history, Ronald Manzer concluded that early state economic policy was primarily based on the principle of "appropriation." That is, the early Canadian state encouraged labor force members to develop business activities by appropriating already existing means of production, such as land, waters, and forests. Given Canada's bountiful natural resources, there were a large number of opportunities to start up businesses. Farmers could appropriate already existing land to grow crops; fishers could appropriate the waters; lumber cutters could appropriate the trees of the forests; fur trappers could appropriate fur-bearing animals.

The result, according to Manzer, was an economy based on small units of production in which workers owned their own means of production and were driven by a strong sense of competitive individualism in their pursuit of resource exploitation. The Canadian state's role in the appropriative period was to facilitate "access to natural resources" and encourage or direct "human effort toward their exploitation." Construction of transportation infrastructure (roads, railroads, canals, ports) to facilitate access to natural resources and marketing of the resulting products was the most tangible of the state's roles during this period.

Accumulation of Capital

The appropriative period, in Manzer's estimation, lasted until approximately 1900, when the state shifted to a capital accumulation strategy. Business activity that was based upon capital-intensive — as opposed to labor-intensive appropriative — means of production was now encouraged and supported. The start-up costs of these types of businesses were much higher than those of appropriative businesses, but their efficiency, productivity, and international competitiveness were much greater. This shift, according to Manzer, has been accompanied by three important consequences for the social organization of production:

First, ownership and control of capital is progressively concentrated in the hands of a relatively small entrepreneurial class, and workers become dependent on capitalists to supply the means of their productive employment. Second, small individual business enterprise is displaced by large corporate business enterprise and the organization environment for work is progressively bureaucratized. Third, both the expansion of business enterprise and the dependency of bureaucratized workers necessitate the development of mass markets and the progressive replacement of production for personal consumption by production for mass consumption.[1]

Manzer's description of the two stages of Canadian development could as easily be applied to the economic history of the United States, where small business activity was progressively displaced in the twentieth century so that it occupies today no more than a marginal position in the economy. As late as 1880, 36.9 per cent of the labor force owned their own businesses. Most were farm owners, followed by owners of commercial establishments, work shops, and professional practices. By 1920, the proportion of self-employed slipped to 23.5 per cent — similar to that of Mexico today — and the decline progressed steadily since to just 11.1 per cent in 2005.[2]

As small business ownership declined, corporations and government economic activities increased. Most of the markets formerly serviced by small businesses are now controlled by large private corporations. State-organized economic activities have also increased dramatically in the last 100 years. At the time of the Civil War, public employees were a very small part of the labor force. By 1970, as much as one-third of the labor force was either directly employed by the state as civil servants, teachers, soldiers, and the like or indirectly as employees of private businesses that were financed by state contracts.[3]

There have also been sweeping changes in the capitalist character of the economy. The period following the Civil War was one in which many different corporations fought for control of particular markets. The logical outgrowth of this intense struggle was the elimination of weaker by stronger competitors so that most markets shifted toward oligopolistic control. Blair concluded that by 1970 two-thirds of all local and national markets were dominated in the United States, that is, that the largest eight firms operating in those markets accounted for at least 50 per cent of sales.[4]

As the power and control of large corporations grew, so too did international expansion of their activities. Before 1900, the vast majority of private corporate activity took place within the confines of the country. Today, a significant component of the activities of virtually all large U.S. corporations takes place outside the country. Foreign activity has thus significantly supplemented domestic activity.

In the nineteenth century, most corporations were identified with single families. Today, control of corporations has diversified among many families through stock sales. Similarly, wealthy families have diversified their stock holdings among many different corporations. Thus, there has been a shift largely from family to class control of corporations.

However, the same shift, or at least the degree of shift, from an appropriative to a capital accumulation economy does not apply to Mexico, where small business activity continues to be a very significant mainstay of total business activity. Just over one-quarter (25.2 per cent) of the Mexican labor force continues to be made up of independent business owners—the vast majority of whom own micro-sized farms and shops—compared to 11.9 per cent in Canada and 9.8 per cent the United States.[5] If, following Manzer's account, economic development has proceeded on a continuum from one pole characterized by appropriative, small, and labor-intensive businesses to another pole characterized by large, capital-intensive businesses, then the Mexican economy remains significantly closer to the former pole than either the Canadian or U.S. economy.

One example will suffice to demonstrate the different timing of the stages of Mexican economic history. In 1917, at the conclusion of the major phase of the Mexican Revolution, the Carranza government instituted an agrarian reform program that over the next several decades distributed small parcels of land to thousands of peasants. In 1917, by contrast, the period of small farm expansion had long since been over in both Canada and the United States, and ownership of farm land was beginning to be concentrated in fewer hands. In other words, at the very time that the Canadian and U.S. governments were pursuing development strategies that discouraged appropriative, small-scale, labor-intensive business activities, the Mexican government was attempting to promote them. The Mexican appropriative strategy conformed to what had been promoted north of the border a century earlier and in different international economic conditions.

The Mexican agrarian reform program was contained in Article 27 of the 1917 Constitution, which mandated the distribution of land to the landless, thereby creating over the next decades both thousands of small landholders and *ejidos* or rural communal organizations that held land which could not be sold. The original designers of Article 27 made *ejido* land non-alienable (that is, forbade its sale). They avoided the disastrous consequences of the Dawes Act in the United States (see Chapter 3) by solving a classic peasant problem. In agrarian conditions, small landowners often must take out loans to finance their operations, frequently putting up their land as collateral. When enough expected returns to retire their loans do not materialize, they forfeit their lands. The non-alienability of *ejido* land thus provided a fail-safe protection to the *ejitario* (farmer). No matter how badly *ejitarios* fared economically, at least the land—their essential means of production—remained secure.

Roger Bartra, in his 1974 study of the Mexican countryside, concluded that the *ejido* and land distribution programs, especially during the Cárdenas period of the 1930s, were economically irrational from the point of view of capitalist developmental needs because they impeded land concentration. But they were politically rational from the point of view of the state's need to build a base of peasant political support. In his words, "Today's bourgeoisie pays a high price for the radical bourgeois populism of the 1930s; of course, it gained something else that was priceless: the famous political stability of the Mexican system."[6]

Technological Development

Accumulation of capital parallels and facilitates technological development. A country's economy technologically develops through agricultural, industrial, and post-industrial stages. In the first stage, the majority of the labor force is absorbed in agriculture and associated primary sector (fishing, forestry, and mining) activities. In the second stage, as farmers become more productive, proportionately fewer of them are needed to feed the country, thereby releasing workers from the countryside who are now available for urban manufacturing and industrial employment. In the third stage, labor-saving technological advances in industry decrease the need for factory workers. This post-industrial stage is marked by tertiary service employment absorbing the majority of the labor force. There are thus two great shifts in labor force distribution in economic development: from farms to factories and from factories to services.

Both shifts have occurred in the United States and Canada but not to the same extent in Mexico. For the first century of the existence of the United States, farming absorbed the majority of its labor force. In 1800, the earliest year for which labor force statistics exist, three-quarters of the labor force was on farms.[7] As agriculture became more productive and capital-intensive, surplus countryside labor shifted to urban factories. In New England in the 1830s and 1840s, textile mills started up with labor forces made up mostly of young women who had grown up on farms. Manufacturing activities grew in fits and spurts up through the 1861-65 Civil War and then accelerated dramatically in its aftermath. Farming and other primary sector activities, though, still continued to absorb the majority of the labor force up through 1880.

The 1880-90 decade was the first decade in which the United States could be properly described as an industrial society in the sense that agriculture and other primary sector activities no longer absorbed the majority of its labor force. Farming continued to account for the largest part—but no longer the majority—of labor force employment. In the industrial period (1890-1920) the majority of the labor force was absorbed in agricultural and industrial employment. The 1920-30 decade drew to a close the properly industrial period as the current post-industrial labor force pattern set in with the majority of workers beginning to be engaged in producing services in offices, hospitals, restaurants, schools, and other locations rather than physical goods on farms or in factories. The distribution of Canada's labor force went through similar historical changes that occurred relatively soon after those of its southern neighbor.

The distribution of the Mexican labor force has not yet fully gone through these stages. Proportionately more workers are engaged in agriculture in Mexico than in the United States or Canada. In fact, Mexico, with under one-quarter of North America's population, has nearly 70 per cent of its agricultural workers. Comparatively high as the proportion of Mexican farm workers is, it began to steeply decline with the advent of the 1994 North American Free Trade Agreement, (to be discussed in the next chapter) which allowed tariff-free food imports from the United States to displace many Mexican farmers.

So Close to the United States

Mexican dictator Porfirio Díaz famously remarked, "Poor Mexico, so far from God, so close to the United States." Whatever one may think of his mock lament, there is no question that because of the great economic and political power of the United States, any country that borders it, including Canada as well as Mexico, will have its destiny, including accumulation of capital, greatly determined by that location.

The U.S.-Mexico Border

Of the two literal borders in North America — the one between Mexico and the United States and the one between the United States and Canada — the 1,945-mile border that separates Mexico and the United States is a sharper dividing line, for it separates, in addition to the two countries, Latin and Anglo America and North America's Third and First Worlds. It was on the Mexican side of the latter of these borders that U.S.-based multinational corporations began in the 1970s a new form of investments that would portend some of the main features of corporate globalization decades later.

Definitions of this border zone vary. Some concentrate on the major twin cities (Brownsville-Matamoros, McAllen-Reynosa, Laredo-Nuevo Laredo, El Paso-Ciudad Juárez, Calexico-Mexicali, and San Diego-Tijuana), where over half the population live. Others have a much broader definition that encompasses everything within 200 miles of either side, including such major U.S. cities as Los Angeles, Phoenix, and San Antonio and the interior Mexican cities of Monterrey, Chihuahua, and Hermosillo. The majority of observers, though, define the border zone as the 26 U.S. counties that touch it to the south and the 35 Mexican *municipios* that touch it to their north.

It is on the border that we can see in unusually sharp relief much of the particular manifestations of class and race in North America. The U.S. border labor force has been traditionally divided along racial lines between Anglos and Mexican-descent members, many of whose living conditions have been among the worst in the country. Average living conditions on the other side of the border are much more depressed, although they compare favorably with Mexican national averages.

An impoverished and marginalized surplus population surrounds the Mexican border cities. Thousands live on illegally squatted land in shacks made out of whatever is at hand. There are whole neighborhoods of houses made from packing cartons. Many survive only by scavenging what is left by the throwaway society on the U.S. side. Each dawn they search the U.S. parks for empty cans to sell, hunt for newspapers in alleys, and comb the city dumps for a piece of board, a broken chair, or perhaps a shirt that can be sewed again or even sold. In the blocks before the border, stores sell clothing by the pound—the absolute last stop of the U.S. cast-off and defective clothing markets.

The desert sun is cruel to the poor in Ciudad Juárez, one of the Mexican border cities. Without air conditioners, many cool off in the Rio Grande, whose muddy calm covers treacherous currents in the summer. Hardly a summer day passes without small items in the El Paso newspapers announcing the washing up of another yet-to-be identified body of a "Mexican national." Water service in Ciudad Juárez varies according to the prosperity of the neighborhood. The higher the income, the more likely there are to be taps in the house that always work; the lower the income, the more likely the water comes from a neighborhood communal pipe or open barrel. In the summer water is scarce, and its availability slows to a drip in many of the poor neighborhoods.

The poor in the Mexican border cities who turn to open begging are immediately evident. Others practice disguised forms of begging—offering to wash windshields (children) or to keep parking meters fed for a tip (adults). Still another indicator of the poverty is the large number of servants on both sides. There are probably many more servants per capita in the U.S. border cities than anywhere else in the country.

The border's traditional economic bases are divided between those derived from the land and those derived from the irrationalities and artificialities of it being a zone separating countries. In the first group are agriculture, ranching, and mining. Large stretches of the border zone are covered by desert, but irrigation practices that date back to pre-Hispanic times and the federally financed reclamation projects of the last century make agriculture possible. This is especially true for the Rio Grande Valley (Texas) and Imperial Valley (California), which are among North America's most productive fruit and vegetable sources. The center of the border, from west Texas to Arizona and from Chihuahua to Sonora, contains the foothills of the Rocky and Sierra Madre mountains, where copper veins run.

The copper economy produced the border's first industrial working class and unions. At the beginning of the twentieth century, U.S. corporations, including the American Smelting and Refining Company (ASARCO), owned by the Guggenheims, and the Cananea Consolidated Copper Company, owned by Colonel William Greene, developed mines and refineries on both sides. In 1906, during the regime of Porfirio Díaz, the workers at Cananea went out on strike. When violence broke out, Colonel Greene sent for 275 Arizona Rangers to protect his interests. The governor of Sonora, Rafael Izábal, gave permission for them to cross the border and patrol Cananea. Within days and after several dozen deaths, the strike was broken. The Cananea tragedy quickly became a leading issue fueling the Mexican

Revolution, since it exemplified Porfiriato's subservience to foreign U.S. interests.[8]

On the U.S. side, mainly Mexican-descent miners and refinery workers organized through a progression of unions, which began with the Western Federation of Miners, an offshoot of the Industrial Workers of the World (IWW) that later reformed itself as the Mine, Mill, and Smelter Workers Union; when the Mine, Mill, and Smelter Workers Union disbanded after being driven out of the Congress of Industrial Organizations (CIO) in the 1950s under the charge of being communist-dominated, its locals affiliated with the United Steelworkers. They fought famous battles in, among other places, Bisbee, Arizona, and Silver City, New Mexico, the latter dramatically portrayed in the blacklisted 1951 classic labor movie, *Salt of the Earth*.

Specifically because it is a zone separating two countries, a large part of the border economy is based on legal and illegal commercial activities and tourism. Trucking and freight train routes converge at the border points of entry and exist. As much as 40 per cent of the vegetables destined for the U.S. winter market pass through Nogales, Arizona. Though many of the goods travel on to interior markets, they still generate a quantity of economic activities to service the trade.

Some large part of the economic prosperity of the twin cities is dependent on the existence of each other as mutual export markets. In terms of relative importance, the U.S. merchants are more dependent on sales to foreigners. Whenever the Mexican peso devalues, Mexican buying power decreases, sending a number of stores on the U.S. side out of business.

The merchandizing of tourism inflates the border's artificial merchant character even more. For many in the United States, Mexico is the only foreign country that they will ever visit, their visits sustaining a service industry of hotels, restaurants, souvenir shops, and the like.

Widespread smuggling is the illegal side of the border merchant economy. The smuggling goes both ways. The highest profits come from smuggling marijuana, cocaine, and heroin into the United States. Lesser profits are made from smuggling more prosaic items such as automobiles, consumer durables, and machinery into Mexico. The large smugglers make prudent investments in the legal and political communities to insure immunity. Profits and violence surrounding the drug smuggling economy increased dramatically beginning in the 1990s, in part as unintended consequences of NAFTA and other neoliberal reforms.

Maquiladoras

Through the 1960s, the border cities were economic backwaters, known mainly for their tourist dives, smuggling, and the Border Patrol's perpetual war on undocumented workers. Since then the border has become a major world industrial center as multinational corporations have rushed in to take advantage of its cheap labor and build assembly plants, called *maquiladoras*, on the Mexican side. A maquiladora is essentially a factory where workers use imported materials to complete the assembly stage of a multinational corporation's production process. The completed product is then exported to the multinational corporation's home country from where it is marketed. Somewhere on the final product or its container can usually be found words such as "assembled in Mexico of U.S. materials." A host of U.S. corporate giants—including General Electric, Zenith, RCA, and General Motors—as well as many smaller subcontractors have set up shop along the border, dominating the formal economies of such border cities as Ciudad Juárez, Tijuana, and Mexicali.

The opening up of the border cities to maquiladoras began in 1965, when Mexican President Gustavo Díaz Ordaz inaugurated the Border Industrialization Program for the announced aims of attracting jobs and technological development to the region. The timing of the program was prompted by the ending a year earlier of the U.S. Bracero Program, which had allowed thousands of temporary agricultural workers into the country since the labor shortage period of World War II. The Mexican government viewed the ending of the Bracero Program as potentially dangerous for the stability of the border cities, where many of the temporary workers lived.

Making the potential crisis more ominous was the 1964 outbreak of guerrilla warfare in Chihuahua. Concluding that the Mexican agrarian reform was a fraud, that the government was giving away rich forest and mineral concessions, and that the Tarahumara Indians were being subjected to increased exploitation, rural school teacher Arturo Gamiz took to the Sierra Madre mountains to launch guerrilla attacks, like the ones occurring at the time in many other parts of Latin America. The Mexican Army was quick to respond, and on September 23, 1965, Gamiz and seven of his followers were killed in battle at Madera, Chihuahua.[9] Though the Gamiz movement was a manifestation of mainly rural problems, it still worried government officials who were in charge of the border cities, which were the destinations for many of the peasants pushed off the land by impoverishment. By 1965, Mexico was fully committed to export-oriented agricultural policies that favored large growers at the expense of these peasants, causing out-migration to urban centers such as the border cities.

Meanwhile, in the board rooms of the multinational corporations to the north, the middle 1960s were experienced as a period of transition from wide-open expansion to renewed competition. The United States had pursued policies during the last year of World War II to make the free movement of commodities and capital a cornerstone for the reconstruction of postwar international relations. Multinational corporations based in the United States were in a unique position to profit because their industrial plants had not been bombed during the war. By the 1960s, however, Japan, West Germany, and other economic powers had rebuilt themselves and were beginning to penetrate U.S. domestic and foreign markets.

In the labor-intensive garment industry, as well as the labor-intensive electronics industry, which was just beginning to expand, labor costs became vital factors in the new world of international corporate competition. Taking advantage of greatly improved transportation networks, multinational corporations began to shift labor-intensive units of production outside of the home country to cheap labor areas of the Third World such as South Korea, Taiwan, Singapore, and the Mexican border cities. If the logic of the first period of Western industrialization was to bring workers to capital, the new logic was to take capital to where cheap workers were.

In choosing among Third World labor areas, U.S. multinational corporations generally considered three factors: labor cost, freedom, and stability. Labor cost in market economies is inversely related to unemployment: the higher the unemployment, the lower the labor cost, since when the supply of a commodity such as labor exceeds its demand, its price drops. High unemployment also acts to increase the productivity of those who are employed because the knowledge of how easily one is replaceable by others desperately seeking employment acts as a psychological whip to work harder. Without even counting the added unemployment caused by the ending of the Bracero Programs, the border cities with 30 to 40 per cent underemployment and unemployment rates easily met the multinationals' first requirement.

Table 6.1: Growth of the Maquiladora Industry

	FACTORIES	EMPLOYEES
1965	12	3,087
1970	120	20,327
1975	532	67,214
1980	600	119,546
1985	n.a.	211,986
1990	2,013	486,723
1995	2,241	680,209
2000	3,590	1,291,232
2005	2,816	1,166,250

Sources: Instituto Nacional Estadística Geografía e Informática [INEGI], Estadística de la Industria Maquiladora de Exportación, 1978-1988; Estadística de la Industria Maquiladora de Exportación, 1991; and Estadística de la Industria Maquilador de Exportación, Febrero 2007 (Aguascalientes: INEGI, 1989, 1992, 2007); El Paso, TX Chamber of Commerce Twin Plant publications, 1968-80.

The multinational corporations' second requirement for foreign investments, freedom, necessitated government policy compliance on both sides. Ideally, multinational corporations want to be able to place their assembly plant in the host country as if it were only a department of a global factory from and to which capital, materials, and products can be moved without tax and customs restrictions. Mexico's Border Industrialization Program obligingly cooperated by designating the frontier area as a free trade zone and waiving special taxes on foreign corporations. On the border the maquiladoras have virtually all the privileges of Mexican-owned corporations.

US government policy complied with the plan by establishing provisions 806.30 and 807 of the Tariff Code for maquiladora products. Upon re-entry into the United States, those products are taxed at a customs duty according to the value of the labor added in Mexico. How the value added is defined makes a great deal of difference. It is not defined as the difference between the value of the raw materials and the market value of the assembled product, as one might think. Rather, it is defined as the wages paid in Mexico, which is a lot less. In effect, the Tariff Code contained a loophole that allowed the free movement of above-average profits back into the United States.

The third requirement, stability, is also eminently a political question. Corporations prefer not to make risky investments. Like any business firm, they like to be able to calculate with reasonable accuracy their short- and long-term returns. Concretely, they want assurances that the government is not going to change from friendly to hostile, the leftist opposition is kept under control, the unions are cooperative, and the workers in general are disciplined.

In Mexico there was both extraordinary government control and sharp rumblings under the surface. The governing PRI's practice was to skillfully co-opt as much as possible the leadership of movements from below and leave the rest to be physically repressed by the state or right-wing terrorist organizations. That governmental control became a more attractive advertising feature after the 1968 Tet Offensive in South Vietnam made it clear that stability in that part of Southeast Asia was crumbling. Not entirely coincidentally, 1968 saw the emergence of the first maquiladora in Ciudad Juárez, which became the largest center of their activities.

The maquiladora operation on the border expanded greatly between 1965 and 1980, from 12 factories with 3,087 workers to close to 600 factories with 119,546 workers (see Table 6.1). By 1975, over three-quarters of all industrial jobs in the Mexican frontier were maquiladora jobs, and Mexico displaced Southeast Asia to become the largest assembler of U.S. components for re-export to the U.S. market.

Employment prospects in the maquiladoras attracted peasants from the impoverished countryside, swelling the populations of the border cities. Over 70 per cent of maquiladora work in the 1970s was in electronics and apparel, both of which required considerable labor for final assembly. The home factory farmed out, or in corporate terminology "outsourced," this work to save on labor costs.

Most of the workers were young women first employed in their middle teens. The corporations believed them to be more dexterous, patient for tedious work, easier to control, and thus more suited to assembly work than men. When maquiladora workers marched in the annual May Day parades behind the names of their companies, they looked like contingents from girls' high schools. RCA dressed its workers up in red and white U.S.-style cheerleader mini-skirted outfits and lined them up behind the "His Master's Voice" corporate insignia as male managers barked out marching orders through megaphones.

Since electronics assembly could only be done in clean, temperature-controlled areas to avoid deterioration of the parts, the new factories were air conditioned—to protect the parts, not the workers—from the dry desert heat, which in most of the border cities can rise to 114 degrees Fahrenheit. Apparel parts are not as vulnerable to the heat. Many of the sewing maquiladoras tended to be scattered about the border cities in older buildings without cooling equipment.

From the point of view of the companies, the maquiladora program was a tremendous success. Richard Michel, general manager of seven General Electric maquiladoras in Mexico during the 1970s, painted a glowing picture. With seven years of experience on the border, GE found the absentee rate to be only 2 per cent compared to the 5 to 9 per cent rate among its U.S. workers, and the productivity of the maquiladora workers was 10 to 15 per cent above that of their U.S. counterparts.[10]

A tenuous labor peace generally reigned within the maquiladoras, but there were isolated confrontations. In 1975 urban guerrillas from the Liga Comunista 23 de Septiembre, whose name was taken from the date on which Chihuahua guerrilla leader Arturo Gamiz was killed by the Mexican army, entered a Sylvania maquiladora in Ciudad Juárez, killed a Mexican manager who tried to stop them, and distributed leaflets. The response of the maquiladoras was to beef up security. The Mexican government in turn speeded up its successful campaign to crush the Liga's presence in Ciudad Juárez and the rest of the country. In one incident the next year, the army opened fire on and killed a number of guerrilla suspects in an outlying Ciudad Juárez neighborhood. The right-wing Brigada Blanca kidnapped and presumably murdered a number of people who had suspected links to the Liga.

Although the pay of maquiladora workers was a pittance compared to the profits that were wrought out of them, it was still enough to make their jobs among the better paying ones on the Mexican side of the border. A major complaint, though, was that while the pay remained constant or increased in terms of its nominal peso value, it fluctuated greatly in terms of its real purchasing power and exchange rate with the dollar. The value of the pay in terms of its convertability to dollars is especially important on the border where maquiladora workers often shop in the United States and U.S. prices influence the price of Mexican goods.

Mexican law requires that senior workers be assured job security, but there are many ways for multinational corporations to get around the requirement. Employers can slash hours or shut the plant down for a period, thereby forcing employees to seek work elsewhere. Companies have also been known to swap workers, eliminating accrued seniority in the process. If a worker does not make production quotas, there is cause for firing which most often will be upheld by the government's Board of Arbitration, which exists to adjudicate labor disputes.

Serious problems also existed off the job. The original practice of hiring almost exclusively young women unbalanced employment patterns in the border cities. Not only were men left unemployed, they were also stripped of whatever traditional identity they had as providers. Women were pulled out of the houses into the factories and men were thrust back into the houses. This dramatic reversal of roles for which neither partner was prepared produced severe consequences.

The idling of the married male working class produced increases in all the social problems traditionally associated with unemployment, including alcoholism, bar fights, and family tensions. In a typical development, a young married couple with children found that only the woman could get a job; she began to work, a grandmother took care of the children, and the husband increasingly felt worthless. He then became tempted to abandon his family and search for work as an undocumented worker in the United States. Both Ciudad Juárez and El Paso Spanish-language radio stations regularly broadcasted during this period appeals from wives searching for husbands. Unmarried teenage men, who looked forward to bleak employment prospects, in turn increasingly sank into gang membership, drug smuggling, and petty criminal activities in general.

Although the border zone competed with similar tax break/cheap labor havens in other parts of Latin America, it had a unique selling point: the "twin plant" concept. The multinational corporation could keep the capital-intensive part of its operation in the United States and the labor-intensive side a short distance away in Mexico. For instance, in apparel manufacture, the cloth could be cut on the U.S. side (a relatively skilled job that required expensive and often computerized capital equipment) and then sent less than a mile way to the Mexican part of the factory where it was sewn, a more labor-intensive exercise. It was then returned to the shipping department on the U.S. side for distribution. For a minimum investment the corporation could thus take advantage of Mexico's cheap labor without major risks to its capital equipment.

The decade of the 1980s saw a further expansion of the border maquiladora economy. Between 1980 and 1991 the total number of maquiladora employees in Mexico nearly quadrupled, rising from 119,546 to 467,454 (see Table 6.1). Maquiladora wages remained very low by U.S. standards but average by Mexican standards. In 1992 maquiladora workers received an average *daily* wage of $6.80,[11] an average that has changed little to the present.

There were two new developments in the 1980s. A number of maquiladoras were located in interior Mexican cities, which by the end of the decade contained nearly one-quarter of all maquiladora employees. However, most of these did not move very far into Mexico since a full 92.4 per cent of all maquiladora jobs were still located in the seven border states of Baja California Norte, Sonora, Chihuahua, Coahuila, Nuevo Leon, and Tamaulipas. The second new development was that male maquiladora employment increased significantly from 22.7 to 39.6 per cent of line workers. That was largely because auto parts became a new branch of maquiladora industry, displacing apparel as the second largest industry after electronics, and about half of its line workers were males. Electronics and most of the other maquiladora branches continued to depend disproportionately on young female labor.

The 1980s also saw the developing of service maquiladoras, that is, factories that assembled a service as opposed to physical product. In one of the more notable cases, Ciudad Juárez became the destination for discount shopping coupons. In the United States, manufacturers of food and other household goods often promote their products by distributing discount coupons through newspapers and other means. Stores accumulated large numbers of these, which they needed to redeem for credit from the manufacturers. In the 1980s, most of these cashed coupons were sent to a service maquiladora in Ciudad Juárez, where they were sorted and counted, with the information being entered on computer tapes for re-export to the U.S. manufacturers. In this case, the cashed coupons were the raw materials and the tabulated information about them the product for export.

The trends of increasing male employment and opening of factories away from the border continued in the 1990s and into the beginning decade of the new century. By 2005, men occupied half of all maquiladora jobs. The border cities and states still had the majorities of all maquiladora jobs but less so, with 59.2 and 82.2 per cent respectively. The period from 2000 to 2005 showed the first, albeit modest, decrease in maquiladora employment as more multinational corporations shifted jobs to even lower cost locations, especially China.

Staples and Branch Factories in Canada

Canadian economic development has been affected by its bordering location with the United States even more than has that of Mexico. Examination of Canadian trade and foreign investment reveal the extent to which the country functions as an appendage of the U.S. economy. International trade, especially with the United States, was and continues to be of much greater importance for Canada than for Mexico. In 2004 the value of all exports accounted for over one-third (37.6 per cent) of Canadian GDP, compared to 10.4 per cent of that of the United States and 20.6 per cent of that of Mexico (see Table 6.2). Of Canadian goods exports, 81.7 per cent went to the United States.[12]

Table 6.2: International Trade (Percent of GDP), 2004

	CANADA	MEXICO	UNITED STATES
Exports	37.6	20.6	10.4
Imports	34.5	21.7	16.5

Source: Calculated from Organization for Economic Cooperation and Development, OECD Stat Extracts, http://stats.oecd.org/WBOS/default.aspx?DatasetCode=CSP2007.

Furthermore, in 2005 over one-quarter (26.9 per cent) of corporate assets were under foreign control in Canada. Of those, the United States had 59.5 per cent. U.S. corporations receive 68.4 per cent of all profits of foreign non-financial investments in Canada. Nearly half (49.2 per cent) of manufacturing is foreign controlled, mainly as branch factories of U.S. corporations.[13]

Because of the high foreign control of its industry and drain of profits, Canada resembles a developing economy. Yet the high average standard of living of its citizens clearly places it among the world's developed societies. Canada thus presents an unusual combination of features associated with both developing and developed economies.[14] Also the high extent of U.S. corporate control raises questions about Canada's very independence as a country. Gary Teeple, in a widely discussed book, concluded that "the American influence in the economy forces the policies of the Canadian government to fall into line more or less with those of Washington (or Wall Street). Thus, this nation has the political trappings of independence but not the reality."[15]

Canadian branch factories are similar to Mexican maquiladoras in that they are foreign-controlled assembly plants for the most part. What differentiates them are, first, that branch factories are in Canada in order to be closer to Canadian consumers while maquiladoras produce for markets outside of Mexico; and, second, that the economics of maquiladoras are based on being able to take advantage of cheap labor, which is not a factor in corporate decisions to set up branch factories in Canada.

Primary goods that have been little processed, such as fur, fish, lumber, wheat, and oil, historically have been an unusually large part of Canadian exports while imports have been industrial goods. The pattern of export of primary and import of secondary goods gave rise to the staple thesis of Canadian development, first advanced in the 1920s by W.A. Mackintosh and Harold Innis. According to it, overall Canadian development has been marked by production of primary goods and little development of indigenous industrialization. Its industrialization, rather, has been largely dominated by foreign control—first by the French, then by the British, and now by the United States. According to critical advocates of the staple thesis, foreign domination of industrial activities, such as through branch factories, in turn severely constrains Canadian economic sovereignty.

The staple thesis resembles Latin American and Third World dependency theory, according to which foreign domination and concentration on export of raw materials inhibit development. Yet, Canada clearly has developed. The question is why, despite existing in an economically dependent status with the United States, Canada still has been able to develop much more prosperity than Third World countries with similar dependency relationships.

One factor that differentiates Canada from all Third World countries with the exception of Mexico is that it, indeed, does border the United States with its voracious demand for natural resource imports. That has meant that Canada has had a market close by for its very valuable — compared to those of typical Third World countries — primary exports. Canada's relatively small population has meant that its per capita actual and potential natural resource value has been exceptionally high, and having a bordering market in which to sell them has been clearly to its advantage.

Bordering the United States has proved to be much more economically beneficial for Canada than Mexico. Despite sharing with Mexico the additional conditions of being dominated economically by the United States and relying on exports of staples such as oil and food, Canada, nevertheless, achieved First World living conditions and Mexico did not.

Canada's ability to benefit from its border location to the U.S. market resulted from other conditions that were not shared with Mexico. As we have discussed in previous pages, Canadian capitalist development was not as much fettered by feudal and pre-existing Indian institutions as was that of Mexico — what Mel Watkins called "an absence of inhibiting traditions."[16] Canada and the United States, born from the same British colony, had similar — though not identical — cultural, linguistic, and economic backgrounds that enabled maintenance and increase of trading relations. Mexico grew out of the Spanish colonial empire with different cultural conditions, including language, and few trading relationships with the United States. As mentioned above, the great majority of the Canadian population has lived close to the border. Mexico's great population centers and overall densities were far south of the border. Most important is that Canada's abundant resources remained within Canada and thus provided the basis for later advantageous trade with the United States. In the 1846-48 Mexican-American War, the United States took Mexico's northern states, which contained its most valuable actual and potential natural resources. Mexico, thus, lost what could have enabled a natural resource export-led development experience that would have been closer to Canada's.

Canada's economic fate has been and continues to be greatly marked by export of staples to and investment of capital from the United States. While the country has been able to use these to its advantage in terms of contributing to its First World level of prosperity, at the same time it is a dependent relationship that constrains its ability to act independently, thereby undermining its economic sovereignty. Among the disadvantages are that there is little public control over foreign corporate decisions that will have an impact on the country. Foreign corporations that operate branch factories in Canada usually retain more desirable and better paying planning and design positions within the home country. In the case of the United States, U.S. corporate branch operations must obey U.S. law regarding their sales and purchases outside of Canada. If U.S. law or foreign policy embargoes a particular country, the U.S. branch operation in Canada must conform even if Canadian law and foreign policy has no such embargo. For example, while Canada has active trade with Cuba, U.S. corporate controlled firms abide by U.S. rather than Canadian foreign trade policy and do not—are forbidden to—participate in it.

Chapter 7

NAFTA

During the 1980 presidential campaign in the United States, Republican Party candidate Ronald Reagan announced his goal of creating a free trade zone "from the Yukon to the Yucatan." By 1988, his last year in office, he had succeeded in negotiating the Canada-United States Free Trade Agreement (FTA). His Republican Party successor, George H.W. Bush, then carried the campaign forward and by the spring of 1990 began negotiating the North American Free Trade Agreement (NAFTA), which would cover Mexico as well as the United States and Canada.[1]

In one sense, the NAFTA negotiations represented the capstone of the increasing tendency for the three countries to become economically interrelated, although the relationship was an asymmetrical one between two First and one Third World countries. It was the seemingly logical and natural consolidation of tendencies that had long been underway, including, most importantly, the establishment of maquiladora industry in Mexico and the steady lowering of Mexican tariffs, begun by the administration of Miguel de la Madrid in 1983.

Free Trade

A free trade agreement is one in which the participants allow each other's commodities to enter their domestic markets duty free. As such, free trade policies are the opposite of protectionist policies. In the latter, countries shield their domestic industries from international competition by charging tariffs on imports, making them more expensive than domestically produced goods.

During the late nineteenth century, the United States facilitated its industrialization in large part by establishing high tariff walls. These enabled its infant industries to grow by shielding them from the competition of already developed and more powerful foreign industrial corporations. Protectionist policies have been followed by other countries seeking to industrialize, most notably Japan. Mexico for a number of decades up through the 1980s followed strict protectionist policies.

Free trade policies have traditionally been advocated by the more industrially advanced and strongest of international competitors in order to give them access to larger markets. They also are consistent with conservative political philosophies, which take the forms of Republicanism in the United States, neo-liberalism in Mexico, and Toryism in Canada. From the point of view of conservatism, state interference with the laws of the market should be eliminated or minimized. In that respect, protectionist policies represented state interference with the laws of the international market, and NAFTA represented the international dimension of Republican Party, neo-liberal, and Tory policies. NAFTA thus coincided with the ascendancy of conservative political philosophies in all three countries during the 1980s.

Obstacles in Mexico

The emergence of the NAFTA project in 1990, though, was not entirely predictable. Mexico had maintained its traditional foreign policy, a correct but distant posture toward the United States, during the 1980s, while from 1981 to 1987 the United States government seriously objected to Mexico's Central America policies. At the same time that the Reagan administration was mounting its campaign to destroy the Sandinista revolution in Nicaragua and isolate the rebels in El Salvador, the Mexican government was sending aid to Nicaragua and tacitly recognizing the legitimacy of the political and military representatives of the Salvadoran revolution. The Mexican government was following two long-standing principles: first, independence (from the United States especially) in its foreign policy and, second, active support of Latin American revolutionaries and revolutions. Mexico, for example, had been the only Latin American country to not bow to the pressure of the United States to break diplomatic relations with Cuba in the 1960s. Mexico had also been the location from where Fidel Castro and Ernesto "Che" Guevara, in exile, had planned the Cuban revolution.

The public perception of the Mexican government in the United States fell victim to the Reagan administration's determination to destroy leftist governments and movements in Central America. The Reagan administration never respected the right of Mexico to have an independent foreign policy and decided to punish the country for Central American policies that were interfering with U.S. goals. The punishment took the form of accusing the Mexican government of being corrupt and undemocratic and of abetting drug smuggling. Moreover, the U.S. government indirectly and the press directly accused the Mexican government of committing massive electoral fraud in the 1986 state elections. A number of television and print media in the United States predicted electoral fraud, concluding that the governing PRI would steal certain victories from the conservative Partido Acción Nacional (PAN).

This coverage was unusual. If the U.S. press generally has taken little interest in Mexican national elections, it has taken even less interest in its state elections. The only possible reason for this new-found interest was that the Reagan administration was orchestrating a campaign to punish Mexico for not joining its Central American campaign. Thus, the U.S. government and press directed public attention to the necessity of democratizing Mexico during the period 1981-87 at the same time that they were hitting the Sandinistas hard for the supposed lack of democracy in Nicaragua. The perception promoted in the United States was that democracy did not exist in either Mexico or Nicaragua.

The Canada-United States Free Trade Agreement

If in the mid-1980s the U.S. government was viewing Mexico as a distant, troublesome neighbor in regards to its foreign policy, it was viewing its northern neighbor, Canada, much more favorably. In early 1985 the governments of conservative President Ronald Reagan and Prime Minister Brian Mulroney held preliminary talks on establishing a Canada-United States Free Trade Agreement (FTA). At the end of that year, Reagan announced that he would pursue the FTA under fast track authority. Under that authority, once a final agreement was proposed, the U.S. Congress would have 90 days to vote on its approval with no amendments allowed. The purpose of the fast track procedure was to allow trade agreements to avoid becoming bogged down by individual senators and representatives amending them according to their own special interests, which would in turn require renegotiation of the agreement with the other country or countries.

In May 1986 formal negotiations began, with the final draft of the FTA completed in October 1987. Following legislative passage in both countries, on January 2, 1988, President Reagan and Prime Minister Mulroney signed the agreement.

Few ordinary citizens in the United States paid much attention to the issue. It did not rate much attention in the U.S. media either. It was different in Canada, though, where the issue was highly contentious and keenly followed. For people in the United States, trade with Canada represents a minority of international trade; for Canadians, it is the overwhelming majority of their trade. Canadians thus have a greater interest in trade issues with the United States than do their counterparts to the south.

A substantial opposition developed in Canada out of fear that the agreement would severely undermine the country's sovereignty, and it became the leading issue of the 1988 election. The Liberal Party and the New Democratic Party strongly opposed the FTA. Prime Minister Mulroney's Progressive Conservative Party, the proponents of the FTA, narrowly prevailed in the election with a plurality of popular votes (43 per cent) and majority of seats (57 per cent) in the House of Commons.

The FTA went into effect on January 1, 1989. It stipulated phasing out all tariffs on trade in goods and services over a ten-year period and removed non-tariff related obstacles to investments in each other's economies. At Canadian insistence, the areas of culture, education, and health were exempted, thereby allowing the Canadian government to continue to protect its own cultural development and social policies from U.S. domination.

With the signing of the FTA, there was speculation in the United States that it would be extended to Mexico. However, many, including high Mexican government officials, believed that to be unlikely. The FTA was signed between countries that were at the same level of development, albeit with dramatically different sizes of their economies. Mexico was at a much lower level of development. If, because of the relatively small size of its economy, Canada was at a disadvantage *vis-à-vis* the United States, Mexico, with an even smaller economy and lower stage of development, was at an even greater disadvantage. It would not be to its advantage to enter into a distinctly asymmetrical free trade agreement with Canada and the United States.

A Dubious Election Prepares the Way

In August 1988, six months after the signing of the FTA, Mexico held its presidential election. Free trade with the United States and Canada was not an issue since the NAFTA project had not yet been launched. However, the dubious results of the election proved to be of crucial importance for the eventual establishment of NAFTA.

The election was held as the Mexican economy was suffering from a decade-long downturn aggravated by low international oil prices, its major export. It pitted Carlos Salinas de Gortari of the long-ruling PRI against Cuauhtémoc Cárdenas, the candidate of a coalition of opposition parties, mostly leftist, and also son of Lázaro Cárdenas, the country's most revered twentieth-century president. The early returns showed a sweeping Cárdenas victory. Then the central vote tabulation computer mysteriously broke down. No more returns were announced for hours. When vote tabulation results finally resumed, they showed Salinas de Gortari to now be in the lead, and he was declared the winner with 50.4 per cent of the vote.[2]

The probable victory of the candidate of the leftist opposition sent shock waves through the United States Embassy in Mexico City. Top embassy officials calculated that a Cárdenas victory would completely destabilize bilateral relations between Mexico and the United States. Most likely that would have included unannounced plans for establishing NAFTA. For that reason, the embassy explicitly decided not to make any direct or indirect statement over the elections as it had in the 1986 state elections. Instead, it let the Mexican authorities resolve the crisis.[3] On this occasion, when it was useful to its interests, the United States adopted a public policy of not interfering in Mexican politics.

The posture of the *New York Times* was curious. On the day after the election, it reported that the PRI had possibly been defeated and detailed the suspicious breakdown of the tabulating computer. For three days the paper's coverage created the impression and perception that the PRI had lost the elections and was preparing a fraud to maintain presidential control. It reported with skepticism the official results that Carlos Salinas de Gortari had won with just over 50 per cent of the votes. On the fourth day after the election, its coverage changed completely. It ceased interpreting the election as fraudulent and began to report the official results as accurate without commentary. Sixteen years later it would describe the election as "rigged."[4]

It is clear that maintaining the interpretive framework that the Mexican electoral process was fraudulent would not have served the national interests of the United States if it had resulted in supporting a significant leftward shift in the Mexican government that would have made agreement on NAFTA doubtful. For that reason, concern over democracy in Mexico began to disappear from the U.S. press in the fall of 1988.

During 1989, officials of the new George H.W. Bush administration tried to convince their counterparts in the new Salinas de Gortari administration of the advantages of a free trade agreement. At first the Mexican government opposed the agreement on the grounds that the country was too weak economically to benefit from such an agreement and that it would open the doors to greater economic penetration and control from its powerful neighbor. However, in the spring of 1990, the Mexican government did a complete about-face and announced that it was enthusiastically seeking a free trade agreement with the United States. NAFTA then became the cornerstone of the Salinas de Gortari administration's modernization project.

Why the Mexican government suddenly changed its economic policies is the subject of considerable debate and speculation. To some degree, the prior de la Madrid administration had already begun to lower tariffs in 1983; hence, acceptance of NAFTA was a logical consequence. However, it is not likely that by 1989 the Mexican government was ready to take as radical a step as entering into a full-fledged free trade agreement. What most likely pushed it over the last doubts was the collapse during that year of the governments in Eastern Europe that had relied on state-led economic policies—as had Mexico.

At the same time, there had been significant opposition in Canada from the beginning to its free trade agreement with the United States. When it was announced that the agreement would be extended to Mexico, opposition increased even further. Economic recession in 1988 and 1989, which was in large part blamed on the free trade agreement, fueled opposition. The economic recession hit earlier and harder in Canada than the United States.

In addition, the New Democratic Party government of Ontario in 1990 had to abandon its election promise to develop public automobile insurance for the province as existed in Manitoba and Saskatchewan because of a provision of the FTA. Article 1605 would enable U.S. automobile insurance companies to demand substantial compensation if the Ontario government developed a plan that was "tantamount to expropriation" of their pre-existing businesses.

In Quebec, however, the bulk of public opinion favored the country's free trade agreement with the United States and NAFTA. Free trade agreements would allow Quebec's independent-minded merchants and producers to develop direct trading links with the United States without the approval of Ottawa.

Selling NAFTA

In order to support the negotiations for NAFTA and win its subsequent approval in the U.S. Congress, the George H.W. Bush administration and its allies in the press began a campaign to establish a new interpretive framework for stories about Mexico. Given the controversial 1988 elections, they could not sustain the thesis that Mexico was a model democracy. In its place, they emphasized the vision of a country that was struggling to modernize itself and was led by a young, able, and, most important, pro-American president. As part of this effort to spread a favorable image of Mexico in the United States, the highly successful art exhibition "Mexico: Splendor of Thirty Centuries" toured the country.

At the same time, the Mexican government for the first time employed a public relations firm in Washington to design another campaign to create positive images and perceptions of the country. One of its most ironic conquests was nominating President Salinas de Gortari for an ecology award, when Mexico undoubtedly had one of the most polluted capitals in the world. Although the award came from a minor environmental organization, it was widely reported in Mexico as being "the equivalent of the Nobel Prize for Ecology."

The campaign to change the image of Mexico and its government in the United States had great success by 1991. It is not coincidental that it was then that the U.S. Senate authorized the fast track process for negotiating NAFTA.[5] During that period, it was common in the United States to describe the Mexican president as "the Mexican Gorbachev" — a problematic analogy given what subsequently occurred: the collapse and dismemberment of the Union of Soviet Socialist Republics.[6]

Very little opposition to NAFTA appeared in the Mexican press. The opposition PRD, headed by Cuauhtémoc Cárdenas, at first equivocated on NAFTA, complaining that the negotiations were secretive and not carried out democratically. Only later did it take a position of opposing the agreement. The press, over which the government exerted indirect control, in general cheered the negotiating process on, seeing NAFTA as the solution to Mexico's economic problems.

The common analysis was that the post-Cold War world was dividing into three economic blocks — the European common market, an Asian block led by Japan, and a North American bloc led by the United States — and Mexico had the historic opportunity to link up with an economic superpower and be a player in the economic big leagues. If Mexico did not, so the taken-for-granted analysis ran, it would remain mired in the Third World periphery. As NAFTA gathered steam, remarkably optimistic press headlines promised that "With NAFTA Mexico Will Leave the Third World for the First" and "Five Years After the Inauguration of NAFTA Mexican Wages will Equal Those of the United States."

In the fall of 1991, the campaign for approval of NAFTA was going very well. Its approval seemed inevitable. So too did the re-election of President Bush, who triumphantly emerged from the Persian Gulf War with a 90 per cent public approval rating. Then the economic recession in the United States deepened, and, what is more important, the U.S. public began to perceive it as such. By the beginning of 1992, it was evident that neither the re-election of President Bush nor a rapid approval of NAFTA in the United States was inevitable.

In the United States the most reliable variable for predicting a standing president's re-election possibilities is the state of the economy. More than anything else, U.S. voters demand of their presidents that the economy be healthy. This gives a standing president a tremendous advantage in an election, as was the situation of Ronald Reagan in 1984. However, when voters perceive that the economy is not going well, as was the case of Jimmy Carter in 1980, the opposition candidate, whether Republican or Democrat, has a good chance to win.

With the economy in full recession in the summer of 1992, it was clear that President Bush would not win an easy re-election. Among the president's vulnerabilities was precisely his sponsorship of NAFTA. During the primary elections, many of the other candidates attacked, or at least questioned, NAFTA, arguing that with it the economy was going to suffer more because it would lead to the exportation of jobs to Mexico, where wage costs were dramatically lower.

In September 1992 the final draft of NAFTA was completed. President Bush delayed signing it until mid-December, well after the conclusion of the election in which he was defeated. The new Clinton administration then inherited the agreement, which still faced ratification by the Congress.

Bill Clinton, during the campaign, had walked a tightrope on support for NAFTA. He was caught between growing grassroots opposition to free trade in the electoral base of the Democratic Party and the counsel of his advisors that failure of the United States to ratify the agreement would likely provoke political and economic crises in Mexico that could pose a security threat to the United States.

Not only was President Salinas de Gortari betting all of his and the PRI's political capital on passage of NAFTA, Mexico had also greatly restructured its economy through privatization of state industry, lowering of tariffs, and, most importantly, delivering a double blow against the 1917 agrarian reform. He initiated legislation to rewrite Article 27 to formally end the distribution of new land to the landless and to allow sale of *ejido* land, thereby removing a key obstacle to capital and land concentration in the countryside.[7] The opposition press was quick to dub the president's reform as the "counter agrarian reform." The World Bank was behind the reform of Article 27, having promoted it in a 1990 policy document as part of its plan to effect a neoliberal modernization of the countryside. Bank policy-makers viewed the *ejido* formation, which accounted for close to half of Mexican land, as an obstacle to market relations in the countryside.[8]

The Mexican government had also maintained a policy of subsidizing the value of the peso *vis-à-vis* the dollar, a policy that resulted in overvaluation of the peso and a growing unfavorable trade imbalance with the United States. All of this was in anticipation of passage of NAFTA before the 1994 Mexican presidential elections.

Candidate Clinton resolved the contradiction between opposition to NAFTA in his party and the perception that non-passage of the treaty would provoke a security crisis on the southern border by pledging both support for NAFTA and the inclusion of new side agreements to address environmental and labor concerns. Once in office he negotiated the side agreements, but these did little to diminish opposition to NAFTA among labor and environmental constituencies at the liberal base of the Democratic Party. Opposition to NAFTA then spread to some leading conservatives, including columnist Pat Buchanan. Making matters still more difficult for the administration was that Ross Perot, the maverick multimillionaire and independent presidential candidate in the 1992 election, mounted a well-financed publicity campaign against passage. It appeared that the left and right of U.S. politics were uniting in opposition to the center. By early fall 1993, many were predicting that Congress would not approve NAFTA. The possible collapse of the agreement sent shock waves not only through Mexico but also through the U.S. State Department, which was facing its greatest potential crisis with Mexico since the 1988 disputed election.

To make matters more problematic, on October 25, 1993 Canadian voters resoundingly voted against the Progressive Conservative Party and elected a Liberal government which ran in part against the FTA and, as a part of its platform, pledged to renegotiate NAFTA. The day before the election, the *New York Times* ran a story under the title "Voting in Canada Can Affect NAFTA," in which it described the opposition to the FTA and NAFTA within the Liberal Party. Two days after the election, however, it published an article titled "U.S. Says Chretien Will Not Undo NAFTA," in which it reassured supporters of the agreement that the incoming prime minister, Jean Chrétien, was actually a supporter of the agreement despite the substantial criticism of free trade within the ranks of his party.[9]

The political situation in Canada paralleled that of the United States. As in the United States a political party that had negotiated NAFTA was turned out of office before it went into effect by a political party that had strong rank-and-file opposition to the agreement, raising speculation that it would be abandoned. The incoming prime minister, like Bill Clinton in the United States, prevailed over critics of NAFTA within his own party and then skillfully steered it toward implementation.[10]

It was clear that in Canada, as in the United States, there was committed support for NAFTA that united the top rank of the leading political party most critical of free trade with that of the party most in favor of it—a support that reflected elite corporate interests and desires.[11] There was still, though, a final political obstacle to be overcome before NAFTA could be implemented.

The fight over the controversial trade agreement reached its critical phase in early November. The new Clinton administration, with significant corporate backing, concentrated all of its energies on legislative passage of NAFTA. In the final days before the crucial show down in the House of Representatives, both sides took to the airwaves. Never before had a proposed *trade agreement* been so controversial in U.S. politics; much of the publicly aired debate was concerned with the specifically class-related issue of whether it would lead to an increase or decrease in jobs. On November 17, 1993, the pro-NAFTA forces prevailed by a small majority (234 to 200) in the House of Representatives. The last serious obstacle to NAFTA had been overcome. The Senate then passed NAFTA by a significantly larger margin.

Disastrous Beginning in Mexico

The proponents of NAFTA hoped that it would bring a peaceful period of economic growth and modernization to Mexico as well as increased prosperity to Canada and the United States. But those hopes were quickly dashed. On January 1, 1994, the day NAFTA went into effect, the Zapatista National Liberation Army (EZLN) launched a revolution in the name of Mexico's impoverished Indians. The timing was intentional. The Zapatistas claimed that implementation of NAFTA would undermine traditional Indian ways of life and further impoverish them.

On March 23 an assassin in Tijuana shot dead Luis Donaldo Colosio, the presidential candidate of the ruling PRI. On September 28, in the second high-profile political assassination of the year, Jose Francisco Ruiz Massieu, who was about to become the PRI's majority leader and who was also an ex-brother-in-law of President Carlos Salinas de Gortari, was gunned down on a downtown Mexico City street.

While the assassinations were not directly linked to NAFTA, an economic development at the end of the year after the presidential election was. The peso, which had been overvalued during the build up to NAFTA, faced its day of reckoning. It spectacularly crashed on December 20, sending the economy plummeting. The public blamed Carlos Salinas de Gortari, the former president and chief promoter of NAFTA, for the economic crisis, and he left the country in March 1995 for self-imposed exile. Meanwhile his brother, Raul Salinas de Gortari, was jailed for masterminding the assassination of Ruiz Massieu and was also accused of massive corruption involving tens of millions of dollars.

In Mexico City a wave of crime broke out. What had been a relatively safe city almost overnight became dangerous. Particularly nerve-racking for the upper classes was that the city became one of the world's capitals for kidnapping. Little of this appeared in official statistics. Many victims did not want to go to the police out of fear that the police themselves were involved in the crimes.

Mexico recovered its short-term political and economic stability but has yet to fully adjust to the long-term social impacts of NAFTA. These are being particularly felt in the countryside, where millions of peasants have lost traditional markets to the flood of cheaper imports, particularly in corn and beans. This in turn is forcing them to migrate to urban areas and the United States.

Lessons from Puerto Rico

Mexico's experience with NAFTA is similar to that of Puerto Rico's with Operation Bootstrap, a policy with similar motivations that 45 years earlier inaugurated Puerto Rico's rapid postwar industrialization. Similar to the *maquiladora* program, Operation Bootstrap enticed U.S. corporations to set up factories on the island by offering them access to cheap labor costs and freedom from paying taxes. At roughly the same time, technological improvements in transportation allowed U.S. corporations on the mainland to increasingly use the island as an export market, particularly for food. No formal free trade policy needed to be enacted because Puerto Rico was a colony of the United States; the technological improvements in the transportation of commodities allowed the already existing de facto free trade relationship between the island and mainland to become a reality.

Operation Bootstrap was in many ways a development policy based on substituting foreign industrial capital for surplus labor. Its proponents and others viewed the island as overpopulated and encouraged unemployed Puerto Ricans to migrate to the United States as they attempted to import corporate capital from the mainland.

Puerto Rico sent relatively few emigrants to the mainland before World War II, but during and after the war two gigantic push-and-pull factors came together to produce within a very short time more emigrants than in the entire previous colonial history combined. On the pull side, the United States emerged from the war as the unchallenged leading industrial country in the world, which put it in position to dominate world markets. Its industrial engine revved up to take advantage of the opportunity and sucked in labor from rural areas, including from its own South and colonial Puerto Rico. Not all Puerto Ricans went into factories; many went into agriculture and services as well. In all cases, relative labor shortages in the context of a rapidly growing U.S. economy became the pull factor that brought waves of Puerto Rican emigrants to the mainland. They, unlike other Latin Americans, had ready access to the U.S. labor market, having been citizens since 1917.

On the push side, Puerto Rico's government encouraged emigration, based largely on the assumption that the island was absolutely overpopulated. Since 1930 various government and private reports had blamed chronic unemployment in Puerto Rico on overpopulation.[12] C. Wright Mills, Clarence Senior, and Rose Kohn Goldsen, in their study of New York's early Puerto Rican community, were among those who assumed that overpopulation had been the root cause of emigration from the island. They asserted that "there remain but two civilized recourses: to control the number of births, or to encourage substantial migration from the island."[13]

Both policies, in fact, occurred. Within two decades of the publication of those words, 35 per cent of women of child-bearing age in Puerto Rico had been sterilized in an excess of neo-Malthusian abuse[14] and one-third of Puerto Ricans were living off the island, producing one of the most geographically and to some extent culturally divided nations in the world. By 2002, over half of all Puerto Ricans were living in the mainland United States.

By most macroeconomic indicators, Puerto Rico became a modern almost First World society by 1990. It had Latin America's highest per capita gross national product and income. Its labor force profile with 3 per cent in agriculture, 24 per cent in industry, and 73 per cent in services was virtually identical to that of the United States and other First World societies.[15] In 2000 its infant mortality rate of 10.5 and life expectancy of 75, while not Latin America's best, was closer to First World than typical Third World standards.[16] Free trade, rapid industrialization, and wholesale emigration appear then to have been a successful development recipe.

But other indicators were not as positive. Puerto Rico began the third millennium with 48.2 per cent of its citizens living below the poverty line, four times as high as that of the United States, and an unemployment rate of 19.3 per cent that was over three times higher than the United States. Only 40.5 per cent of persons 16 years old and older were in the labor force, compared to 67.2 per cent in the United States.[17] If the United States had the normal participation rate for a developed society, then the difference between the two rates indicated that in addition to the 19.3 per cent officially unemployed, another 26.7 per cent are permanently unemployed outside of the labor force. The real rate of unemployment may thus be closer 46 per cent.

To maintain a poor and unemployed population that large, the United States must continually transfer public assistance funds to the island. In 2000 the United States transferred $8.4 billion in assistance. It received $2.8 billion in taxes and revenues, indicating a net subsidy to the island of $5.6 billion.[18] At the same time U.S.-based corporations have been allowed to operate tax free. It is arguable as to which is the greater sum: the amount of private profits that leave the island for the mainland or the amount of public assistance funds that enter it to maintain the surplus population, which in part serves to depress wages and thereby inflate private profits.

Thus, Puerto Rico's development has been marked by extreme dependency on the United States to the point that if that relationship were stopped, it is doubtful that the island could maintain its relative economic advantage over other Caribbean nations. It is also largely for that reason that political independence, while culturally attractive to many, is not considered to be a serious option by the vast majority of the electorate. There is evidence that independence had more popular support in the 1930s before the island's economic dependency on the United States became so complete. Operation Bootstrap may have, wittingly or unwittingly, contributed to dampening popular enthusiasm for independence.

Transforming Mexican Agriculture
NAFTA has many of the same goals and means to achieve them as Operation Bootstrap. It relies on encouraging foreign investment and free trade to transform

Mexico from a poor traditional society in which agriculture absorbed one-quarter of the labor force into a modern industrial society. NAFTA gives U.S. and Canadian corporations free access to Mexico's low-cost labor force and domestic market.

Unlike Operation Bootstrap, however, there has been no official attempt to encourage Mexican emigration, in large part because of political sensitivities in the United States. Mexican President Carlos Salinas de Gortari and U.S. Ambassador to Mexico John Negroponte went out of their ways to assure U.S. public opinion that there would be no increase in illegal migrants by alleging that NAFTA would actually result in fewer emigrants from Mexico. President Salinas de Gortari stated that with NAFTA Mexico intended to "export goods, not people."[19] Ambassador Negroponte[20] then repeated the same formulation, which was repeated again by Democratic Party President Bill Clinton during the final campaign to pass NAFTA.[21] However, increased Mexican emigration was as inevitable a consequence of NAFTA as Puerto Rican emigration was of Operation Bootstrap because fundamental to both policies was the goal of modernizing agriculture so that it could be more efficiently accomplished with fewer laborers.

As Table 7.1 indicates, there were striking similarities between the labor forces and population distributions of Puerto Rico in 1950 and Mexico in 1990, the census years closest to the inaugurations of Operation Bootstrap and NAFTA respectively. Agricultural employment absorbed a relatively large part of both labor forces. More striking was the nearly identical relatively small proportion of emigrants from both countries at those times: in 1950, 88.9 per cent of all Puerto Rican-descent persons in the world lived on the island; in 1990, 86.4 per cent of all Mexican-descent persons in the world lived in Mexico. Correspondingly, most of the balances of each population lived in the United States. Within a very short time, both Puerto Rican distributions would shift dramatically as the Mexican ones are now.

Neither Operation Bootstrap nor NAFTA represented as much radical innovations as formalizations and accelerations of developments already underway. Puerto Rican small farmers and agricultural laborers were already being squeezed off the land as were Mexican peasants before 1994, and both countries had already produced emigrants to the United States.

NAFTA, like Operation Bootstrap, was based on the assumption that it was more feasible to attract U.S. investment to provide manufacturing jobs than to continue to attempt to build up a domestically controlled industrial base. As a corollary, NAFTA, also like Operation Bootstrap, allowed U.S. agricultural surpluses to enter the country tariff free. The justification for this was partly to encourage modernization and efficiency. Free trade proponents argued that protective tariffs functioned to protect inefficient industries and agriculture while free trade acted to force them to keep up with competitors or be driven from the market. In this respect, Mexico's inefficient manufacturers are being forced out by competition from U.S. producers who can produce the same products at lower costs with fewer laborers, in many cases at offshore plants in Mexico itself as well as the United States.

Table 7.1: Comparative Labor Force Distributions and Migration: Puerto Rico at the Beginning of Operation Bootstrap (1950) and Mexico Just Before the Beginning of NAFTA (1990)

	Puerto Rico 1950	Mexico 1990
Labor Force Distribution in percentages		
Agriculture and other primary	37.8	24.7
Manufacturing and other secondary	21.8	27.0
Services	40.4	48.3
Total	100.0	100.0
Number	586,587	22,599,000
Population Distribution in percentages:*		
In country	88.9	86.4
In United States	11.1	13.6
Total	100.0	100.0
Number	2,512,078	98,393,000

* Includes both the populations of Puerto Rico and Mexico and all Puerto Rican- and Mexican-descent persons living in the United States.

Sources: U.S. Bureau of the Census, *Census of Population: 1950,* Vol. II, Part 54, *Characteristics of the Population* (Washington, DC: U.S. Government Printing Office, 1953) Table 69; Instituto Nacional de Estadística Geografía e Informática (INEGI), *XI Censo General de Población y Vivienda 1990* (Aguascalientes: INEGI, 1992).

Mexico's peasant farmers have been particularly vulnerable. The United States produces an enormous agricultural surplus each year, much of it under the cost of producing comparable products in Mexico. Mexican peasant farming is much more labor intensive. Despite having less than one-quarter of North America's population, Mexico before the advent of NAFTA had 58 per cent of its combined agricultural labor force. In 1991 Under Secretary of Agricultural Planning Luis Tellez stated bluntly, "It is the policy of my government to remove half of the population from rural Mexico during the next five years."[22]

Phased in over 15 years, NAFTA eliminated all tariffs on agricultural imports so that by 2008 all would be tariff free. During the negotiations, products were placed in five categories: those that were already tariff free; those that would immediately have tariffs completely eliminated in 1994; those that would have tariffs eliminated in five equal annual stages beginning in 1994 and be duty free by 1998; those that would have tariffs eliminated in ten equal annual stages beginning in 1994 and be duty free by 2003; and those that would have tariffs eliminated in 15 equal annual stages beginning in 1994 and be duty free by 2008. Hence, by 2004, most formerly protected agricultural products had lost all of their protection from imports and the remaining ones had lost at least two-thirds of their protection, with all of it scheduled to be lost within the remaining four years of the phase-out period.

In 1999 the Mexican Senate held a series of hearings and commissioned studies on the impact of NAFTA on the Mexican economy, including the agricultural sector. Among their conclusions was that though Mexican commercial agricultural exchanges with the United States grew significantly in the first five years of NAFTA, the size of the country's agricultural sector shrank. In 1990, the closest census year to the 1994 inauguration of NAFTA, 23.5 per cent of the Mexican labor force was in agriculture compared to less than 3 per cent in the United States and less than 5 per cent in Canada. Ten years later in 2000, the percentage of the Mexican labor force in agriculture had declined by nearly one-third to just 15.8 per cent. However, the absolute number of workers in Mexican agriculture, some 5.3 million, did not decline.[23] Rather, that number did not keep up with increases in the sizes of the population and labor force.

Thus, whereas the population increased by 15 million persons and the labor force by 10 million, the size of the agricultural labor force remained roughly the same. That meant that overall the sector did not absorb new workers coming into the labor force. Children could not work in the occupations of their parents.

There were "winners and losers" in the sector, the winners being those in fruits and vegetables and the losers being those in grains and food oils. The greatest losers, according to one authority who testified, were the poorest of the farmers in grains and food oils.[24]

The fate of corn, the greatest staple of poor peasant diets and crops, was indicative of the NAFTA-induced pressures. As many as 18 million Mexicans depend on corn production for their livelihoods.[25] Between 1994 and 2000, as Mexican tariffs declined incrementally, the volume of corn imports from the United States tripled.[26] The impact on corn-growing peasants was devastating.

Economic Displacement and Migration

The cumulative result of NAFTA was to squeeze people, particularly the coming-of-age children of peasants, off the land. Some moved into Mexico's urban areas; others emigrated to the United States and, to a much lesser extent, Canada. Also, a new flood of manufactured imports undercut domestic manufacturing and the jobs that it supported.

There is considerable dispute over just how large this migrant stream has been. While the agricultural labor force was 5.3 million, the population that lived in the countryside was larger, since it included children, other non-working family members, and other workers and families whose economic activities, such as stores, restaurants, and repair shops, depended on the existence of an agricultural labor force. The number of people in the countryside who were impacted by NAFTA policies thus was much larger than just those who worked in agriculture. NAFTA may have driven as many as 15 million people from the countryside.

Table 7.2: Total Puerto Rican and Mexican Origin Populations with Percents Living in the United States

| | Puerto Rican Origin | | Mexican Origin | |
	Number	% in U.S.	Number	% in U.S.
1910	1,120	0.1	15,542	0.2
1920	1,312	0.9	14,880	4.9
1930	1,597	3.3	17,833	7.2
1940	1,939	3.6	21,221	7.4
(1948 – beginning of Operation Bootstrap)				
1950	2,512	12.0	28,072	8.1
1960	3,237	27.4	39,515	8.8
1970	4,103	33.9	55,222	8.2
1980	5,201	38.5	78,029	11.1
1990	6,174	43.0	98,393	13.6
(1994 – beginning of NAFTA)				
2000	7,215	47.2	118,124	17.5
2005	7,450	50.8	130,045	20.6

Note: Numbers in thousands.

Sources: Compiled from U.S. Bureau of the Census, *Census of Population* for years 1950, 1960, 1970, 1980, 1990, 2000; and *2005 American Community Survey* (Washington, DC: U.S. Government Printing Office); Frank D. Bean and Marta Tienda, *The Hispanic Population of the United States* (New York: Russell Sage Foundation, 1987); James W. Wilkie, ed., *Statistical Abstract of Latin America* (Los Angeles, CA: UCLA Latin American Center Publications, 1992); A.J. Jaffee, Ruth M. Cullen, and Thomas D. Boswell, *The Changing Demography of Spanish Americans* (New York: Academic Press, 1980); Instituto Nacional de Estadística Geografía e Informática (INEGI), *XII Censo General de Población y Vivienda, 2000* and *II Conteo de Poblacón y Vivienda 2005* (Aguascalientes: INEGI).

There is dispute over the number of migrants who have gone to the United States. The problems of estimating the size of this population are obvious since it is a population whose survival depends upon not being detected by immigration officials. The most careful demographic estimates indicate that the size of the undocumented Mexican population residing in the United States nearly doubled between

1996 and 2001 from approximately 2.35 million to 4.51 million.[27] In 2004 they numbered 5.9 million.[28]

Just as the percentage of Puerto Ricans living in the United States more than doubled in the decade after the beginning of Operation Bootstrap, between 1990 and 2000, the decade that includes the beginning of NAFTA, the percentage of Mexicans living in the United States jumped from 13.6 to 17.5 per cent. While not as dramatic as the Puerto Rican emigration surge, it nevertheless was the largest emigration increase in Mexican history (see Table 7.2).

One of the obvious reasons why the increase was not higher is that, unlike with Puerto Ricans who are U.S. citizens, Mexicans cannot move freely to the United States. At the same time, large numbers of peasants have resisted the economic pressures and voluntarily remain in the countryside, in part supported by increasing remittances sent by those who have migrated to the United States. The reform of Article 27 to promote land privatization and concentration in NAFTA's first ten years did not prove to be a significant factor in promoting outmigration. There was no initial rush among *ejidatarios* to sell and lose newly privatized land, as proponents and critics alike of the reform had assumed would happen.[29] The core of the Mexican peasantry has proved to be resilient in the face of this and other neoliberal pressures. In assessing the pressures to leave the land and the cultural and other factors that promote determination to stay on it, economist David Barkin writes, "It is not surprising that large numbers of peasants and their children are leaving the countryside .... What is surprising is the large number of people who do return to their communities, the volume of resources they are transferring to these communities, and the lengths to which they are going to implement new strategies to consolidate their social and productive systems."[30]

Nevertheless, the dramatic increases of undocumented Mexican workers and documented Mexican-origin persons residing in the United States confirm that NAFTA, contrary to the claims of its early proponents in Washington and Mexico City, stimulated a significant surge in migration from Mexico to the United States.

In 2000 there were approximately 25 million Mexican-origin persons residing in the United States. Of those about half had been born in Mexico and 17.9 per cent were in the country illegally.[31] If NAFTA continues to stimulate the same level of emigration, then the decades ahead will see tens of millions of persons swelling the ranks of the Mexican-origin population in the United States.

Death and the Wall

On October 26, 2006, President George W. Bush signed legislation to construct 698 miles of additional fencing along its southern border to block the entry of illegal migrants from Mexico and other Latin American countries. Constructing such a wall had long been advocated by the most nativist, right-wing sectors of the Republican Party. No previous administration, though, had taken the idea seriously.

It was thought that it was easier and less expensive to simply step up patrolling of the main illegal crossing points.

Traditionally, the issue of border security comes and goes in U.S. politics. Often it becomes an issue when unemployment rates rise, with undocumented migrants being used as scapegoats for "taking jobs from Americans." Both Democratic and Republican administrations responded to such political pressure by making public announcements that they were increasing vigilance of the border to stop illegal crossings. The 2006 wall project, though, did not come as the result of pressure about unemployment but came as a result of heightened security fears, encouraged by the Bush administration, in the wake of the September 11, 2001 terrorist attacks in New York and Washington.

The Bush administration found itself after the attacks facing a contradictory policy dilemma. On the one hand, it firmly embraced NAFTA and had been turning a largely blind eye toward the increased migration associated with it. Mexican President Vicente Fox, also a firm NAFTA supporter, wanted to develop a bilateral plan to legalize much of the increased migration and the Bush administration was receptive. After 9/11, however, the centerpiece of all government policy became the so-called War on Terror and increasing security. In that rhetorical climate of its own making, the Bush administration became vulnerable to pressures from the most right-wing nativist bases of the Republican Party, which had never embraced economic integration with Canada and Mexico through NAFTA. They turned the security rhetoric of the president against him: if the country was to become truly secure, it had to secure its southern border with a wall. To force the issue, right-wing vigilante groups, including the Minutemen, began patrolling part of the border in search of undocumented crossers. Bush capitulated with the symbolic gesture of additional fencing to appease the right-wing base of his party. The symbolism of the gesture, though, has cost the United States dearly in terms of its image among Latin Americans. The fencing is universally referred to in Latin America as a wall, invoking the symbolism of the Cold War's Berlin Wall. Additionally, constructing a wall on the southern but not northern border is a symbol well understood and resented in Mexico and the rest of Latin America.

A consequence of increased security on the border will be to increase an already increasing toll of migrant deaths. The number of undocumented workers who died crossing the border doubled to 472 between 1995 and 2005,[32] the first ten years of NAFTA. This increase has been caused by, first, the increasing size of the migrant flow as a result of the economic displacement caused by NAFTA; and, second, by the increasing effectiveness of U.S. security measures. The latter, including the fencing of more of the popular crossing areas, have pushed migrants to long unsafe treks across remote desert areas in blistering heat.[33]

Chapter 8

COMPARATIVE ECONOMIC AND SOCIAL CLASSES

A half millennium of uneven development in North American has produced economic class structures in the United States and Canada that are similar and distinctly different in Mexico. The similar economic class structures of the United States and Canada, however, does not carry over to their social class profiles, which are noticeably different, as is that of Mexico. Put differently, North America contains two types of economic class structures and three types of social class profiles.

As stated earlier but worth reiterating, from one angle classes have to do with the different categories of people who constitute the labor forces of particular production systems. They are made up of people who perform different roles within divisions of labor. Polar class roles in historical production systems have been slaves and owners in slavery, peasants and landlords in feudalism, workers and capitalists in capitalism. From another angle, classes suggest the different levels at which people live as rich, poor, and all shades in between. The first angle is that of economic classes, the second of social classes.

The contemporary labor forces of Canada, Mexico, and the United States are divided into the *economic* classes of workers, small business owners, middle-class professionals and managers, and capitalist owners. At the same time, the populations of North America are divided into lower, working, middle, and upper *social* classes.[1]

There is undoubtedly correspondence between economic and social class positions, but it is far from complete. Social middle-class incomes, for example, can come from prosperous working-class, new middle-class professional or managerial, or small business class positions.

Economic Classes

Given Mexico's significantly lower level of economic development compared to the United States or Canada, which is reflected in the configuration of its labor force, it is not surprising that it would have a significantly different economic class profile. Uneven development produces different economic class profiles as well as different labor force bases from which they arise.

Official statistics in the United States, Canada, and Mexico categorize their labor forces into the general "classes of activities" of the self-employed, the employed, and unpaid employees. Though the statistics clearly separate these categories, they do not distinguish economic classes within them. Therefore, in order to estimate proportionate sizes of economic classes in labor forces, it is necessary to employ operational definitions for each of the classes and regroup official governmental statistics according to these categories.

The self-employed class of activity consists of the economic classes of capitalists and small business owners in all three countries. In Mexico until relatively recently, it also included peasants in the economic sense of the term, that is, small landowners who operated largely outside of the market by directly consuming rather than selling most of what they produced. The employee class of activity includes the new middle class of professional and managerial employees and the working class. Unpaid employees are members of the working class.

The first class of activity to be examined for its division into internal economic classes is the self-employed, who can be divided between capitalists and small business owners. In the most general of terms, what distinguishes a capitalist from a small business owner is that the former is an employer in addition to being an owner, while the latter is not. At what point, though, is a business owner enough of an employer to constitute a capitalist? Clearly an owner with only unpaid family workers or at most a few paid laborers does not constitute a capitalist. Theoretically, we must conclude that a business owner becomes a capitalist when the majority of his or her income derives from profits made from the labor of employed workers. Unfortunately, there is no source of information on the exact number of capitalists in any of the North American countries who conform to this definition. Most researchers, therefore, have counted as capitalists those employers who have more than a certain minimum number of employees. Some include as capitalists employers with as few as five employees; others require higher thresholds. I have, instead, counted as capitalists those high-income labor force participants who derive most of their income from ownership profits, capital gains, dividends, interest, and rents rather than from employee salaries or wages

Among the employee classes, what distinguishes a new middle-class member from a worker is that the former occupies a position that requires the exercise of a professional skill or managerial ability for which the employer is willing to pay a significantly higher salary. The new middle class exists in the employment hierarchy between, on the one hand, owners and top managers and, on the other, ordinary workers. In brief, relatively highly paid employed professionals and managers make up the new middle class. For calculation purposes, employed professionals, managers, and supervisors were included as members of the new middle class. Once the size of the new middle class has been estimated, the remainder of paid and unpaid employees in each of the labor forces can then be counted as workers.

With these definitions in mind, we can proceed to portray the economic class structures of each of the North American countries.

For the United States, income tax return distributions reveal that the first bracket at which profits, capital gains, and other ownership incomes exceed employee compensation is those received in excess of $500,000 — 0.8 per cent of tax filers. Thus, according to this estimation, the capitalist class makes up 0.8 per cent of the labor force.

Members of the highest stratum of the capitalist class have yearly incomes of over $10 million. An examination of this stratum is revealing. In 2004, 9,677 returns from the highest stratum of the capitalist class were filed with $10 million dollar or more incomes. Eighty per cent of the income of this stratum came from capital properties (stocks, bonds, business profits, rents, etc.). By far, the largest single source of capital income came from the sale of capital assets. That is, speculation on the rise in value of capital properties remains the largest single source of income for the richest stratum of the labor force in the United States.

Subtracting capitalists from self-employed members yields the estimate that the small business class makes up approximately 9 per cent of the labor force (see Table 8.1). Independent professionals, such as physicians and lawyers, represent the largest occupational fraction of small business owners, followed in descending order by craft workers, such as plumbers, electricians, mechanics, and carpenters; store keepers; farmers; and owners of service establishments, such as barber and beauty shops, restaurants, and the like.

Among the employee classes, new middle-class professionals and managers constitute approximately 30.2 per cent of the labor force, a proportion that has been rising rapidly in the last decades. Professionals account for 60 per cent of the class. The distinction between managers and professionals refers more to position that occupation. That is, many middle- and top-level managers began as professionals and then were promoted into managerial positions. They thus occupationally combine both managerial and professional characteristics in their positions.

The majority, 60 per cent, of the labor force is made up of workers. Unskilled and semiskilled workers constitute the largest occupational fraction of the working class, followed in descending order by clerical workers, sales persons, crafts persons, and technicians. If we follow the traditional blue-collar/white-collar distinction, then the majority, 56.8 per cent, of the working class is still made up of blue-collar workers. These represent 37.7 per cent of the entire labor force.[2]

In sum, the economic class structure of the United States is made up of 0.8 per cent capitalists, 9 per cent small business owners, 30.2 per cent new middle-class professionals and managers, and 60 per cent workers.

Table 8.1: Labor Forces and Economic Classes, 2000-2001

	UNITED STATES	CANADA	MEXICO
A. Labor Forces			
Self-Employed	9.8	11.9	25.2
Employed	89.9	87.7	70.6
Unpaid	0.3	0.4	4.2
Total	100.0	100.0	100.0
Number (in 1000s)	129,721	15,577	32,670
A. Economic Classes			
Capitalist	0.8	.3	.2
Small Busines	9.0	11.6	25.0
New Middle Class	30.2	21.0	5.0
Working	60.0	67.1	69.8
Total	100.0	100.0	100.0

Sources: Estimates based on data in U.S. Bureau of the Census, Census 2000, Summary File 3, Tables P50 and P51; Statistics Canada, "Paid Work, Occupation," 2001 Census (http://www.stat-can.ca/); and INEGI, *XII Censo General de Poblacion y Vivienda 2000.*

Application of the same techniques of estimation to the Canadian labor force reveals the existence of an economic class structure that resembles, with notable differences, that of the United States — 0.3 per cent capitalists, 10.9 per cent small business owners, 21 per cent new middle-class professionals and managers, and 67.1 per cent workers.

The most notable difference is the proportionately smaller size of the Canadian capitalist class. The highest income stratum identified by official Canadian tax data was $250,000 ($236,585 U.S.), which accounted for 0.6 per cent of filers. The majority, 58.4 per cent, of income for that stratum was made up of employment income. Thus, capitalist income begins at a higher level and for a smaller minority than identified by official data. Most likely, not more than 0.3 per cent of the Canadian labor force is made up of capitalists, which is proportionately less than half the size of their U.S. counterparts.

The 2000 Mexican Census identified the self-employed members of the labor force but did not provide a clear basis for distinguishing the capitalist and small business classes among them. Capitalists, as indicated earlier, have the double identity of both being business owners and employers. In this respect, the Census found 854,166 business owners, 2.5 per cent of the labor force, who had employees, but it did not subdivide those individuals according to the numbers of their employees.

Business owners with as few as one employee were included as employers. It is thus impossible to directly distinguish capitalist from small business employers. The Census distinguished employers according to the amounts of their income. In its highest income category, equivalent to $9,927 a year, it found 205,354 employers.[3] If that were the number of capitalists, it would represent 0.6 per cent of the labor force, but we can safely assume that capitalists receive far more income. Unfortunately, though, the official statistics do not distinguish employers that have those higher incomes. At most, capitalists probably represent no more than one-third of those employers who receive $9,927 a year or more. They therefore make up no more than 0.2 per cent of the entire labor force.[4]

The remainder of the self-employed, 25 per cent of the total labor force, is made up of small business owners. However, that is a very highly stratified class, ranging from itinerant sellers of foods on the streets to owners of fixed places of business. All technically operate profit-oriented small businesses, but the livings they can derive from them vary greatly. It would be a mistake, therefore, to view small business ownership in Mexico as necessarily conferring a middle-class standard of living or social status.

The new middle class of employed professionals and managers makes up 5 per cent of the labor force. However, this figure should be treated with caution. Half of the country's professionals are schoolteachers whose very low average wages are not sufficient to afford a socially middle-class standard of living. If we define new middle-class members as those who had both an employed professional and managerial position and a middle-class salary, then the size of that class would shrink to no more than 2 to 3 per cent of the labor force. The remaining 69.8 per cent of the labor force is made up of the working class.

In sum, the Mexican economic class structure is made up of approximately 0.2 per cent capitalists, 25 per cent small business owners, 5 per cent new middle-class professionals and managers, and 69.8 per cent workers.

As in the case of the labor force configurations, there are dramatic differences between the economic class structures of Mexico and those of the United States and Canada. In relative terms, there are significantly more capitalists and new middle-class members in the United States and Canada, while there are more small business owners in Mexico.

These differences occur because Mexico is at a different stage of capital accumulation than the United States and Canada. On the one hand, capital accumulation is more advanced in the United States and Canada in the simple sense that quantitatively more of it has been formed, on the basis of which relatively larger capitalist classes can subsist. However, it is also more advanced in these two countries in the sense that capitalist businesses have been able, as we have seen earlier, to take over greater percentages of economic activity at the expense of small businesses than have their Mexican counterparts. As a result, the small business class continues to control very significant parts of the Mexican economy, while in the United States and

Canada most of the professional and managerial skills formerly exercised in small business contexts are now exercised in corporate and state bureaucracies. Put differently, because there is a relatively much smaller accumulation of private capital in Mexico than the United States or Canada, the relative sizes of both the capitalist and new middle classes are correspondingly much smaller.

The relatively smaller accumulation of private Mexican capital has meant that there has been less possibility of financing large-scale capitalist businesses, hence the fewer the number of capitalists that can be supported. The existence of fewer large-scale businesses has also resulted in there being fewer positions for a new middle class of middle-level managers and professionals.

Despite its proportionately small size, however, the Mexican capitalist class contains some spectacularly wealthy and powerful members by world standards. In 2007, *Fortune* magazine concluded that the world's wealthiest man was Carlos Slim Helú, the owner of Telmex, the Mexican telecommunications monopoly.[5] Slim's estimated fortune of $59 billion surpasses that of even Bill Gates, the owner of Microsoft. Slim was one of the principle beneficiaries of the neoliberal privatization policies of the 1990s that included the signing of NAFTA. President Carlos Salinas de Gortari sold him the national telephone company in 1990. Altogether in the 1990s ten Mexican capitalists joined the ranks of the world's 946 billionaires.

Table 8.2: North America's Billionaires, 2007

	UNITED STATES	CANADA	MEXICO
Number	403	23	10
Total Wealth	$1,317.1	$84.4	$74.1
Total Wealth as % of GDP	11.2	8.4	7.3

Note: The top five for each country are: United States—William Gates III, Warren Buffett, Sheldon Adelson, Lawrence Ellison, and Paul Allen; Canada—David Tompson, Galen Weston, James Arthur and John Irving, Edward Rogers, and Bernard Sherman; Mexico—Carlos Slim Helú, Alberto Bailleres, Ricardo Salinas Pliego, Jerónimo Arango, and Emilio Azcárraga Jean. Five Walton family members, owners of Wal-Mart, have smaller fortunes that do not rank in the top five in the United States; however, together the fortunes add up to $83.3 billion, which is the largest fortune of any individual or family in the world.

Source: Calculated on the basis of information in Lisa Kroll and Allison Fass, eds., "The World's Billionaires," *Forbes*, 8 March 2007.

The great difference in the relative sizes of the self-employed components of the North American labor forces has far-reaching consequences for the economic class profiles of the three countries. The small business class, because of the large number of self-employed in the labor force, is much larger in relative terms in Mexico than the United States or Canada. The capitalist class of large business owners is smaller, though. Large businesses in the United States have been more successful than their Mexican counterparts in monopolizing markets, as is indicated by the relatively small amount of small business activity that continues to exist on the margins of the national economy. As a result of medium- and large-size private and public units monopolizing the economic landscape, close to 90 per cent of both Canadian and U.S. labor force members are employees. Because large units in Mexico have not absorbed as much of the economic landscape as have those in the United States or Canada, there is relatively more economic space to operate a small business, and consequently over one-quarter of the labor force is still self-employed.

The comparatively high percentage of self-employed workers in the Mexican labor force also affects the profiles of the employee classes, that is, the new middle and working classes. Because of the large number of small businesses in Mexico compared to the United States or Canada, the economic space occupied by businesses, either public or private, that are large enough to have significant numbers of employees is relatively smaller. As a result, both the new middle and working classes are relatively smaller. Put differently, because of the disproportionately large size of the small business class in Mexico, all other classes — capitalists, new middle-class professionals and managers, and workers — are disproportionately smaller in relative terms.

Thus, the most dramatic difference between the labor force of Mexico and those of its continental neighbors is the larger number, in relative terms, of small business owners and, consequently, the smaller number of wage and salary workers that it has. As mentioned above, over one-quarter (25.2 per cent) of Mexican labor force members draw their main incomes from business profits compared to just 9.8 per cent in the United States and 11.9 per cent in Canada. The Mexican self-employed are proportionately over two and one-half times as many as their United States and Canadian counterparts. With a population only one-third the size, Mexico has almost as many self-employed persons as the United States.

The self-employed in all three countries are highly stratified, ranging from extremely poor street vendors to billionaire capitalist owners. Mexico's self-employed are much more likely to have only micro-sized businesses and to be poorer than their U.S. or Canadian counterparts. The vast majority of the Mexican self-employed (86.2 per cent) operate businesses that are too small to have any paid employees.[6] In contrast, 89.1 per cent of the business establishments in the United States are large enough to have paid employees.[7]

A substantial part of the Mexican self-employed population consists of itinerants who peddle their wares or services from place to place. The existence of this very large itinerant floating labor force reflects two facets of Mexican underdevelopment. First, there has not been a sufficient accumulation of either private or public capital to create enough regular paying jobs to absorb them. Second, there is little or no public assistance or welfare to serve as an alternative source of income for that part of the labor force that cannot find regular employment. Many members of this itinerant population prefer to work as employees when and for as long as such regular jobs in the formal labor force can be found. When they cannot find jobs, they must hustle livelihoods as best they can as itinerant peddlers of goods and services. It is typical for a worker to be laid off, be unemployed for a period, and then start some type of itinerant business in order to generate an income. The business will then be abandoned if a better paying position as an employee opens up.[8] There is also a substantial part of the itinerant population that earns an income higher than the low average wages prevailing in Mexico and thus prefers to remain in that position.[9] These itinerants constitute a lumpen bourgeoisie. They are bourgeois by virtue of being owners of independent businesses but lumpen (from the German "rag") by virtue of their businesses being so small. Their massive existence reflects structural conditions in the nature of Mexican capitalism that are different, at least in degree, from those of the United States and Canada.

Somewhat similar itinerant sellers exist in large U.S. cities such as Washington, New York, and Los Angeles, and Canadian cities like Toronto and Vancouver. The growing existence of weekend flea markets indicates that many people are at least part-time itinerants, but the significance of itinerancy is not nearly as great as in Mexico. Itinerant sellers are one of the largest components of the Mexican labor force. In the contemporary United States and Canada, they are a distinctly marginal phenomenon, although they were not always so. In the late nineteenth and twentieth centuries, many neighborhoods, especially immigrant neighborhoods, contained street markets and itinerant sellers. The relatively large Mexican itinerant population is thus a reflection of the country's stage of development, a stage surpassed in the United States, Canada, and other First World countries decades ago.

Because of the sporadic type of employment pattern of a substantial part of the Mexican labor force, it is difficult to estimate the true size of unemployment in the country. Depending on whether they are counted as employed, underemployed, or unemployed greatly affects overall estimates of unemployment in the country. Mexican government statistics do not count itinerant sellers as unemployed or underemployed which results in unrealistically low estimates of underemployment. The Organization for Economic Cooperation and Development (OECD), for example, uncritically reported that for 2005 Mexico had an unemployment rate of only 3.5 per cent compared to 5.2 per cent in the United States and 6.8 per cent in Canada.[10]

The relatively large percentage of mainly small — most often micro — business owners in Mexico explains a second difference in labor force compositions. Because there are proportionately so many more family-owned businesses in Mexico than in the United States or Canada, there are more family members working without pay. In Mexico, 8.1 per cent of the labor force is made up of unpaid workers, compared to 0.3

per cent in the United States and 0.4 per cent in Canada (Table 8.1). There are thus proportionately more than 20 times as many unpaid workers in the Mexican labor force. The large part of the labor force accounted for by unpaid workers is a logical consequence of farming and self-employment, which are still predominant in the Mexican economy. There is a high correlation between the existence of family small business ownership in a sector and the use of unpaid family labor. Traditionally, the family members, including children, of both farmers and urban small business owners have been called upon to supply labor when hired workers could not be afforded. To the degree that farms and small businesses decrease, as they have in the United States and Canada, such opportunities for employment of unpaid family labor decrease.

The relatively large percentage of family business owners and unpaid laborers in the Mexican working population results in part, but not fully, from agriculture continuing to absorb 15 per cent of the labor force, compared to 1.6 per cent in the United States and 2.7 per cent in Canada.[11] Over one-fifth (21.8 per cent) of Mexican small business owners are farmers.[12]

However, as any citizen of or visitor to Mexico knows, the nation's urban streets and markets are also filled with small businesses—family-owned stores, restaurants, and repair and workshops. And significant numbers of independent itinerants peddle their goods or services from place to place—or subway car to subway car in the case of merchants who work the Metro. Mexicans are more likely to eat out in the thousands of small independently owned family restaurants than at chain operations such as MacDonald's (which exists in Mexico but is not as omnipresent as it is in the United States or Canada). They have their mufflers repaired or replaced in independent curbside shops rather than Midas-type franchises. They are more likely to buy their clothes off impromptu rods in market stalls than in department stores.

As is well known, Mexican labor is cheap compared to labor in Canada and the United States. The minimum wage in Mexico in 2007 was between 55 and 58 cents (U.S.) per hour, depending on the zone of the country. That compares to the U.S. federal minimum wage of $7.25 and the Canadian of between $6.59 and $8.00 (U.S.), depending on the province. Calculations from the two most recent surveys of the Mexican labor force offer different estimates of income averages, but both are significantly lower than those prevailing in the United States or Canada. According to figures from the Mexican Census, the median daily wage of the labor force in 2000 was between two and three times the minimum wage or between $8.80 and $14.01 U.S.[13] According to the national survey of households, the median monthly income of households in 2004 was $402 while its mean income was $685.[14] Medium incomes in Canada and the United States are over ten times as high as that in Mexico.

That difference of incomes, though, does not mean that the differences in standards of living are as severe. Substantial parts of the Mexican labor force receive forms of income that do not appear in the census estimations. Undoubtedly the over one-quarter of the Mexican labor force that is self-employed under-reports its income to avoid taxes. Many of those who are employees receive forms of non-monetary income such as free medical care, subsidized loans for purchasing houses at below market rates, and coupons that can be exchanged for food. While there is no question that the standard of living of the Mexican labor force is, on the average, much lower than those of the United States and Canadian labor forces, it is not as different as the disproportions in direct monetary incomes reported in official statistics seem to indicate.

The current distribution of the Mexican labor force bears a resemblance to that of the United States before the full brunt of industrialization, monopolization, and urbanization had set in before World War II. In 1940, for example, 15.9 per cent of the U.S. labor force was still occupied in primary sector agricultural and mining activities, which is close to what exists today in Mexico.[15] Correspondingly, small family-owned businesses lined and, in some cases, filled urban streets in the United States and Canada, as they do today in Mexico. The great difference is that the United States with that labor force distribution in 1940 was still a rich society by world standards while Mexico today with the same distribution is a poor society.

What is striking is that in the wake of implementation of NAFTA in 1994, agricultural employment in the labor force declined dramatically from 23.5 to 15 per cent but small business employment remained at the same proportion of 26 per cent. A shift occurred in activities but not in class relations. Where people work changed more than their class membership.

Managerial Power and Corruption

In all three North American economies the role of managers within labor forces has been increasing. The growth of a separate role for managers is the result of long-term trends in all market societies. The earlier the period of capitalist development and the smaller the company, the more likely ownership and management roles were fused, that is, the owner ran the company directly. But as companies developed into large-scale corporate bureaucracies, the roles became divided and were occupied by different people. Generally, the role of management increases as corporations grow larger and direct ownership control declines. It becomes increasingly impossible for owners to be involved in all decisions. They must delegate those powers to trusted managers. This inevitable development has given rise to two questions: What is the class position of managers? And have managers displaced owners as the real holders of corporate power?

Managers in general terms are employees who organize and direct other employees. The larger and more complex the economic organization — either public or private — the more the need for the coordinating function of management. In one sense, managers are simply coordinators in the production process who exist under all complex systems — be they capitalist or socialist, public or private sector. For that reason, there is some circulation of managers between top public and private positions in the United States, Mexico, and Canada. In another sense, though, they are intermediaries between centers of economic power and workers. In formerly socialist societies, managers transmitted the directives of central plans that had been developed by ruling communist parties. In market societies, managers in the public sector transmit the general directives of those who control the state. Managers in the private sector transmit the directives of the owners of the corporations for which they are employed. Private corporations are thus organized as bureaucracies with managers in the top positions of presidents, vice-presidents, treasurers, and so on, but above them are boards of directors who represent the interests of owners. The whole occupational role of managers is highly stratified, rising in positional terms from foremen on factory assembly lines and managers of franchised convenience stores to top officers of transnational corporations.

In economic-class terms, the bottom rungs of the managerial hierarchy exist in the working class, its middle levels are in the new middle class, and it peaks in the capitalist class. Many working capitalists identify themselves in occupational terms as managers. Many top corporate managers, who did not start out as capitalists, become capitalists in the course of their career developments by virtue of receiving very high salaries that are invested in profit-making activities. Many professionals, as they advance in their careers, take on managerial responsibilities.

The expansion of the separate role of private-sector management, that is, separate from that of ownership, in the United States and Canada is one of the reasons why the occupants of its top positions often receive multimillion-dollar incomes that are sufficient to propel them into the ranks of the capitalist class itself. In 2005 the average compensation for the chief executive officers (CEOs) of the 350 largest U.S. corporations was $11.6 million.[16] The separation of the roles of owner and manager is much less advanced in Mexico, where the private manager is much more likely to be the working owner. Overall, because accumulation and concentration of capital are less advanced in Mexico, the proportion of Mexican labor force members who identify themselves as managers is less than in the United States or Canada.

While it is clear that more and more decisions in the private sector are completely within the prerogatives of managers, it is also clear that hiring and firing power over managers is still held by owners. The top manager survives only so long as he or she carries out the management role to the satisfaction of the owners. If profit rates begin to slide dangerously or the corporation begins to lose its competitive footing, owners, as represented by boards of directors, will replace top managers.

To some extent, managers and owners thus have different interests. Managers, like any other employee, would like to receive as much compensation as possible; owners want the company to be as strong and profitable as possible. To the extent that managers are able to use their day-to-day power to overcompensate themselves with high salaries, stock options, and the like, they divert funds that would otherwise go into stock dividends and capital accumulation that would favor shareholders.

Overcompensation of CEOs at the expenses of shareholder dividends and worker pay has become an issue in the United States in the last decades. The ratio between total compensation for CEOs and average worker pay went from 42-to-1 in 1980 to 525-to-1 in the peak year of 2000. In 2005 the ratio was 411-to-1.[17]

The three countries differ in the extent to which appointments to state managerial posts are politically determined. Politically based appointments reach further down into the administrative hierarchies of national and local governments of the United States than Canada.[18] They reach much further down in Mexico, where patronage appointments, even for clerical positions, are customary. Middle-level managers in Mexico attach themselves as team members to particularly powerful or upwardly mobile individuals. As the patrons change positions, they take along their team members. The patron can arrange for the appointment of the relatives of the managers to other positions.

In the United States and Canada, very few managers in the public sector become wealthy. Those are generally new middle-class positions whose incomes peak in the top ranks of the social middle class. In Mexico, however, management within the public sector has for many been the source of capital formation, which later financed private ventures. Thus, Mexican state managerial positions have been sources of capital accumulation for a significant number of capitalists. Salaries, which are not high, have not been the sources of this accumulation. Rather, what have made state managers in Mexico into wealthy men have been the opportunities that their positions afforded to make money.

In the most crass of cases, state managers received large payoffs for special uses of the powers of their positions. The famous payment of the *mordita* ("small bite") to traffic police to avoid larger fines and problems is only the most visible base of a pyramid of corruption that reaches into the heights of the state apparatus. Kickbacks are a second type of corrupt profit-making opportunities from state positions. A state manager can facilitate the awarding of a contract to a private company that will then show its appreciation financially. The most spectacular profits come from insider knowledge that allows top managers to turn small investments into fortunes. It would be naïve to believe that top state managers did not reap super profits for themselves during the wave of the sale of state-owned companies to the private sector initiated by the Salinas de Gortari government's privatization policies in the 1990s.[19]

Corruption of public managers and officials has not been unknown in the history of the United States, the Tammany Hall scandals being just one example. Payoffs of public officials for special favors and the use of insider knowledge for private ends continue. The difference, however, is one of scale. Payoffs of public officials for favors continue to be taken for granted in Mexico, whereas they are now considered to be exceptional in the United States. This corruption occurred most when the United States was at a stage of economic development similar to Mexico's today. However, it would be a mistake to assume that corruption is an inevitable feature of particular stages of development, since Canada's history with corruption was not nearly as scandalous.

According to Transparency International, on a scale of 1 to 10 with 1 having the most and 10 the least reputation for corruption, Mexico 3.3, the United States 7.3, and Canada currently scores 8.5.[20]

The real economic difference between the countries lies in the respective balances of public and private capital. Mexico, unlike the United States or Canada, developed a form of state capitalism in which the state was the main accumulator and director of development. That system continued to give opportunities for public corruption because the state was where money and power were. In the United States and Canada, most of the money and power were in private corporations. Corruption can be used to bilk public monies in Mexico without causing the state itself to collapse economically no matter how much public cynicism it might leave in its wake. However, continual embezzlement of a private corporation can lead to bankruptcy. Hence, private corporations have a greater purely economic interest in controlling corruption than does the state. The private corporation can bilk the public as much as it wants without directly undermining its own financing, but it cannot allow embezzlement. Thus, if we are to seek out an economic explanation for the greater public sector corruption that has existed in Mexico, we would have to conclude that it rested in the greater use of the state as an accumulator of capital and director of the economy. At the same time, stating this conclusion is not the same as concluding that state-directed economic development inevitably produces corruption. A general anti-corruption cultural ethic can act to keep opportunities for corruption in check, as can strong political or accounting control measures.

Nor is this conclusion a prediction that Mexico's recent neo-liberal privatization policies will inevitably lead to a lessening of corruption. Indeed, privatization undoubtedly led initially to an increase in corruption as insider knowledge allowed powerful individuals to profit handsomely from it. Transparency International's Corruption Index, cited above, showed very little change in Mexico's reputation for corruption between 1995 and 2006.

Social Classes

In each of the North American countries, there are four general social-class standards of living: upper, middle, working, and lower. In addition to shared standards of living, the concept of social class also indicates popular recognition; that is, unlike the concept of economic classes which refers to research categories of analysis, the concept of social classes refers to labels that are widely recognized and identified with by populations. Because popular conceptions are at the core of the meanings of social-class terms, in order to define a social class for measurement purposes, it is necessary to begin with such meanings.

The popular conceptions of upper and lower class are fairly straight forward. By "upper class" most people mean the rich and by "lower class" they mean the poor. We will assume that upper-class incomes are high incomes that are primarily based on property ownership rather than employment. The proportionate size of the upper class in a population is equivalent to the proportionate size of a capitalist class in a labor force. For the estimation of the proportionate size of the lower class in each country, we can accept the estimations of government studies of the number of poor in their populations.

By middle class most people assume a standard of living that is supported by an average professional or managerial income — we consider the average income because very high professional and managerial incomes support upper-class standards of living and low professional and managerial incomes only support working-class standards of living. In a related sense, the highest paying positions of working-class occupations support middle-class standards of living.

We will consider the average professional and managerial income to be the average middle-class occupational income. To estimate the proportionate size of the middle class in the population, we will determine how much higher average professional and managerial occupational incomes are than average overall occupational incomes. Using that figure as a threshold for middle-class income, we will calculate the percentage of households that receive that amount of income. Thus, if the average professional and managerial occupational income is 50 per cent higher than the average occupational income, we will determine the percentage of households that received incomes 50 per cent or more than the national average. From that percentage we will subtract the percentage of upper class households to arrive at the middle-class size.

Once the proportionate size of the middle class has been determined, the social working class will then be estimated by process of elimination. That is, the working class equals the proportion of the population that is not in the upper, middle, or lower classes.

We can begin by estimating the proportionate sizes of the upper and lower class extremes in the United States. If we consider rich or upper-class families to have a minimum income of $500,000 — where property income begins to exceed employment income — they are, according to 2004 income tax returns, the top 0.8 per cent of the population.[21] Those who receive this upper-class income almost always identify their occupations as either managers or professionals. The lower class of the poor constitute, according to official government estimates, the bottom 12.6 per cent. For the middle class, our method yields a figure of 44 per cent. By process of elimination — that is, by subtracting the sizes of the upper, middle, and lower classes from the total — the relative size of the social working class was then estimated to be 41.6 per cent of the population.

Employment of the same procedure to Canada yields an upper class of 0.4 per cent, a middle class of 46.9 per cent, a working class of 45.3 per cent, and a lower class of 7.4 percent.

Table 8.3: Distribution of Income, Poverty, and Social Classes, 2001-2007

	UNITED STATES	CANADA	MEXICO
A. Income Classes[1]			
Poorest 10 percent	1.9	2.6	1.6
Poorest 20 percent	5.4	7.2	4.3
Second 20 percent	10.7	12.7	8.3
Third 20 percent	15.7	17.2	12.6
Fourth 20 percent	22.4	23.0	19.7
Richest 20 percent	45.8	39.9	55.1
Richest 10 percent	29.9	24.8	39.4
Total	100.0	100.0	100.0
Gini index	0.408	0.326	0.461
B. Poverty Rates			
Relative[2]	17.7	12.1	20.2
Absolute[3]	12.6	7.4	50.0
C. Social Classes[4]			
Upper	0.8	0.3	0.2
Middle	44.0	47.0	30.0
Working	42.6	45.3	19.8
Lower	12.6	7.4	50.0
Total	100.0	100.0	100.0

Sources: 1. World Bank, *2007 World Development Indicators* (Washington, DC: World Bank, 2007): Table 2.7.

2. Luxembourg Income Study (LIS) Key Figures, http://www.lisproject.org/keyfigures.htm.

3. Carmen DeNavas-Walt, Bernadette D. Proctor, Cheryl Hill Lee, "Income, Poverty, and Health Insurance Coverage in the United States: 2005," *Current Population Reports* P60-231 (2006): Table 4; United Nations Development Programme, *Human Development Report 2006*, Table 4; Miguel Székely, *Pobreza y Desigualdad en México entre 1950 y el 2004* (Mexico City: Secretaria de Desarrollo Social, 2005) Table 1.

4. Estimates based on above sources and U.S. Bureau of the Census, Census 2000, Summary File 3, Tables P50 and P51; Statistics Canada, "Paid Work, Occupation"; and INEGI, *Encuesta Nacional de Ingresos y Gastos de los Hogares 2002* (Aguascalientes: INEGI, 2003) Tables 2.8 and 2.9.

The Canadian social-class profile is somewhat similar to that of the United States, but there are significant differences at the extremes: the Canadian upper and lower classes are proportionately smaller because there is a more equal distribution of income. Canada does not contain proportionately as many poor people as does the United States. The Canadian poor make up 7.4 per cent of the population compared to the 12.6 per cent in the United States.[22]

Mexico has a social-class profile of 0.2 per cent upper class, 30 per cent middle class, 19.8 per cent working class, and 50 per cent lower class.

The most dramatic difference between the social class structures of Mexico and those of the United States and Canada is the disproportionately large size of the lower class in the former—50 per cent of the Mexican population—compared to 13.6 per cent in the United States and 7.4 per cent in Canada. As in the case of the disproportionately large size of the economic small business class in Mexico affecting the relative sizes of all other economic classes, the disproportionately large size of the lower class of the poor in Mexico results in all other social classes being disproportionately smaller. Hence, the Mexican working, middle, and upper classes are relatively smaller than their counterparts in the United States or Canada.

The Mexican poverty rate cited here is based on absolute rather than relative criteria. Absolute poverty is a condition in which individuals or families do not have enough income to afford basic necessities; relative poverty is a condition in which individuals or families do not have enough income to consume at normal levels for a particular society. The Mexican absolute poverty rate of 50 per cent is much higher than its relative rate of 20.2 per cent. Many people consume within the normal levels for Mexico. The problem is that the normal level is depressed, especially compared to that of the United States and Canada. Nearly half of all Mexicans, for example, do not live in homes with indoor plumbing. The median annual income of poor children in Mexico is $940 compared to $6,900 and $8,700 for poor children in Canada and the United Stares respectively. [23]

Chapter 9

RACIAL CONTOURS OF NORTH AMERICA

The South Side of Chicago stretches for miles. Its inhabitants are almost all black, evoking the title of St. Clair Drake and Cayton's 1945 classic, *Black Metropolis*. One can board the El, Chicago's major public transportation system, on the southern edge of the South Side. The train rolls through the black ghetto until it reaches the downtown Loop and then passes into north Chicago, which is mostly white. As it passes through the Loop, white passenger faces systematically replace black faces. Black passengers feel a certain uneasiness if they stay for the white section of the run, and white passengers feel a corresponding uneasiness if they ride through the South Side.

Some Canadian cities also contain neighborhoods where particular racial minorities predominate. In Toronto and Montreal, recent black immigrants from Jamaica and Haiti have established their own neighborhoods, but there is nothing in Canada that approximates the scale of U.S. black ghettos, in large part because the black population is infinitesimally small by comparison.

In large Mexican cities, there can be racial differences between residential areas. Some areas have relatively more whites than others, but there are no areas in which whites alone reside. The racial complexion of Mexican neighborhoods can differ, with rich areas being relatively whiter, but the racial tension that exists is much more latent than in the United States.

The cities of North America today thus reflect in different ways the legacy of a half millennium of racial contact and inequality. These urban ecologies of race reflect the racial composition of each society and how each has institutionally structured its particular diversity.

Racial Compositions

The national populations of each of the North American countries a half millennium after the conquest are composed of indigenous-, European-, African-, and Asian-descent individuals, but in different proportions and combinations, resulting in significantly different overall racial textures. In the parts of the continent that became the United States and Canada, as we know, the indigenous populations were relatively small, allowing white European immigrants to establish numerical superiority quickly. That numerical superiority continues today, with white European-descent people predominating in Canada (87 per cent) and the United States (70 per cent).[1] Because the part that became Mexico was densely populated by indigenous peoples, white, mainly Spanish, European immigrants were never able to establish numerical superiority. Today, whites do not make up more than 5 per cent of the Mexican population.

The United States experienced slavery in its history to a much greater extent than either Mexico or Canada. For that reason, blacks are a sizeable minority in the United States (13 per cent) but very small minorities of less than 1 per cent in Canada and Mexico.

Asians have migrated to all three countries, but their numbers are slight compared to Europeans. Most live in the United States, but they are proportionately the largest minority in Canada, where they constitute 8 per cent of the population compared to 4 per cent in the United States and much less than 1 per cent in Mexico. At the same time, Asians are the fastest growing immigrant race in North America as a whole.

Three historically overlapping events produced surges in Asian emigration to the United States and Canada since the 1950s. The United States has had a large number of troops stationed in Korea since the 1950-53 war. The first Koreans to enter the U.S. were brides of these troops, who were later able to send for family members. Today, there are over 1 million Koreans living in the U.S. There are 95,000 in Canada, which also had troops stationed on the Korean peninsula.

In 1965 and 1967, respectively, the United States and Canada liberalized their immigration laws. The new law in the United States, which took effect in 1968, allowed large numbers of Asians who had been previously blocked to enter by giving preference to relatives of people already in the country and to persons who had needed job skills. The Canadian law removed racial and geographical biases in its immigration quotas, thereby allowing large numbers of new Asian immigrants who qualified on the bases of other criteria to enter the country. There was no comparable development in Mexico. The demographic effects of the U.S. and Canadian changes of immigration policy on the Chinese and Filipino communities have been dramatic. Chinese has now displaced Nahuatl as the fourth largest spoken language in North America after English, Spanish, and French.

In the United States, the Chinese population had grown at a rate proportionate to that of the population as a whole until 1968, when the 1965 law liberalizing immigration quotas took effect. Since then, the number of Chinese in the United States has nearly doubled every ten years, from 436,000 in 1970 to 812,000 in 1980 to 1,645,000 in 1990 to 2,432,545 in 2000.[2] Over three out of every four Chinese in the United States today are now immigrants; less than one in four is a descendent of the original nineteenth-century immigrant communities. In Canada, between 1971 and

2001, the proportion of Chinese in the total population increased nearly six-fold from 0.55 to 3.2 per cent.[3]

Over 90 per cent of the nearly 2 million Filipinos in the United States today came after the initiations of the immigration liberalization, as did most of the 266,000 currently in Canada.

Because there was no comparable immigration development in Mexico, the number of Chinese-Mexicans remains very small, far less than 1 per cent of the population, and they are dispersed throughout the country. We cannot assume that the Chinese population has had the same rate of increase as the Mexican population, because of the sexual imbalance whereby more than 90 per cent of immigrants were males.

There seems to be little doubt that the Chinese-descent population in Mexico does not exceed 100,000 today. There are no Chinatowns of the size of those in a number of U.S. and Canadian cities. There had been some small Chinatowns in the early part of the twentieth century, but these were abandoned as the Chinese population dispersed, leaving only traces to indicate their original identity. Along the Calle Álvaro Obregón of the Colonia Roma in Mexico City, for example, there are a number of buildings with clear oriental architectural features, indicating that they had once been the heart of a small Chinatown in the 1920s. By the 1950s, though, the Chinese had sold out and left. Large numbers of Chinese Hispanicized their names in the same way that immigrants from southern and eastern Europe to the United States were pressured into Anglicizing their names.

The period of immigration reforms also has had little effect on the Japanese-North American population. With Japan rapidly moving to the top rank of First World countries in the 1960s, there has been little incentive for its citizens to migrate. There are today a little under 1 million Japanese-descent residents in North America. Over 90 per cent live in the United States, and over two-thirds of these live in just two states, Hawaii and California. In Canada, Japanese-descent residents are a small percentage not only of the total population but also of the Asian population. The 53,000 Japanese-descent Canadians make up less than 3 per cent of Asian-descent Canadians. Five other Asian-descent populations—Chinese, Indians, Filipinos, Vietnamese, and Koreans in order—are larger. In Mexico, there are approximately 30,000 Japanese-descent residents. As in the United States, the Japanese communities in Canada and Mexico distinguish themselves according to generations since arrival— *Issei, Nisei, Sansei,* and *Yonsei.*

Since the 1960s, in addition to the original Asian-North American Chinese, Filipino, and Japanese communities and the postwar Korean community, sizeable Asian Indian and Indochinese communities have developed. Relatively few Indians migrated to the United States or Canada before the 1960s' period of immigration reform.[4] Today, there are 1,679,000 Asian Indians in the United States and 582,000 in Canada, disproportionate numbers of whom have entered already possessing university degrees.

U.S. losses in the Indochinese wars of the 1960s and 1970s — not the period of immigration reforms themselves — produced Vietnamese, Cambodian, and Laotian communities in North America. Thereafter, as with other immigrant communities, the communities became magnets for additional migrants. There are now 1,633,000 Indochinese settled in the United States and some 146,000 in Canada.

In addition to the main racial trunk lines of the North American population — Europeans, Indians, Africans, and Asians — a half millennium of coexistence has produced a very statistically and socially significant fifth race population of combined racial descent. Nearly 80 per cent of the Mexican population exists somewhere on a continuum between the poles of fully indigenous and fully European descent. There are also significant mestizo minorities in the United States and Canada. Most Mexican-origin individuals in the United States — the largest of its Latino minorities — are mestizos, along with those produced through contacts between domestic whites and Indians. In Canada, there is a significant cultural as well as racial minority of Métis who combine Indian and French or English ancestry. In the total North American context, mestizos are the largest racial minority, making up just more than one-quarter of the continent's population. In a parallel sense, much of the continent's population that is socially identified as black is in reality technically mixed, combining both European and African ancestry. A much smaller population of Eurasians also exists.

Table 9.1: Estimates of North America Racial Groupings, Percents of Populations, 2000-2001

	UNITED STATES	MEXICO	CANADA	NORTH AMERICA
European	70	5	87	56
Indigenous	2	15	2	5
African	13	< 1	1	9
Asian	4	< 1	8	3
Mixed				
Indo-European	9	79	3	25
Afro-European	1	<1	<1	<1
Other	<1	<1	<1	<1
Total	100	100	100	100

Sources: Estimates extrapolated from U.S. Census Bureau, Census 2000 Summary File 1, Tables P8, PCT11; Statistics Canada, "Population by Selected Ethnic Origins" *2001 Census* (http://www.statcan.ca/); Instituto Nacional Indigena, *Estimación de la población indígena y vivienda, 2000 INEGI* (http://www.cdi.gob.mx/ini/), cuadro 1 and estimates.

Notes: Estimates for the United States based on assumptions that 79 per cent of Mexican- and Central American-ancestry residents in the United States are mixed race, 15 per cent are indigenous, and 5 per cent European; 25 per cent of Puerto Rican- and Cuban-ancestry residents are mixed race; and 50 per cent of Dominican Republic-ancestry residents are mixed race.

Table 9.2: Estimates of Distribution of North America Racial Groupings, 2000-2001

	EUROPEAN	INDIGENOUS	AFRICAN	ASIAN	MIXED
United States	86.3	26.9	98.7	80.8	26.4
Mexico	2.1	70.3	0.5	1.4	72.6
Canada	11.6	2.7	0.7	17.8	1.0
North America	100.0	99.9	99.9	100.0	100.0

Note: Because of rounding, percentages may not total 100.

Sources: See Table 9.1.

Racial interaction patterns differ in the three countries because of the different racial compositions of the respective national populations. Mexicans become minority members only when they travel to the United States and Canada. Canadian and U.S. whites become minorities only when they travel to Mexico. In the United States, blacks are the largest racial minority, with domestic Indians being far less than 1 per cent of the population.[5] (The overall proportion of Indians, though, has more than doubled with the arrival of immigrant Indians from Mexico and Guatemala.) In Mexico, Indians are the largest minority, with blacks being far less than 1 per cent.

The United States could promote legal segregation of races in education, housing, public transportation, and public accommodations until 1964 in large part because it was a segregation imposed against a demographic minority. Canada also segregated blacks from whites at various times in its history. Mexico, during its colonial period, largely segregated Indians, mestizos, Afro-mestizos, and blacks from the white minority, but it was very difficult for Mexican whites to maintain that segregation after independence since they were the demographic minority. To do so, they would have had to develop a social system along the lines of South Africa's former apartheid, but they did not.

The experiences of race, racial interaction, and racism differ in the three countries, therefore, because of these different racial proportions and compositions. They differ also because they are culturally perceived differently, with each national culture containing a set of norms and values that filter the perceptions of racial relations.

As a result, there is no common definition of racial identity in North America. In the United States and Canada, racial identity tends to be defined genetically according to biological descent, in Mexico, by appearance, that is, according to skin color. The issue is further complicated for African-origin individuals in the United States, who have a social definition that overrides their actual biological identity. Most U.S. blacks, as we saw in Chapter 5, are actually mixed race, with a number of these carrying more European than African genes. Nevertheless, these predominantly white individuals are socially defined as blacks. In Mexico, a number of very light-skinned individuals, who are biologically mestizos, define themselves and are defined by others as whites.

Legacies of Slavery, War, and Colonialism in the United States

The history of race relations in the United States is intimately connected with conquest and labor exploitation. It began, as we have seen, in the colonial period with the violent usurpation by European settlers of the lands of indigenous peoples and the importation of African slaves to work many of those lands. Up through independence, race relations were played out between a dominating white majority, conquered and resisting Indians, and enslaved blacks.

The 1848 U.S. victory in the Mexican-American War opened up the Southwest for exploitation. It also resulted in the formation of two new racial minorities: mestizos and Asians. The takeover of Mexican territory meant that its mainly mestizo citizens became a racial minority under white domination. Exploitation of that land required the importation of Chinese contract laborers, the origin of the Asian minority, to work mines and build railroads. The 1898 U.S. victory in the Spanish American War added colonial subjects—Puerto Ricans and Filipinos—to the already existing categories of dominated racial minorities. Voluntary immigration from the 1870s to the present, especially of Latin Americans and Asians, also contributed significantly to the formation of the minority populations. Most came as a result of voluntary immigration, but it was migration in the context of international inequality.

The directions of international migration patterns are almost always from poorer to richer regions. Regions become richer for a variety of reasons, including their ability to out-compete poorer regions in production and trade. In this sense, the ability of the United States to out-compete economically most of the countries of the world has had the unintended effect of stimulating many of the citizens of these poor countries to attempt to migrate there. Economic deprivation, in part caused by the economic success of the United States, has thus driven many Latin Americans and Asians in the last few decades to leave their countries for perceived better economic opportunities in the United States. Because of this history of conquest and exploitation of minority labor forces as well as the attractiveness of the country to Third World immigrants, the United States has been and continues to be the most racially heterogeneous of the North American countries. The relations between these different groups, therefore, have been one of the most critical problems in U.S. history.

Racism developed as strongly as it did in the United States because it had an ideal climate within which to grow. The white majority rationalized its harsh treatment of first Indians and blacks and later Latinos and Asians by accepting the belief that these were inferior races. With racism being a vital component of the belief system or ideology embraced by most of the white majority, it is no wonder that up through the first half of the twentieth century the United States evolved and institutionalized an elaborate system to separate and segregate the races in housing, schooling, and other areas.

With the passage of the 1964 Civil Rights Act the United States made an official break with legally sanctioned racial segregation. Most interpretations of the end of legally sanctioned segregation in the United States have focused on the role of the Civil Rights Movement and its leaders, such as Martin Luther King. The major organizations of the civil rights movement — the Southern Christian Leadership Conference, the National Association for the Advancement of Colored People, the Congress of Racial Equality, and the Student Nonviolent Coordinating Committee — used law suits, lunch counter sit-ins, boycotts, marches, and other tactics to nonviolently protest and eventually bring down the legal edifice of segregation. But there is an additional, often overlooked, reason why overt segregation ended in the United States: after World War II, as large parts of Africa and Asia became decolonized, newly independent Third World countries entered and began voting in the newly formed United Nations and, at the same time, were being wooed by the United States and the Soviet Union as Cold War allies. Thus, segregation became an increasing liability for U.S. foreign policy objectives. A number of embarrassing incidents occurred in the late 1940s and 1950s involving African diplomats stationed in the United States who were refused service and even arrested as vagrants when they traveled between Washington and New York. It was obviously difficult to enlist their support for the U.S. campaign against communism when they knew from personal experience that the "free world" was not as free as it purported to be. Elites in the United States began to see segregation as an increasing liability in the Cold War and joined in the efforts to end it. The tacit allowance of segregation by northern elites, which began with the end of Reconstruction in 1877, thus ended in part, and ironically, as a result of the Cold War in the 1950s.

With the main goals of the Civil Rights Movement accomplished with the passage of the Civil Rights Act in 1964, nonviolent protest actions declined rapidly. At the same time, however, riots and rebellions began to break out in black northern ghettos outside of the South. Between 1965 and 1970, such major cities as New York, Philadelphia, Detroit, Cleveland, Newark, Los Angeles, Chicago, and Washington, DC experienced serious breakdowns of law and order in black areas. During 1967 alone, 87 people lost their lives in racial disturbances.[6] The largest violent outbreaks occurred during the week after the assassination of Martin Luther King in 1968 when more than 50,000 U.S. troops were deployed in black ghettos. For the most part the riots were spontaneous outbreaks that were easily ignited because of the charged atmosphere that existed in those years.

The traditional divide between integrationist and nationalist orientations was present in the 1960s black social movement. In many ways the 1964 Civil Rights Act was the triumph of the integrationist organizations, which believed that the solution to racial injustice in the United States lay in removing the barriers to full and equal participation of blacks *within* the institutions of the society, including schooling, housing, electoral politics, and the work force. These organizations, the oldest of which was the National Association for the Advancement of Colored People, had fought a long battle since the nineteenth century for blacks to be accepted and recognized as equal citizens of the United States.

Not everyone in the black activist and intellectual community agreed with the underlying assumptions of the integrationist-oriented organizations. Many questioned whether blacks should want to become a part of the fundamentally white-defined institutions of the United States. They believed that the country was in a period of decadence as anticolonial revolutions of non-white peoples were redefining the world order. The novelist James Baldwin questioned whether blacks wanted to be integrated into "a burning house."[7] Separatist-oriented organizations, such as the Nation of Islam, believed that the racial division within the United States could not be reconciled within the near or medium future. Given this irreconcilability, they urged that blacks develop their own institutions to the point of achieving substantively equal standards of living. At that point, perhaps, the question of racial integration could be reopened but on the solid basis of an agreement between races with substantively equal economic and social living conditions.

Throughout the late 1960s and 1970s the federal government was actively engaged in both implementing the mandates of the Civil Rights Act and attempting to ameliorate the conditions of economic deprivation in the ghettos. However, in the 1980s, the administration of President Ronald Reagan began to decrease its involvement in redressing the problems of African-Americans. This was a part of the conservative Republican philosophy of reducing governmental regulation of the economy and addressing social issues. During these years, therefore, the gap between African-Americans and whites, which had been narrowing in the previous decade, began to increase again.

As a result, throughout the 1980s there were sporadic violent outbreaks in some black communities, the most notable being Liberty City in Miami, but these did not come close to the scale of violence that occurred in the late 1960s. However, in Los Angeles on April 29, 1992, a jury that contained no blacks acquitted four white policemen who had savagely beaten Rodney King, a black. The beating had been secretly videotaped, and millions around the world had seen the irrefutable proof of police brutality. The acquittal touched off nights of pent-up rage among blacks in

South Central Los Angeles, causing deaths, injuries, and millions of dollars in damage. The disturbance was not suppressed until 6,000 National Guard troops were called in to patrol the mostly black areas of Los Angeles.

The most conventional way to interpret these events is to see the violence as a tragic and self-defeating response to injustice. There is, though, another interpretation. Frances Fox Piven and Richard A. Cloward have noted that social welfare spending in the United States generally expands after periods of threatened or real violence by the poor and contracts during periods when the poor are quiescent. In this respect, the New Deal social programs of Franklin Delano Roosevelt developed as a response to mass mobilizations of the unemployed, some of which were led by the Communist Party, during the early part of the Depression. After the Depression, the scale of social welfare programs decreased until the urban black eruptions of the late 1960s. The federal government then expanded old programs and developed new ones in an attempt to ameliorate desperate living conditions in the black ghettos.[8] By the 1980s, when the federal government began to cut back social welfare programs, black activism was at a low point. If this line of interpretation is valid, then the most important consequence of urban riots, which few political leaders want to acknowledge, may well be the forcing of politicians to increase governmental social spending in the communities where the rioters live.

Politically, blacks vote significantly to the left of the national pattern with the black vote being firmly in the Democratic Party. In each of the presidential elections between 1972 and 2004, 86 per cent of blacks on average cast their votes for the candidate of the Democratic Party. Only 12 per cent on average voted for Republican Party candidates.[9] Part of the reason why blacks vote in that direction is because they have disproportionately low incomes and, like other low-income classes, believe that the Democratic more than the Republican Party will support social programs, such as subsidized housing and welfare, that will directly benefit them. In addition, blacks perceive the Democratic Party to be more willing than the Republican Party to use the powers of the federal government to remove discriminatory barriers in jobs, education, housing, and the like.

In sum, while racism and racial discrimination did not come to an end with the passage of the 1964 Civil Rights Act, they did cease to be officially promoted and tolerated despite continuing to permeate de facto economic and social life in the United States. It is not surprising that the institutionalized racism that developed during over 300 years of colonial and post-colonial history—89 per cent of the history of the United States—would not immediately end and completely disappear with the passage of a bill. The Civil Rights Act was an absolutely necessary but not a sufficient step for achieving racial justice. The relations between whites and the other racial minorities—Latino mestizos, Asians, and Indians—also continue to be problematic, though not as contentious as they were in earlier historical periods.

143

Table 9.3: Race and Per Capita Income in the United States and Canada, 2000-2001

| | UNITED STATES | | CANADA | |
	Income	% of white income	Income	% of white income
White	$24,819		$24,038	
English			$24,913	103.6
French			$21,904	91.1
Asian	$21,823	87.9	$18,147	75.5
Black	$14,437	58.2	$15,876	66.0
Indian	$12,893	51.9	$10,100	42.0
Hispanic	$12,111	48.8	$14,437	60.0

Note: Income in U.S. and Canadian dollars respectively.

Sources: U.S. Bureau of the Census, Summary File 3 (P157), 2000 Census; calculated on the basis of information in Statistics Canada, "Income of Individuals, Families, and Households."

At the same time, there is no question that there have been significant changes in relations between whites and racial minorities in the United States. Whites perceive blacks and other racial minorities very differently than they did before the achievements of the Civil Rights Movement. Most white politicians are careful not to make directly racist statements. When former Secretary of Agriculture Ezra Benson told a racist joke that was overheard and reported by reporters, he created a public furor and was obliged to resign from office. Popular talk show host Don Imus lost his program in 2007 after a similar public furor over a racist reference. Before 1964, blacks appeared in television programs only as happy-go-lucky menials and not at all in commercials. There are now a number of programs with blacks in dignified leading roles, and they regularly appear in commercials.

The civil rights movement opened up opportunities for blacks with higher education to move into new middle-class economic roles. One of the unintended consequences, however, was that many then moved out of the traditional black communities and into integrated suburbs, leaving a dearth of leadership and role models in those communities. In a sense, the solidarity that was forced by common racial oppression on all classes of the black community broke down. William Julius Wilson thus argues that class inequality is becoming a more important issue for most blacks than racial oppression per se.[10]

Mestizos, *Indians, and* Criollos *in Mexico*
The logic of racial relations in Mexico began, as described, with the Spanish conquest of the large indigenous population. From that time on, European-descent

whites, either first-generation Spaniards or their criollo full descendants, though always a small minority, have exercised economic and political dominance over the majority non-white population. During the colonial period, the Spanish authorities practiced clear discrimination and segregation against the non-white population and, in official records, carefully categorized it into castes according to its proportions of European, indigenous, and African ancestry.

Following independence in 1821, in reaction to the caste system under colonial rule and to black slavery in the United States, Mexico adopted the liberal position that all citizens regardless of race or ethnic background were equal. That position has continued to exist in virtually unaltered form ever since. A number of Mexicans point with pride to the fact that the country's most revered president, Beníto Juárez, was a full Indian as indicating that racism either does not exist in Mexico or exists least there of all of the countries of North America.

In general terms, mestizos, Indians, and whites make up in order of size the racial groupings in Mexico, although estimates of their exact sizes vary widely because official statistics are not collected according to race. The government considers the very compilation of public statistics on racial minorities to be racist. If all Mexicans are equal regardless of skin color, according to the official position, then it is a contradiction to divide them by skin color for statistical purposes. In the 1921 Census, however, the government did include a question about racial identification. Some 60 per cent of the population identified themselves as being of mixed racial descent, 29 per cent as indigenous, 10 per cent as white, and 1 per cent as other.[11] Projecting from those and other statistics, we can estimate that today approximately 79 per cent of the population is mestizo, 15 per cent indigenous, 5 per cent white, and less than 1 per cent predominately black or Asian.

The failure of the Mexican government to distinguish racial groups in its contemporary statistics frustrates research attempts to document the degree to which discrimination and inequality exist or do not exist in the country.[12] At most, the government admits that its indigenous population constitutes minorities—but cultural minorities. Indians exist in official discourse as a socially definable group primarily because they practice cultures that differ from the national culture. The color of their skin is theoretically irrelevant as a definer. The official view of the country's small black population, on the other hand, is that it does not practice a culture that is significantly different from the national culture. Blacks therefore are not officially recognized as a distinct minority.

The problem with the official view is that it is belied by everyday experience.[13] Racial differences, in fact, do matter in Mexico. One Mexican psychiatrist states offhandedly, "All you need to get ahead here is blue eyes." A Mexican economist makes the observation that people with dark skin who have professional or managerial positions dress better than people with light skin. The reason, she states, is dark-skinned people feel subtly obliged to compensate for the low status of their skin color with high-status clothing. Everyday terms in the country, such as *negritos* and *chinos*, carry at least some racist connotations.

On the level of official discourse, Mexico scrupulously takes pride in its Indian foundations. Unlike Canada or the United States, the sense of history in Mexico begins with the large Indian civilizations that preceded the arrival of Europeans. Mexican schoolchildren are taught to take pride in the accomplishments of these civilizations. In reality, however, the predominantly European-descent population continues to be disproportionately represented in positions of power and the middle and upper classes. It maintains its position of racial privilege by practicing considerable discrimination against the predominantly Indian-descent population, and it is not immune from indulging in racist-tinged discourse against them too. The term *nako*, which has somewhat the same connotations that "nigger" has in the United States, is often used in discourse among the predominantly European-descent population as a code word for dark-skinned Indians. *Nakos* are usually described, in addition to being dark-skinned, as uncouth, dirty, and ignorant. Expressions such as *nuestros inditos* are also common and condescending.

Mexican sociologist Jorge A. Bustamente reported that there are more cases of Mexican police brutality against undocumented workers waiting to cross the border in Tijuana (across from San Diego, California) than Ciudad Juárez (across from El Paso, Texas). He believed that the reason is racial. Most of the undocumented that pass through Ciudad Juárez are from northern Mexico and light-skinned while those passing through San Diego are from central and southern Mexico and are darker skinned. In his estimation, the relatively light-skinned Mexican police in San Diego and Ciudad Juárez are more likely to abuse the dark-skinned Indians than those that are somatically light-skinned and more like themselves.[14] Bustamante sees a link between the historical racism against Indians and widespread indifference in the middle and upper classes to the problems of laborers who are forced to migrate to the United States in search of work.[15]

The consciousness of race permeates everyday life not only between people of different skin colors and shades, but also possibly in the psychology of individuals. Mexican authors, such as Samuel Ramos and Octavio Paz, have long argued that the mixed Indian and European descent of most Mexicans has been problematic for their psychological identities. Despite the official pride in the Indian descent, there is in fact a complex of inferiority because of it. Mexican racism, therefore, is in part a racism of self-denigration, according to this view, with the mestizo majority feeling shame about the Indian part of its descent and somatic appearance.[16]

Not surprisingly, race is often associated with class in generalizations about Mexican society. In a half-century debate over the Mexican national character that included Samuel Ramos, Octavio Paz, and Roger Bartra, the class structure was presented in tripartite Indian, mestizo, and criollo terms. These writers either associated the Indian with the rural peasantry or as being marginalized and outside of the main drift of modern Mexican history—"like a chorus that silently accompanies the drama of Mexican life."[17] Mestizos make up the urban proletariat—Ramos's and Paz's *pelados* who suffer from inferiority complexes and excesses of violence in the *cantinas* (bars). The bourgeoisie in these accounts is assumed to be—if not openly stated to be—essentially white. Although this description cannot be taken as absolutely or literally true, it does highlight the tendency, taken for granted in Mexico, for racial and class positions to cohere. The existences of poor whites and rich Indians are exceptions that do not invalidate the main tendency.

However, because official statistics in Mexico are not categorized according to race, they cannot be directly used to document the extent to which race and social class are correlated, that is, the extent to which whites, mestizos, and Indians have different social class standards of living. Not only can they not be used to document the inequality of non-whites, they cannot be consulted to document the extent to which white criollos continue to dominate. White domination is both officially denied and statistically hidden.

Visible Minorities and First Peoples in Canada

In Canadian history, the main axes of racial relations have been between whites and Indians and between whites and Asians. The dynamics begin with French trappers and farmers establishing a toehold on the continent by adapting themselves to the reality that this was land occupied by Indians. The first generations of Europeans, who also soon included the British, were minorities, but because the number of Indians in the area that would become Canada was relatively small and because the promise of free land lured so many British and French immigrants, within a short period of time Europeans became the majority. Canadian history then became the history of greater and greater white domination over the Indian peoples. As described earlier (see Chapter 3), unlike in the United States and Mexico, the establishment of white domination proceeded relatively peacefully, though, not without injustices. There were no large-scale frontier wars. Today, Indians—referred to variously as first peoples, Aboriginal peoples, and First Nations, among other terms—make up a proportionately larger minority in Canada than in the United States, and they continue to adhere to separate identities and press for land and cultural rights.

Canada considers as "visible minorities" persons of Asian, African, Latin American, and Arab descent. The largest visible minority today is Asian, Chinese and Indians being the largest components. These began to arrive in Canada in the middle and late nineteenth century, and they encountered considerable racist hostility from the European-origin population.

Canada also has other less pronounced racial axes. As in Mexico, but not the United States, mestizos—known in Canada as the Métis—have a defined identity as described in Chapter 5 that is neither Indian nor European. As in colonial Mexico, relatively few women accompanied the first European inhabitants and so French set-tlers and trappers took Indian wives of necessity. In time, sizeable communities of Métis developed. They often established separate communities and identities and in the nineteenth century attempted rebellions of secession from Canada. Today, the Métis continue to be recognized as a separate minority.

The number of blacks in Canada has always been very small. There was a long period of slavery, but it was nowhere near as significant as it was in the history of the United States or Mexico. There were never plantations, mostly because of the unsuit-ability of climate and soil conditions. Most blacks who entered Canada entered as free persons, often fleeing slavery in the United States. Nevertheless, it would be a mis-take to believe that whites in Canada necessarily welcomed blacks. Throughout Canadian history, there have been acts of hostility toward the black minority. In the nineteenth and twentieth century, immigration officials attempted to discourage and block black immigrants. In the nineteenth century, Nova Scotia and Upper Canada segregated their schools.[18] The Ku Klux Klan was active at various times in Canada as well as in the United States. Labor unions have in the past barred blacks from membership or accepted them only in separate segregated locals.[19]

Perceptions of race in Canada tend to follow the pattern in the United States—but not entirely. This is because of the different protagonists—Indians and Asians rather than blacks have been the main minorities. More importantly, it is because post-indigenous Canada was established by two European populations rather than one. The necessity of accommodating the separate cultural identities of French- and English-origin citizens was then extended to racial and other European minorities.

Because Canadians use the metaphor of a mosaic rather than a melting pot to evoke the image of the type of multicultural society that they wish to preserve and promote, there is now more sensitivity toward preserving the separate cultural sources, including languages, of the identities of all minorities in Canada than in the United States or Mexico.

Nationality and Ethnicity

At the same time that many North American cities spatially manifest to different degrees underlying racial inequalities, many also often reveal ethnic and nationality differences as well, with ethnic or national minorities that share the same racial identity living in different neighborhoods. San Francisco has a Japantown as well as Chinatown. The New York metropolitan area has both predominantly Irish and Italian neighborhoods. Where ethnic differences within racial groupings have not generated distinct ecological patterns within cities, they have been sufficient to gen-erate subcultures within and sometimes cross-cutting racial groupings.

A common racial position thus does not necessarily produce a common cultural outlook. Italian- and British-origin Americans, while sharing the same racial group-ing, are culturally different. It would be a mistake to assume that a common racial position unites Chinese- and Japanese-Americans. In 1906, the Japanese community of San Francisco protested vigorously when a racist and culturally ignorant school board attempted to segregate its children in Chinatown schools.[20] And, certainly, no one could maintain that common racial position makes English Canadians and French Canadians culturally indistinguishable.

What differentiates the concepts of ethnicity and nationality is the degree of separateness. The concept of nation is intimately related to the concept of state. A nation is a people that shares a common identity that is or has the potential of being manifested in the formation of its own separate government.[21] In this respect, minority nationality identities have existed in North American history among recently arrived immigrants who still carried the identities of their originating countries. They also exist among those minorities, such as the French in Canada, for whom the possibility of formation of a separate state exists.

Ethnicity, as opposed to nationality, refers more to the identities of immigrant groups that are on their way toward being integrated into one multi-ethnic identity and for which formation of a separate state or society does not appear to be likely. Contemporary Italian-Americans or Chinese-Mexicans, in this respect, can be considered more ethnic than national minorities. Whether a minority is defined as being an ethnic or a national minority is a pre-eminently political issue, since the latter implies separate loyalty. In either case, ethnic and national minorities are cultural minorities.

What race and ethnicity or nationality share in common as categories of analysis is that they are bases from which groups develop senses of common identity. By being black, one shares a common racial identity with other blacks that is not shared with whites and other racial groups. By being Polish-American, one shares a common and distinct identity that is not shared with other European-, Asian-, Native, or African-Americans. However, the degree to which a common racial or ethnic position evokes a common identity and consciousness varies historically and socially.

Racial and ethnic differences are sometimes directly related, as when blackness in the United States is associated with both a common racial and ethnic subculture. However, sometimes one racial grouping contains a number of culturally different ethnic groupings. Race and ethnicity can also crosscut each other, as when black and white Puerto Ricans in the United States feel a common ethnic and nationality bond despite their racial differences. The Latino population of the United States is a culturally heterogeneous combination of Mexican, Puerto Rican, Cuban, and other nationalities. The same can be said for the Asian populations, which have originated for the most part in China, Japan, and the Philippines. The indigenous population is also culturally heterogeneous, containing many different language and tribal groups. Only the African-origin populations in the United States and Mexico lack major internal ethnic or nationality differences.

For most of its history, the United States excluded blacks, Indians, Latinos, and Asians from its melting pot cultural homogenization process. They were thought to be inassimilable for largely racial reasons and subjected to discrimination and prejudice. At one time or another all of the racial minorities were subjected to segregation, with blacks being the most systematically segregated.

The metaphor of a melting pot applies to Mexico as well as the United States, but with important differences. The United States experienced a *cultural* melting pot among its dominant white population in which southern and eastern European immigrants submerged their separate cultural identities and adopted the dominant British-origin cultural characteristics of the white majority. The products of this melting pot became the dominating racial majority. In Mexico there was a *racial* melting pot among substantial portions of the indigenous and immigrant European populations, resulting in the creation of a mestizo majority. The products of this melting pot became a dominated rather than dominating racial majority.

Chapter 10

A NORTH AMERICAN SOCIAL MODEL?

The power structures of the three North American countries reflect in different ways the underlying realities of their respective economic and social class systems. Those who exercise economic power seek at the least to influence if not directly control the exercise of political power. In all three countries there are institutional mechanisms by which economically powerful individuals and corporations influence state policies.

Power Structures

C. Wright Mills's *The Power Elite*,[1] published in 1956, included the most influential postwar sociological explanation of the relationship between economics and state power in the United States. According to Mills, in the United States power is exercised by an elite composed of the occupants of the command positions of the economic, political, and military institutional bureaucracies: the members of the boards of directors and top managers of the largest corporations; the president, vice-president, members of the cabinet, governors of important states, and powerful members of the Senate and House of Representatives; and the Joint Chiefs of Staff and other top military officials.

Mills proposed that these individuals be studied sociologically like any other group in terms of their family backgrounds and values. Among his findings were that individuals often moved in their careers from one type of elite position to another. A military leader could move to a top political position, as did General Eisenhower when he became president. A corporate manager could be appointed to a cabinet post, as was Robert MacNamara. Mills also concluded that the majority of the power elite came from upper-class families, attended exclusive private prep schools and private colleges, and belonged to the same private clubs. Their common socialization experience, which was different from that of ordinary members of the population, produced common values and outlooks that they carried with them into the command positions of the power elite.

Mills's study and theory of power initiated subsequent studies and debates. Ralph Miliband and G. William Domhoff have been the most prominent followers of his approach in studying the individuals who occupy powerful positions.[2] Among Domhoff's many useful contributions has been his uncovering of the role of private foundation think tanks, such as the Council on Foreign Relations and the Heritage Foundation, in grooming corporate leaders for assuming top political leadership positions. According to his portrayal, think tanks play the crucial intermediary role in translating corporate into state power by bringing together corporate, academic, and political leaders to study political problems. These seminars perform the functions of developing working and social relations among powerful individuals who come from geographically dispersed cities and providing an atmosphere within which corporate leaders with political potential can develop. The contacts necessary to launch serious presidential campaigns are developed within the think tanks as are the pools from which subsequent cabinet appointments are drawn.

What Mills's *The Power Elite* was to subsequent power structure studies in United States, John Porter's *The Vertical Mosaic*, published in 1965, was to subsequent power structure studies in Canada. Porter followed Mills's general approach by concentrating on elite wielders of power in Canadian institutional orders, including economy and politics, as had Mills for the United States, but not the military. In addition, he also included the federal bureaucracy, labor unions, mass media, higher education, and religion, which he considered to be other key functional parts of the society. Unlike Mills, who saw the various elites in the United States as coalescing into one power elite, Porter allowed for much more contention within and between Canadian elites because of the English-French divide and problems between the economic, political, and other elites.

In terms of the class origins of elite members, Porter found upper-class descendants to be heavily overrepresented in the corporate elite. By his calculation, at least 37.8 per cent and possibly as much as 50.1 per cent of the 611 members of the economic elite came from upper-class backgrounds, 32.2 per cent came from the middle class, and 17.7 per cent possibly rose from working- or lower-class backgrounds.

As in the United States, Porter found that members of the economic elite formed a common world view through attending the same private schools, where they developed friendships and kinship ties with each other. However, the upper class was not as heavily overrepresented in the other institutional elites (politics, education, etc.), which tended to draw their recruits more from the middle class.

On the key question of how economic elites influenced state policy and action, Porter concluded that this influence was usually achieved when members of the economic elite were appointed to various political boards and commissions, and when elite individuals moved back and forth between economic and political positions in the courses of their careers, as in the United States.[3]

The Vertical Mosaic, like *The Power Elite* for the United States, continues to be the classic analysis of the power structure of Canada. It was replicated in 1975 by Wallace Clement, who found a stronger relationship between upper-class background and economic elite membership—upper-class background grew from 50 to 59 per cent—than had Porter and an increase in French-Canadian members.[4] Most studies since then have concentrated on the economic elite and have not been as comprehensive as Porter in terms of studying multiple elites and their interrelationships.[5]

Mills continues to be widely read and studied in Mexico for two reasons. First, his popularity results from his critical portrayal of power in the United States. Secondly, it comes from the relevance to his method of analysis to the study of power in Mexico itself. The focus on a tripartite elite of political, economic, and military leaders can be usefully applied to an interpretation of twentieth-century Mexican history. The 1910-17 Revolution was carried out against the political elite that surrounded the Porfirio Díaz dictatorship. It produced a new military elite that essentially ran the country for two decades before institutionalizing itself into a political elite as a monolithic political party, which today is the PRI. The Mexican political elite thus grew out of a military elite. The holders of state power, in both their military and political incarnations, have built strategic alliances with the country's economic elite.

The Mexican upper class can also be studied in the same way that Mills studied their counterparts in the United States. They send their children to exclusive private schools such as the American School and belong to clubs such as the Club Alemán. Up through the 1970s, the upper class sent its offspring to the two Mexican private universities, the Colegio de México in Mexico City and the Instituto Tecnológico de Estudios Superiores de Monterrey in Monterrey, and the public Universidad Nacional Autónoma de México in Mexico City. Now the preferred path is to send them outside of the country to universities in the United States, Britain, or France.

The general orientation of power elite research represented by Mills, Miliband, and Domhoff was not without its critics. To their right, pluralists accused them of erroneously conceptualizing monolithic power in the United States. On the left, Paul Sweezy, the dean of Marxian economists in the United States, praised Mills's study but found its theoretical framework lacking. Instead of seeing the military, corporate, and political components as being co-equal in power, Sweezy argued the classic Marxist position that power was ultimately held by a capitalist-based ruling class.[6] Nicos Poulantzas argued that emphasis on the individual occupants of powerful positions ignored the systemic features of power.[7] That is, no matter who occupied positions of state power in capitalist societies, even if they were committed to socialist reforms, the economic logic of the capitalist system would institutionally constrain their actions. Hence, state power was directed in the way it was not just because of the upper-class values of the occupants of its top positions but also because it functioned within a specifically capitalist institutional environment.

Political Systems

Despite the common influencing of state policies in all three countries by holders of economic power, it functions differently due to the differences in party politics. The United States functions with two parties, the Republicans and Democrats. Other parties exist but rarely attain political office because Congress and the state legislatures have mandated winner-take-all elections. That is, each occupant of a legislative seat is the winner of the most votes in an election from a particular district. There is no representation of losing parties, even if their candidates win as much as 49 per cent of the vote, as there is in countries that have proportional representation.

The winner-take-all provision of U.S. elections has effectively blocked the emergence of third parties leaving the two major parties to compete for the votes of centrist voters. This provision works doubly against third parties that maintain consistent ideological positions. First, they are less likely to attract the majority of voters to attain representation, since they do not change their programs to go after other voters. Second, even voters who agree with their programs may not vote for them out of fear that the vote will be wasted, since there is little likelihood of them winning.

Politics in the United States are also based on very loose relationships between parties and ideologies and parties and candidates. Because each party, as mentioned, seeks to win over centrist voters, it is willing to significantly modify its ideological position. With each of the two major parties fighting for the center, it is often difficult to distinguish them ideologically. Once the candidates win, the parties have little control over their votes within the various legislative bodies. Democratic and Republican legislative office holders often vote with the other side on particular issues. Money also influences politics in the United States in this individualistic climate in two ways. First, running an effective electoral campaign is expensive. Hence, candidates must raise large sums of money from donors, who see their donations as investments in having the candidate, if he or she wins, support their particular concerns. Second, corporate and other special interest groups pay lobbyists whose job it is to convince legislators to vote in particular ways.

Despite the relatively loose ideological basis of politics in the United States, though, there are clear class voting patterns with support for Republican candidates rising with income. In every presidential election since 1976, the earliest year for which this information was available, there has been a direct relationship between social class and voting behavior: the higher the family income class, the greater the proportion of Republican Party votes and *vice versa* for Democratic Party votes.[8]

The Canadian system is constitutionally organized to be relatively more pluralistic and ideological than that of the United States. There are three major political parties that offer voters clear choices between conservative (the Conservative Party), liberal (the Liberal Party), and social democratic (the New Democratic Party) options. Canadian voters choose among candidates for legislative seats to represent their districts. They do not vote directly for national leaders. This provision of the

Canadian Constitution has favored the emergence of third parties within districts. Since there are no national candidates on the ticket, the Canadian voter is not as influenced by the strongest national parties as is the voter in the United States. Third parties can thus develop within particular provinces. Canadian national governments with their prime ministers are then formed by the party or coalition of parties that has the majority of seats within the national Parliament. Unlike in the United States, there is firm party discipline over the voting of legislators.

Mexico was until recently essentially a one-party state. However, it was not so much a question of one party controlling the state as the state being a self-reproducing institution that used one party for its electoral and legitimacy needs. This is not to argue that the Mexican state party, the PRI, was without ideological differences. The Mexican state and the PRI were composed of a number of ideological currents. For example, the ideological difference between the nationalistic somewhat social democratic government of Luis Echeverría (1970-76) and the conservative Salinas de Gortari (1988-94) governments were greater than anything witnessed in recent U.S. governments.

Nor is it to argue that the PRI was the only party represented within the Mexican state during its period of near total domination. There were a number of oppositional parties, the two most important being the Partido Acción Nacional (PAN), to the right of the PRI, and the Partido de la Revolución Democrática (PRD), to the left.

Most people assumed that the Mexican state, when needed, altered electoral results. The 1988 presidential election was the most well-known example, and there continues to be considerable belief that the actual results were reversed to avoid a victory by PRD's Cuauhtémoc Cárdenas over the PRI's candidate, Carlos Salinas de Gortari.

The presidential victory of PAN candidate Vincente Fox ended the PRI monopoly over the presidency. The PRI, though, remains the strongest and most organized of Mexico's political parties, and it controls many state and local offices. In 2006, according to official results, PAN Candidate Felipe Calderón won the presidency by the razor-thin margin of 0.6 per cent of votes cast (35.9 per cent to 35.3 per cent) over PRD candidate Andrés Manuel López Obrador with PRI Candidate Roberto Madrazo in third place with 22.2 per cent.

The results were contested by months of public demonstrations, with many seeing a repeat of the 1988 election scandal. López Obrador demanded a recount of all the votes. The recount was never held, and Calderón was declared the victor and took office in December of that year. According to the interpretation of a dissident former general José Francisco Gallardo, Calderón by not supporting a recount undermined his own legitimacy and has had to develop close relations with the Mexican military to insure his hold on presidential power in the face of substantial public opposition. General Gallardo believes that because of both the legitimacy crisis and the growing use of the military to fight drug trafficking, political power has been more militarized than at any other time since the last decade of the rule of Porfirio Díaz just before the outbreak of the 1910 revolution.[9]

One of the problems is that Mexico, like the United States, has a one-round presidential election that can be decided by a plurality rather than majority of votes. Thus, Bill Clinton was elected president in 1992 with only 41 per cent of votes when independent candidate Ross Perot siphoned significant votes from both the major parties.[10] Calderón won officially with an even smaller minority of just under 36 per cent of votes. Canada also does not have run-off elections.[11] Inevitably any candidate who obtains office with a minority of votes, regardless of whether they are counted correctly, will lack full legitimacy. For that reason, multiparty countries such as Brazil and Peru automatically schedule a second round of run-off elections if no candidate receives a majority in the first round.

All three governments faced armed uprisings in the 1960s and 1970s. The most serious was in Mexico where a number of small groups attempted through armed actions to ignite a general revolution. The most significant rural guerrilla groups operated in Guerrero (the Party of the Poor, led by Lucio Cabañas) and Chihuahua (Popular Guerrilla Group led by Arturo Gámiz and Pablo Gómez); there were also urban groups, the largest being the Liga Comunista 23 de Septiembre and the Movimiento de Acción Revolucionaria, operating in Mexico City, Monterrey, and Guadalajara. The Mexican Army, after several years of counterinsurgency warfare, in which as many as 3,000 were killed and 500 disappeared, largely extinguished the rebellion.[12]

Carlos Montemayor, in the late 1980s, traveled through the mountains of Guerrero, where most guerrilla activity took place, and interviewed witnesses. He then wove those reminiscences into an impressive novel that depicts guerrilla leader Lucio Cabañas, the group that he led, and the war.[13] Also in the novel are descriptions of other guerrilla groups active in Mexico during that period. Among other long-suppressed facts brought to light by Montemayor's research is that the Mexican army in its counterinsurgency campaigns pushed suspected guerrilla prisoners from helicopters high above the Pacific. Their bodies washed ashore just north of the beaches of Acapulco, the international resort, and were discovered by fishermen.

Guerrilla organizations still exist in Mexico. They range from the Ejécito Zapatista de Liberación Nacional (Zapatista National Liberation Army) that led violent confrontations in Chiapas in 1994 but now engages in non-violent challenges to clandestine groups, such as the Ejército Popular Revolucionario (People's Revolutionary Army), that from time to time surface to confront the state.[14]

In Canada the Front de Libération du Québec (FLQ) in the 1960s and 1970s attempted through bombings, kidnappings, and other revolutionary acts to secure independence for Quebec and establish a workers' government. The organization reached its highpoint in 1970 and then declined but not entirely to extinction.

In the United States, the urban black ghetto uprisings of the 1960s gave way in the 1970s to attempts by small, black, Puerto Rican independence and white militant organizations to advance their goals with bombings, robberies, and kidnappings.

A North American Social Model?

Growing economic integration in Europe through the European Union produced conceptions of a common European social model. The question is whether similar economic integration in North America through NAFTA will also produce a common social model and, if so, what its nature will be.

At present, two social policy models confront each other in North America: a conservative market model based on *laissez-faire* capitalist principles and a welfare state model — closer to the European social model — based on promoting state-sponsored social programs and redistribution of income. Mexico functions closest to the conservative pole, Canada to the welfare state pole. At the same time, the Canadian welfare state is less developed than Western European welfare states.[15]

All three societies incorporate elements of each model but in different proportions. What differentiates the models is the extent to which governments use taxes and tax-funded programs to resolve social problems and promote human development of their citizens. Conservatives seek to minimize such efforts, arguing that they are misconceived, harmful, and interfere with market development. Liberals and social democrats argue that they are necessary to offset the negative outcomes, such as poverty and inequality, of market and individual competition.

The models incorporate different goals and means. For conservatives, the purpose of government and goal of public policy is to insure conditions in which private businesses can prosper. The proper roles of government, according to conservative doctrine, include providing police protection, building roads so that commodities can flow freely to markets, and creating minimal laws to insure property rights. Liberals and social democrats argue that governments should, in addition, promote human welfare. They have an obligation to deliver products and services that citizens cannot obtain through work and market participation.

The major means for government action are taxation and development of tax-funded social programs. The governments of North America, like all governments, collect taxes to fund their activities. They differ in the amount they collect. The more they collect, the more possibilities they have to fund programs. Mexico proportionately collects the least. Its taxes account for 19.8 per cent of its GDP, compared to 26.8 per cent in the United States and 33.5 per cent in Canada.[16] The governments also differ in how they collect taxes. Overall Canada has the most progressive taxation, Mexico the least. The more progressive the taxation, the more the very act of tax payment serves to redistribute income downward.

The governments differ again in what they choose to fund with their tax revenues. Social spending, as defined by the OECD, in 2001 accounted for 5.1 per cent of GDP in Mexico, 14.7 per cent in the United States, and 17.8 per cent in Canada.[17] The OECD includes under social spending provision of health care, old age, and poverty services and support.[18] A broader definition of social expenditure includes spending on education, cultural support, and parks. Thus, social programs, broadly conceived, include those that are available as rights to all citizens — public education, parks, subsidized cultural services such as museums in all three countries, health care in Canada, and programs that transfer funds to groups in need such as the elderly and the poor.

At the crux of public policy is the relationship between market and disposable income. Market income is income from all sources except government transference programs (Social Security, poverty relief, etc.). Disposable income is market income plus transference payments minus taxes. The more conservative the approach, the more market and disposable income distributions are equivalent — the rich have the same percentage of national disposable income as they do of national market income. The more liberal and social democratic the approach, the more disposable income is more egalitarian than market income.

In all three countries, market income distributions are highly unequal. As a result of taxation and social programs, those inequalities are lessened for disposable income, but this is so to different extents. They are barely lessened in Mexico, lessened somewhat more in the United States, and lessened the most in Canada.

Most of the reason for the smaller proportionate numbers of the poor in Canada than the United States is that the Canadian government more aggressively favors them through use of redistributive taxation and transfer policies than does the U.S. government. In terms of relative poverty, for example, in 2006 21.1 per cent of Canadians were deemed to be poor in term of their shares of national market income. However, that rate was lowered to 11.4 per cent by transfer payments financed through redistributive taxes, a reduction of 46 per cent. In the United States, the poor were counted as 23.1 per cent before taxes and transfers. Their rate lowered to 17 per cent after taxes and transfers, a reduction of 26.4 per cent. U.S. policies were thus significantly less aggressive and successful in lowering the rate of disposable income poverty.[19]

Canada's more comprehensive social policy reflects a long-standing cultural predisposition to entrust government to rectify social problems with social programs. Canada is the only country in North America that has achieved universal health care, and that was accomplished through state spending.[20] Nearly 70 per cent of Canadian health care is publicly funded compared to 44.7 per cent in the United States and 46.4 per cent in Mexico — the only two OECD-member countries for which the majority of health care is private.[21]

There has been a deep anti-statist tradition in the United States that has been suspicious of government social activities. A substantial number — but by no means great majority — of its citizens remain hostile to paying taxes to develop government social programs to resolve social problems. Mexico's recent experience with a one-party authoritarian state characterized by significant patronage and corruption has proved to be fertile ground for conservatives (in and out of the country) to maintain its very low state social spending compared to Canada and the United States.

No issue is more indicative and financially more significant of the different approaches to social policy than support for retirement. At the end of 1993, just before the inauguration of NAFTA, all three North American countries had public social security systems in place for providing retirement income. The systems all functioned in the same way: current workers and employers paid taxes into a public fund that was then used to provide income for the retired. They were pay-as-you-go systems; there were no individual accounts. Rather, the systems rested on an intergenerational compact — called in Mexico a principle of solidarity[22] — in which working adults supported the retired. Workers paid into the systems throughout their working lives with the knowledge that they would become beneficiaries when they retired.

The intergenerational compact is related to the distinction of three ages in Spanish and Latin American social policy discussions: the first is made up of those too young to participate in the labor force, the second of labor force participants, and the third of the retired. The first and third ages in all societies traditionally have lived off support provided by the second age. In the nineteenth century, for example, active farmers took care of their own children and aged parents and grandparents within the same household. Twentieth-century social policy, especially in Europe, socialized the support of the second for the first and third ages through the creation of child support and social security programs.

Thus, the United States, Mexico, and Canada all had programs in place in which current labor force participants — the second age — paid taxes to support the retired or third age. Beginning in 1981, though, with the ascendancy of the conservative Reagan and Thatcher governments into power in the United States and Britain, there was a concerted effort to transform public social security systems from the principle of intergenerational solidarity to individualism. Instead of basing retirement income on the pay-as-you-go principle of taxing the second age to support the third age, each worker would save up to finance her or his individual retirement without regard for others.

In the United States, this began with the creation of Individual Retirement Accounts, which allowed workers to save tax-free for their retirements. Corporations then began to discontinue defined benefit pay-as-you-go pensions by setting up 401K defined contribution accounts. Chile, in 1981 under a right-wing military dictatorship that was influenced by conservative economists from the United States led by Milton Freedman from the University of Chicago, transformed its entire public pension fund from the defined benefit to the defined contribution basis. Britain enticed workers to change from their public pensions to a new privatized system in 1985. Throughout the 1980s and 1990s the World Bank successfully urged Latin American and post-communist eastern and central European countries to follow suit. By 2000, ten Latin American and such European countries as Hungary and Poland had followed the Chilean lead.

Transforming the public pension system created an enormous windfall for private capital. Instead of the social security taxes going into a public account to finance retirement, they went into private accounts that were available for private investment. Billions of dollars were diverted from public channels to private capital markets. At the same time, private retirement account managers siphoned off as much as 30 per cent in fees.

The greatest fiscal fallacy of the new privatized approach was that it undermined the principle of social insurance. In the traditional defined benefit approach, the funds are dedicated to the sole purpose of providing support for those who cannot support themselves due to old age or disability. In this sense, the short-lived subsidized the long-lived just as with health insurance the healthy subsidize the sick and injured. If a worker pays taxes her or his whole working life and then dies the day after retirement, nothing is collected. The funds that would otherwise be collected are then available to support surviving retired workers.

In the defined contribution systems, to the contrary, if a worker dies the day after her or his retirement begins, the accumulated funds go to relatives who do not need them because they are of working age. Hence, funds to support the third age are siphoned out to the second age, thereby undermining and subverting the principle of social insurance.

By the 1990s it was apparent in Britain that the new privatized system would result in much poorer retirement incomes for workers, and the government allowed people to re-enter the public system. By the end of the decade, the Chilean system was in crisis as the first workers under that system came into retirement. For most of them, their incomes turned out to be much less than they would have been under the former system. The government then had to step in with additional support.

In December 1995, the same year as the peso crisis, the Mexican Chamber of Deputies and Senate, over heavy public protest and with the active encouragement of the World Bank,[23] passed the most sweeping privatization of a public social security system since that of Chile in 1981. What made the unpopular move possible was that the PRI under President Ernesto Zedillo still had semi-authoritarian control of the state with disciplined majorities in the Chamber of Deputies and Senate.

The purported purpose of the privatization was to increase the country's savings rate and thereby decrease its reliance on foreign capital for development.[24] That was putting highly regressive legislation in its most publicly palatable form. It would be hard to argue against allowing the country to find a way to finance its own development and be less vulnerable to foreign control, but beneath the manipulated appearance was a deeper purpose.

What the privatization did was to transform collective workers' savings for retirement to a new source of capital accumulation for investment in the Mexican and other stock markets that private capital could control. Meanwhile, workers assumed all of the risks of the investments and lost the guarantees of retirement income that they had. The risks included those of any market investment due to unfavorable market conditions. In addition, private managers of the retirement accounts were able to charge considerable fees for administering the accounts.

In Mexico, where there has been an historic culture of public and private corruption and lax controls over consumer fraud, social security privatization shifts one of the ways in which the powerful can take advantage of the weak. Instead of corrupt officials pilfering public accounts, in the new neoliberalized Mexico, corporate managers—a number of whom formerly had been public officials—now have access to largely unprotected workers' private accounts to use to their advantage.

In 2005 President George W. Bush attempted a much less ambitious partial privatization of Social Security in the United States, his most audacious domestic social policy goal. With public support for the president high in the aftermath of the September 11, 2001 attack on the Twin Towers in New York and the initial Iraq invasion and fresh from his second-term election victory, the president thought that he had enough public backing to carry out the partial privatization. To his surprise, public reaction was fiercely opposed and the plan had to be abandoned. Social Security is the U.S. federal government's most popular and successful program. Undoubtedly many members of his most socially conservative Christian base themselves or members of their families benefited from the program. Despite supporting the president on most or all other issues, they were not willing to support the beginning of the end of a system that they thought had served them well.

In Canada there has been no significant move to privatize its social security system. The fate of the conservative project to privatize the social security system in North America thus has been correlated with the degree of welfare state development in the respective countries. The greatest success at transformation occurred in Mexico, the country with the weakest social policy and least democratic participation. It was attempted by the Bush administration in the United States but stopped because of democratic opposition. In Canada, the country with the strongest social policy and welfare state development, privatization has not become an issue because of high support by both the public and governing class for the current pay-as-you-go system.

The questions facing North American social and public policy are whether in the long run a converged social model will emerge to complement the economic integration brought forth by NAFTA. And if so, what type of social model will it be? Will Canada be the standard and common continental social protections move closer to those prevailing in the Western European welfare states? Or will conservatives in all three countries succeed in producing a continental *laissez-faire* social model with minimal social protections?

The countries of North America can move—collectively or individually—toward more social security, equality, and solidarity or toward more individual competition, inequality, and social insecurity. Either model can function economically but with greatly different social consequences.

NOTES

Chapter 1

1. World Bank, *World Development Report 2007* (Washington, DC: The World Bank, 2006) 289.

2. United Nations Development Programme (UNDP), *Human Development Report 2006* (New York: Palgrave Macmillan, 2006) 283.

3. UNDP, *Human Development Report 2006*, 315; calculated on the basis of data in United Nations Statistical Office, *Demographic Yearbook 2004* (New York: United Nations Publications, 2004) Table 9.

4. Calculated on the basis of data in the World Bank, *World Development Report 1990* (New York: Oxford U P, 1990) 179 and 231.

5. Seymour Martin Lipset, *Continental Divide: The Values and Institutions of the United States and Canada* (London: Routledge, 1990).

6. Lipset, *Continental Divide*, 92.

7. Samuel Ramos, *El Perfil del Hombre y la Cultura en México* (1934; Mexico City: Colección Austral, 1990) 159. Surprisingly, it is my impression that there are relatively fewer accidents in Mexico City despite the seeming traffic disorder than in the large orderly cities of the United States and Canada. The reason may be that to survive in Mexican traffic full alertness at all times is required. Drivers learn to always expect the unexpected. The wide lanes and orderliness of U.S. and Canadian freeways, on the other hand, tend to have a lulling effect that can precipitate accidents. As one Mexican motorist admitted, "We drive very badly, but with a great deal of skill." This impressionistic hypothesis, though, cannot be empirically verified because of the lack of reliability of the comparative data. In all three countries, many motorists involved in accidents prefer to settle privately to avoid insurance rate hikes. Such accidents, therefore, are never recorded for statistical purposes. Many motorists in Mexico have an additional motive to settle privately: they do not wish to get involved with the police, who often require the payment of a bribe.

8. The metaphor is far from perfect. Canadians are relatively orderly but like hockey, which resembles soccer on ice.

9. For example, William Julius Wilson, *The Declining Significance of Race: Blacks and Changing American Institutions* (Chicago, IL: U of Chicago P, 1980).

10. I have elaborated the distinction between economic and social classes in *Modes of Production in World History* (London: Routledge, 1989) 137-54 and *Societies and Social Life* (Cornwall-on-Hudson, NY: Sloan Publishing, 2006) 166-68.

11. Robert Miles, *Racism* (London: Routledge, 1989).

12. Richard T. Schaefer, *Racial and Ethnic Groups*, 4th ed. (Glenview, IL: Scott, Foresman, 1990) 13.

Chapter 2

1. "The enemy of the human race ... have not hesitated to publish abroad that the Indians of the West and the South, and other people of whom we have recent knowledge should be treated as dumb brutes created for our service, pretending that they are incapable of receiving the Catholic Faith. We ... consider, however, that the Indians are truly men ..." *Sublimus Dei*, 29 May 1537. Available online at http://www.papalencyclicals.net/Paul03/p3subli.htm.

2. Charles C. Mann, *1491: New Revelations of the Americas before Columbus* (New York: Vintage, 2006) 18.

3. The Neolithic revolution of the Americas occurred about 3,000 years after that of the Middle East; Mann 19.

4. Thomas D. Hall, *Social Change in the Southwest, 1350-1880* (Lawrence, KS: U P of Kansas, 1989) 40.

5. R. Douglas Francis, Richard Jones, and Donald B. Smith, *Origins: Canadian History to Confederation* (Toronto: Holt, Rinehart and Winston, 1988) 15.

6. Roger Bartra, "Tributo y Tenencia en la Tierra en la Sociedad Azteca." in Roger Bartra, ed., *El Modo de Producción Asiático* (Mexico City: Ediciones Era, 1969) 215.

7. Jared Diamond, *Guns, Germs, and Steel: The Fates of Human Societies* (New York: W.W. Norton, 1999) 292.

8. Michael Meyer and William L. Sherman, *The Course of Mexican History* (New York: Oxford U P, 1979) 89.

9. Marc Bloch, "Feudalism, European," *Encyclopedia of the Social Sciences* (New York: Macmillan, 1933) and *Feudal Society*, trans. L.A. Manyon (1940; Chicago, IL: U of Chicago P, 1961).

10. Roger Bartra, *La Jaula de la Melancolía: Identidad y Metamórfosis del Mexicano* (Mexico City: Grijalbo, 1987).

11. Alfred M. Crosby, *The Columbian Exchange: Biological and Cultural Consequences of 1492* (Westport, CT: Greenwood Press, 1972).

12. See Carey McWilliams, *North from Mexico* (1949; Westport, CT: Greenwood Press, 1968).

13. Robert Boyd, *The Coming of the Spirit of Pestilence: Introduced Infectious Diseases and Population Decline among Northwest Coast Indians, 1774-1874* (Seattle, WA: U of Washington P, 1999) 3.

14. George W. Ellis and John E. Morris, *King Philip's War* (New York: Grafton Press, 1906) 274; James Truslow Adams, *The Founding of New England* (Boston: Atlantic Monthly Press, 1921) 362.

15. Dee Brown, *Bury My Heart at Wounded Knee* (New York: Henry Holt and Company, 1970) 4.

16. George Brown and Ron Maguire, "Indian Treaties in Historical Perspective," in James S. Frideres, ed., *Native People in Canada* (Scarborough, ON: Prentice-Hall Canada, 1983) 49.

17. Brown and Maguire 40.

18. Francis, Jones, and Smith 47.

19. I have discussed the similarities and differences of the feudal and state modes of production in *Modes of Production in World History* (London: Routledge, 1989) 50-51.

20. Max Weber, *The Protestant Ethic and the Spirit of Capitalism* (1905; New York: Scribner's, 1948).

21. Karl Marx and Max Weber initiated the polar sides of this debate in classical social theory. Marx, in *Capital*, vol. 1 (Moscow: Progress Publishers, n.d., originally published in 1867) 703, maintained that "the discovery of gold and silver in America, the extirpation, enslavement and entombment in mines of the aboriginal population, the beginning of the conquest and looting of the East Indies, the turning of Africa into a warren for the commercial hunting of black-skins, signaled the rosy dawn of the era of capitalist production. These idyllic proceedings are the chief momenta of primitive accumulation." But in contrast, Weber in *General Economic History*, trans. Frank H. Knight (1923; New York: Collier Books edition, 1961) 223, concluded that though "the profits of the slave labor were by no means small ... this accumulation of wealth ... has been of little significance for the development of modern capitalism."

22. For a description, see Guillermo Bonfil Batalla, *México Profundo* (Mexico City: Grijalbo, 1990).

23. Cf. "During these first years after the conquest the Spanish simply substituted themselves for the old indigenous sovereigns and took advantage of the native systems of exploitation." Roger Bartra, "Tributo y Tenencia en la Tierra en la Sociedad Azteca," in Roger Bartra, ed., *El Modo de Producción Asiática* (Mexico City: Ediciones Era, 1969) 216.

24. Angel Palerm Vich, "Factores Históricos de la Clase Media en México," in Miguel Othon de Mendizábal *et al.*, eds., *Ensayos sobre las Clases Sociales en México* (Mexico City: Editorial Nuestro Tiempo, 1968) 93-94.

25. Palerm Vich 93-94.

26. Gonzalo Aguirre Beltrán, *Cuijla: Esbozo Etnográfico de un Pueblo Negro* (Mexico City: Fondo de Cultura Económica, 1958) 8.

27. Rolando Mellafe, *Negro Slavery in Latin America* (Berkeley, and Los Angeles U of California P, 1975) 69.

28. David M. Davidson, "El Control de los Esclavos Negros y su Resistencia en el México Colonial, 1519-1650," in Richard Price, ed., *Sociedades Cimarronas* (Mexico City: Siglo Veintiuno Editores, 1981) 87.

29. José L. Franco, "Rebeliones Cimarronas y Esclavas en los Territorios Españoles," in Price, *Sociedades Cimarronas* 43.

30. Mellafe 105.

31. See Aguirre Beltrán, *Cuijla*.

32. Aguirre Beltrán, *Cuijla* 59.

33. Alexander von Humboldt, *Ensayo Político sobre el Reino de la Nueva España*, vol. 1 (Paris, 1822) 262, cited in Aguirre Beltrán, *La Población Negra de México*.

34. Aguirre Beltrán, *La Población Negra de México*; Othon de Mendizábal *et al.* 9.

35. For an introduction, see the excellent issue of *Artes de México* (Mexico City) 8 (Summer 1990), which is devoted to paintings of the castes.

36. Edward J. Sullivan, "Ún Fenómeno Visual de América," in *Artes de México* 8 (Summer 1990) 60-71.

37. The etymological origin of the Spanish term *mulato* is based on the racist analogy of a

mule, which is a cross between a horse and a donkey. Presumably the horse in the analogy is the European, who is superior to the donkey, who is the African. The mulatto product then is inferior to the horse, or European, and superior to the donkey, or African.

38. Cf., Colonization of the north involved "exploration and possession of new lands, founding of population centers, exploration for natural resources, forced submission of the Indian, and once the enterprise was consolidated, defense of the acquired possessions." María Teresa Huerta Preciado, *Rebeliones Indígenas en el Noreste de México en la Epoca Colonial* (Mexico City: Instituto Nacional de Antropología e Historia, 1966) 103.

39. Francis, Jones, and Smith 78-79; Allan Greer, *Peasant, Lord, and Merchant: Rural Society in Three Quebec Parishes 1740-1840* (Toronto: U of Toronto P, 1985).

40. Francis, Jones, and Smith; also Robin W. Winks, *The Blacks in Canada* (New Haven, CT: Yale U P, 1971).

41. Until 1783 the British colonies of North America were referred to as British America. The term "British North America" came into use to refer to Britain's remaining North American colonies after the independence of those that became the United States. To avoid confusion of terms, I am referring to them simply as the British Colonies.

42. Herbert S. Klein, *African Slavery in Latin America and the Caribbean* (New York: Oxford U P, 1986) 53.

Chapter 3

1. Frances Paul Prucha, *The Great Father: The United States Government and the American Indian* (Lincoln, NB: U of Nebraska P, 1984) 40.

2. Quoted in Francis, Jones, and Smith 209.

3. See Lawrence Douglas Taylor, *El Nuevo Norteamericano: Integración Continental, Cultura e Identidad Nacional* (Mexico City: Universidad Nacional Autónoma de Mexico, 2001) chap. 2, for an interpretation that U.S. expansionism, including in the War of 1812, contributed to consolidating Canadian national identity. Taylor sees a parallel consolidation of Mexican national identity in reaction to U.S. expansionism in the Texas and Mexican-American Wars of 1836 and 1846-48.

4. Bruce Johansen and Roberto Maestas, *Wasi'Chu: The Continuing Indian Wars* (New York: Monthly Review Press, 1979) 27.

5. Francis, Jones, and Smith 218.

6. For a description, see Hall 217-30.

7. James E. Officer, *Hispanic Arizona, 1536-1856* (Tucson, AZ: U of Arizona P, 1987) 306.

8. Johansen and Maestas 32.

9. David J. Weber, *Myth and the History of the Hispanic Southwest* (Albuquerque, NM: U of New Mexico P, 1988) 141.

10. Rosalie Schwartz, *Across the Rio to Freedom: U.S. Negroes in Mexico*, Southwestern Studies monograph 44 (El Paso, TX: Texas Western Press, 1975) 11.

11. See Jack Jackson, ed., *Texas by Terán: The Diary Kept by General Manuel de Mier y Terán of his 1828 Inspection of Texas* (Austin, TX: U of Texas P, 2000).

12. Weber, *Myth and the History* 141.

13. Randolph B. Campbell, *An Empire for Slavery: The Peculiar Institution in Texas, 1821-1965* (Baton Rouge, LA: Louisiana State U P, 1989).

14. U.S. Bureau of the Census, *Statistical Abstract of the United States* (Washington, DC: U.S. Government Printing Office, 1989) 193.

15. Quoted in Weber, *Myth and the History* 139.

16. Calculated from data in Tables 654 and 868 of U.S. Bureau of the Census, *Statistical Abstract of the United States 2006* (Washington, DC: U.S. Government Printing Office, 2005).

17. W.E. B. Du Bois, *Black Reconstruction in America* (1935; New York: Russell and Russell, 1962).

18. For example, James S. Allen, *Reconstruction: The Battle for Democracy* (New York: International Publishers, 1937). Also, in 1944, Howard Fast published *Freedom Road* (New York: Duell, Sloan and Pierce), a best-selling historical novel about blacks struggling for land, equality, and democracy during Reconstruction. Fast based his work on the Communist Party's interpretation, and the book contained a forward by Du Bois.

19. Eric Foner, *Reconstruction: America's Unfinished Revolution, 1863-1877* (New York: Harper and Row, 1988).

20. Cf., Henry Louis Gates Jr. ("Forty Acres and a Gap in Wealth," *New York Times*, 18 November 2007) examined the family trees of 20 successful African-Americans and found that three-quarters contained at least one former slave who had managed to obtain property by 1920 when only one-quarter of African-American families owned property. He concluded that "if there is a meaningful correlation between the success of accomplished African-Americans today and their ancestors' property ownership, we can only imagine how different black-white relations would be had '40 acres and a mule' really been official government policy in the Reconstruction South."

21. Foner 140.

22. Foner 581.

23. The use of lynch law to establish the "Jim Crow" South in the 1870s and 1880s was similar to the use of death squads to terrorize the Salvadoran peasantry in the 1980s. In both cases a rural lower class was threatening a traditional order, and the rural upper classes used terrorist means to intimidate into submission their challengers. In both cases members of the state apparatus took part unofficially in the terrorist repression, and the state was an accomplice to the terrorism. Its agents—the local sheriff and his deputies in the case of the South, military officials in the case of El Salvador—unofficially took part in the terrorism. As a result, the respective state apparatuses took little or no action against the perpetrators of the violence.

24. Brown and Maguire 78.

25. Lipset, *Continental Divide* 91-92.

26. Lipset, *Continental Divide* 64.

27. Lipset, *Continental Divide* 72.

28. Lipset, *Continental Divide*.

29. James W. Walker, *A History of Blacks in Canada* (Ottawa: Minister of State and Multiculturalism, 1980).

30. B. Singh Bolaria and Peter S. Li, *Racial Oppression in Canada*, 2nd ed. (Toronto: Garamond Press, 1988) 190.

31. Robin W. Winks, *The Blacks in Canada* (New Haven, CT: Yale U P, 1971); Headley Tulloch, *Black Canadians* (Toronto: NC Press, 1975).

32. Walker 56.

33. Winks.

34. Agnes Calliste, "Canada's Immigration Policy and Domestics from the Caribbean: The Second Domestic Scheme," in Jesse Vorst, ed., *Race, Class, Gender: Bonds and Barriers* (Toronto: Between the Lines, 1989).

35. See Friedrich Engels, "Letter to Sorge (September 12, 1888)," in Karl Marx and Friedrich Engels, *Letters to Americans* (New York: International Publishers, 1963).

36. Aguirre Beltrán, *La Población Negra de México* 234.

37. For descriptions and documents, see Leticia Reina, *Las Rebeliones Campesinas en México, 1819-1906* (Mexico City: Siglo Veintiuno Editores, 1980).

38. Hall 160-63.

39. Cf., "By the time of Mexican independence it was widely recognized that some Apaches and Comanches, and probably Wichita bands such as the Taovayas, stole horses and mules from Tejanos and exchanged them for guns and ammunition with traders in Louisiana." Weber, *Myth and the History of the Hispanic Southwest* 122.

40. Guillermo Bonfil Batalla, *México Profundo* (Mexico City: Grijalbo, 1990) 151; Hall 161; James E. Officer, *Hispanic Arizona, 1536-1856* (Tucson, AZ: U of Arizona P, 1987) 150.

41. For a description, see Officer.

42. Hall 104.

43. The Yaquis also inhabited land that is now a part of the United States. There is a small Pascua Yaqui reservation in Pima County, Arizona.

44. Ramon Eduardo Ruiz, *The People of Sonora and Yankee Capitalists* (Tucson, AZ: U of Arizona P, 1988) 180.

45. Samuel Ramos, *El Perfil de Hombre y la Cultura en México* (Mexico City: Colección Austral, 1990, originally published in 1934).

46. Aguirre Beltrán, *La Población Negra de México* 234.

47. Aguirre Beltrán, *Cuijla* 59.

48. Aguirre Beltrán, *Cuijla* 59.

49. Most of the information reported here on slave escapes to Mexico was obtained from Rosalie Schwartz's impressively researched *Across the Rio to Freedom: U.S. Negroes in Mexico* (El Paso, TX: Texas Western Press, 1975).

50. Schwartz 26.

51. Schwartz 40.

52. María Luisa Herrera Casasus, *Presencia y Esclavitud del Negro en la Huasteca* (Mexico City: Porrúa, 1989) 25.

53. Schwartz 33.

Chapter 4

1. See Hyon B. Shin and Rosalind Bruno, "Language Use and English-Speaking Ability: 2000,"

U.S. Bureau of the Census (Census Brief 2000, October 2003); Instituto Nacional de Estadística Geografía e Informática (INEGI), *Il Conteo de Población y Vivienda 2005* (http://www.-inegi.gob.mx/); Statistics Canada, "Language Composition of Canada: Highlight Tables," *2001 Census,* http://www.statcan.ca/.

2. French troops with the support of Britain and Spain invaded and occupied Mexico in 1862 after liberal President Benito Juàrez suspended interest payments on loans from foreign countries. In 1864 Napoleon III of France prevailed upon Ferdinand Maximilian Joseph von Habsburg to take the position of Emperor of Mexico. Mexican liberals under the leadership of President Juàrez fought to expel the French troops and impòsed government. In 1867 French troops withdrew, and Maximilian was captured, sentenced to death, and shot by firing squad. Along with U.S. invasions during the 1845-48 war and later during the early twentieth-century revolution, the French invasion stimulated a strong political principle in Mexico of opposition to foreign military interventions of any type. Among the visible legacies of the French invasion and occupation today are the broad avenues and boulevards in the center of Mexico City, built during that period to resemble those of Paris, and a number of bakery goods modeled after French ones such as the *cuervo,* which is a copy of the French croissant.

3. Stanley Feldstein and Lawrence Costello, eds., *The Ordeal of Assimilation: A Documentary History of the White Working Class* (Garden City, NY: Anchor Press, 1974) 4.

4. Information on the Saint Patrick's Battalion was taken from Robert Ryal Miller's *Shamrock and Sword: The Saint Patrick's Battalion in the U.S.-Mexican War* (Norman, OK: U of Oklahoma P, 1989). His was the first extensive and well-documented study of the events. Prior to its publication, many of the existing accounts were largely based on legend and suffered accordingly in terms of their accuracy. In addition to establishing that the majority of the members of the battalion were not Irish, Miller cast doubt on whether persecution of Catholics in the United States and views of the U.S. invasion as unjust were the main motivations for the desertions of the San Patricios.

5. U.S. Bureau of the Census, *Statistical Abstract of the United States, 1989* (Washington, DC: U.S. Government Printing Office, 1989) 40.

6. For the classic study, see W.I. Thomas and Florian Znaniecki, *The Polish Peasant in Europe and America,* 4 vols. (1918-20; New York: Dover, 1958). For an account of second, third, and later generation Polish Americans, see Mary Patrice Erdmans, *The Grasinski Girls: The Choices They Had and the Choices They Made* (Athens, OH: Ohio U P, 2005).

7. Cf., "Your great obstacle in America, it seems to me, lies in the exceptional position of the native-born workers. Up to 1848 one could speak of a permanent native-born working class only as an exception. The small beginnings of one in the cities in the East still could always hope to become farmers or bourgeois. Now such a class has developed and has also organized itself on trade-union lines to a great extent. But it still occupies an aristocratic position and wherever possible leaves the ordinary badly paid occupations to the immigrants, only a small portion of whom enter the aristocratic trade unions. But these immigrants are divided into different nationalities, which understand neither one another nor, for the most part, the language of the country. And your bourgeoisie knows much better than the Austrian government how to play off one nationality against the other: Jews, Italians, Bohemians, etc., against Germans and Irish, and each one against the other, so that

differences in workers' standards of living exist, I believe, in New York to an extent unheard of elsewhere." Friedrich Engels, "Letter to Hermann Schliter (March 30, 1892)," in Karl Marx and Friedrich Engels, *Letters to Americans* (New York: International Publisher, 1963).

8. Statistics Canada, "Mother Tongue, 2001 Counts," *2001 Census* (http://www12.statcan.ca).

9. The francophone population voted heavily yes and everyone else heavily no. Yet even with the expected no votes, the referendum would have passed if a greater majority of French speakers had supported it. Part of the explanation for why a minority of French speakers opposed separation can be found in the Canadian Census's statistics on ethnic identification. While 81.2 per cent of Quebec are francophone, only 30.9 per cent identify themselves as either French or Québécois. The balance identify themselves as Canadian, indicating that a significant minority of French speakers consider themselves to be within the overall Canadian national identity and not separate from it. See Statistics Canada, "Mother Tongue" and Statistics Canada, "Ethnocultural Portrait of Canada," *2001 Census* (http://www12.statcan.ca/) Table 1. Parti Québécois Premier Jacques Parizeau blamed the defeat on "money and the ethnic vote." It is true that immigrants voted overwhelmingly against independence and had they not the referendum would have passed. But an even larger number— though not proportion—of francophones voted against it. A large majority of francophone voters over 55 years old voted against it and significantly fewer francophone women than men supported it. For an analysis of the vote, see Gilles Gagné and Simon Langlois, *Les Raisons Fortes: Nature et signification de l'appui à la souveraineté du Québec* (Montreal: Les Presses de l'Université du Montréal, 2002).

10. John Porter, *The Vertical Mosaic* (Toronto: U of Toronto P, 1965).

11. Calculated on the basis of information in Statistics Canada, "Income of Individuals, Families, and Households," *2001 Census,* http://www12.statcan.ca.

12. Weber, *The Protestant Ethic and the Spirit of Capitalism.*

13. Porter, *The Vertical Mosaic,* 95

14. McWilliams, *North from Mexico.*

15. U.S. Bureau of the Census, *Migration between the United States and Canada* (Washington, DC: U.S. Government Printing Office, 1990) 7.

16. Howard Palmer, "Reluctant Hosts: Anglo-Canadian Views of Multiculturalism in the Twentieth Century," in R. Douglas Francis and Donald B. Smith, *Readings in Canadian History: Post-Confederation,* 2nd ed. (Toronto: Holt, Rinehart and Winston of Canada, 1986).

17. Calculated from Statistics Canada, "Ethno-Cultural Portrait."

18. Palmer 185. There is some evidence though that, in contrast to policies prevailing in the United States, Canadian officials in the late nineteenth and early twentieth centuries unofficially assured non-English-speaking immigrants that they could retain their languages and cultures. See Palmer 157. See also Lawrence Douglas Taylor, *El Nuevo Norteamericano* 114, who concludes that the groups who form the "Canadian mosaic have resisted forming part of a melting pot as did immigrant groups in the United States."

19. Palmer 185-86.

20. See Lipset, *Continental Divide.*

21. Cf., "The very diverse origins of Canadians and their integration into the English-speaking majority probably constitute the most powerful force leading to a new self-definition in Canada.

Not being of British stock, new immigrants do not see themselves as English Canadians, but simply as Canadians." Simon Langlois, "Canada and Québec: An Update," *Footnotes*, American Sociological Association (March 2006).

22. Consejo Nacional de Población (CONAPO), *Población y Desarrollo en México y el Mundo*, vol. 4, *Anexo Estadístico* (Mexico City: CONAPO, 1988) 1099.

23. Campbell J. Gibson and Emily Lennon, "Historical Census Statistics on the Foreign-born Population of the United States: 1850-1990," Population Division Working Papers No. 29, U.S. Bureau of the Census, Washington, DC (February 1999) Table 1.

24. Instituto Nacional Estadística e Geografía (INEGI), *Los Extranjeros en México* (http://www.inegei.gob.mx/, 2007) 10.

25. United Nations Population Division, *The World at Six Billion* (New York: United Nations, 1999) Table 29.

26. Victor G. Nee and Bret de Barry Nee, *Longtime Californ': A Documentary Study of an American Chinatown* (New York: Pantheon Books, 1973) 41.

27. Nee and Nee.

28. Carey McWilliams, *Factories in the Field* (1935; Santa Barbara, CA: Peregrine Smith, 1971) 69.

29. McWilliams, *Factories in the Field* 68.

30. Bolaria and Li 114.

31. Moises González Navarro, *La Colonización en México, 1877-1910* (Mexico City: Talleres de Impresión de Estampillas y Valores, 1960) 84.

32. José Jorge Gómez Izquierdo, *El Movimiento Anti-Chino en México, 1871-1934* (Mexico City: Universidad Nacional Autónoma de México Facultad de Ciencias Políticas y Sociales, 1988) 53.

33. Gómez Izquierdo; Charles C. Cumberland, "The Sonora Chinese and the Mexican Revolution," *Hispanic American Historical Review* 40 (May 1960): 191-223.

34. Evelyn Hu-DeHart, "Immigrants to a Developing Society: The Chinese in Northern Mexico, 1875-1932," *Journal of Arizona History* (Autumn 1980) 275-313.

35. Hu-DeHart; Cumberland; Gómez Izquierdo 85.

36. Hu-DeHart.

37. Gómez Izquierdo 124.

38. Gómez Izquierdo 138.

39. Hu-DeHart.

40. Gómez Izquierdo 127.

41. Campbell Clark, "PM Offers Apology, 'Symbolic Payments' for Chinese Head Tax," *Globe and Mail*, 23 June 2006.

42. K. Victor Ujimoto, "Racism, Discrimination, and Internment: Japanese in Canada," in Bolaria and Li 130.

43. Carey McWilliams, *Prejudice–Japanese Americans: Symbol of Racial Intolerance* (Boston, MA: Little, Brown, 1944).

44. By 1916 the labor movement had reversed its position and disassociated itself from anti-Asian agitation, arguing the need instead to organize all immigrants.

45. McWilliams, *Prejudice–Japanese Americans*.

46. Ujimoto 130.

47. Edna Bonacich and John Modell, *The Economic Basis of Ethnic Solidarity: Small Business in the Japanese American Community* (Berkeley, CA: U of California P, 1980).

48. McWilliams, *Prejudice — Japanese Americans.*

49. Schaefer 396.

50. Schaefer 401.

51. Ujimoto.

52. Blanca Torres, *Historia de la Revolución Mexicana, 1940-1952* (Mexico City: El Colegio de México, 1979) 80n.

53. María Elena Ota Mishima, *Siete Migraciones Japonesas en México, 1890-1978* (Mexico City: El Colegio de México, 1982) 95-102.

54. See Aguirre Beltrán, *La Población Negra de México.*

55. H. Brett Melendy, *Asians in America: Filipinos, Koreans, and East Indians* (Boston, MA: Twayne, 1977).

56. McWilliams, *Factories in the Field* 104.

57. Carey McWilliams, *Brothers under the Skin* (Boston, MA: Little, Brown, 1964) 43.

58. Melendy.

59. Ricardo Trumper and Lloyd L. Wong, "Canada's Guest Workers: Racialized, Gendered, and Flexible" in *Race & Racism in 21st-Century Canada: Continuity, Complexity, and Change*, ed. Sean P. Hier and B. Singh Bolaria (Peterborough, ON: Broadview Press, 2007) 162.

Chapter 5

1. The term "mulatto" for this population, though conventional, is considered racist and offensive by many because of its zoological origin and implications. As noted earlier, it is based on the analogy of the mule, which is a mixture of a horse and donkey, with the former being superior to the latter as racists consider Europeans to be superior to Africans. I will use the term "biracial" for persons who have one black and one white parent and "mixed race" for those who are descended in any combination from both blacks and whites.

2. Overall, the numbers of Eurasians in North America are slight, but in Hawaii, which contains significant numbers of Japanese-origin as well as white citizens, there are significant numbers. Forty-two per cent of Hawaiians identify themselves as Asian, 24.3 per cent as white, 9.4 per cent as native Hawaiian or other Pacific Islander, and less than 2 per cent as either black or Indian. The proportion of Eurasians is indicated by the 22.7 per cent, much higher than the national average, who identify themselves as either "Other" or as having two or more races (U.S. Bureau of the Census, Census 2000 Summary File 1, http://www.factfinder.census.gov', Table QT-P5 Hawaii).

Hawaii, according to F. James Davis in *Who is Black? One Nation's Definition* (University Park, PA: Pennsylvania State U P, 1991) 109, is the one area in the United States where racially mixed persons enjoy complete social equality. It is the area where there is the least correlation between race and class; there is no noticeable whitening of faces as the social ladder is climbed.

The U.S. military presence in Asia continues to result in the births of a number of mixed-race children. During the Korean War, U.S. soldiers, both white and black, fathered thousands of mixed-race children. During the Vietnam War, the number fathered was estimated to be 80,000. Most of these children, though, remained in Korea and Vietnam, where, according to Davis (86), they have suffered considerable discrimination as outcasts. A much smaller number now reside in the United States, where they are generally referred to as Amerasians.

3. Most of Mexico's population that is socially perceived to be black (see Chapter 3) is in reality a mixed population of African and indigenous descent. For that reason a number of contemporary researchers call it an *Afromestizo* population. In the United States a number of Indian tribes welcomed escaped slaves and other blacks into their ranks; resulting marriages produced children with Indian and black descent. Overall, according to Thomas F. Pettigrew in *Racial Discrimination in the United States* (New York: Harper and Row, 1975), one-fourth of blacks in the United States have some Indian ancestry.

4. Magnus Mörner, *El Mestizaje en la Historia de Ibero-América* (Mexico City: Instituto Panamericano de Geografía e Historia, 1961) 29-30.

5. Magnus Mörner, *Race Mixture in the History of Latin America* (Boston, MA: Little, Brown, 1967) 30.

6. Moises González Navarro, "*Mestizaje* in Mexico during the National Period," in Magnus Mörner, ed., *Race and Class in Latin America* (New York: Columbia U P, 1970).

7. Mörner, *Race Mixture in the History of Latin America* 59-60.

8. Mörner, *Race Mixture in the History of Latin America* 40.

9. Quoted in Agustín Basave Benítez, *México Mestizo: Análisis del Nacionalismo Mexicano en torno a la Mestizofilía de Andrés Molina Enríquez* (Mexico City: Fondo de Cultura Económica, 1992) 27.

10. González Navarro, "*Mestizaje* in Mexico during the National Period."

11. Vasconcelos is most remembered as a philosopher, man of letters, and one of Mexico's most controversial post-revolutionary politicians. He occupied such posts as minister of public instruction, secretary of public education, and rector of the National University. He saw his mission as overseeing the development of public education and a revolutionary nationalist culture for the nation as a whole. Vasconcelos infused his work with his own commitment to revolutionary nationalist values. He was responsible for the Mexican government's financing of the production of murals by Diego Rivera, David Siquieros, José Orozco, and other artists to portray Mexico's history on public walls so that it could be seen and learned by the masses. In 1929 he ran and lost as an oppositional candidate for the presidency. After finding himself on the losing side of this power struggle over post-revolutionary Mexican development, he became a bitter critic of the government.

12. José Vasconcelos, *La Raza Cósmica* (1925; Mexico City: Espasa-Calpe Mexicana, Colección Austra, 1992) 27.

13. English novelist Graham Greene's racist portrayal of a mestizo in *The Power and the Glory* (New York: Viking, 1940) exemplified the Anglo abhorrence of race mixing. The character—referred to only as "the mestizo" or, alternatively, as "the half-caste," itself indicative of a racist narrative—is disgusting, thieving, and traitorous. "He wondered whether the mestizo had stolen his mule .... Then the door opened and the man came in—the two yellow canine teeth, the finger-nails scratching in the armpit" (105). Graham implies that whites and Indians are natural races while "the mestizo" is an abomination.

14. Cited in José Jorge Gómez Izquierdo, *El Movimiento Anti-Chino en México 1871-1934* (Mexico City: Universidad Nacional Autónoma de México Facultad de Ciencias Políticas y Sociales, 1988) 116.

15. Ramos, *El Perfil del Hombre y la Cultura en México.*

16. Octavio Paz, *El Laberinto de la Soledad* (Mexico City: Fondo de Cultura Popular, 1950).

17. Roger Bartra, *La Jaula de la Melancolía: Identidad y Metamórfosis del Mexicano* (Mexico City: Grijalbo, 1987). See also, Bartra, ed., *Anatomía del Mexicano.*

18. Emile Durkheim, *The Division of Labor in Society,* trans. G. Simpson (1893; New York: Free Pres, 1964).

19. Quoted in Lilian Alvarez de Testa, *Mexicanidad y Libro de Texto Gratuito* (Mexico City: Universidad Nacional Autónoma de México, 1992) 14.

20. Paul W. Bennett and Cornelius J. Jaenen, *Emerging Identities: Selected Problems and Interpretations in Canadian History* (Scarborough, ON: Prentice Hall Canada, 1986) 268.

21. Bennett and Jaenen 275.

22. Jean H. Lagassé, *The People of Indian Ancestry in Manitoba* (Winnipeg, MB: Department of Agriculture and Immigration, 1959). Cited in Nicole St-Onge, "Race, Class and Marginality in a Manitoba Interlake Settlement, 1850-1950," in Jesse Vorst, ed., *Race, Class, Gender: Bonds and Barriers* (Toronto: Between The Lines, 1989).

23. Joel Williamson, *New People: Miscegenation and Mulattoes in the United States* (New York: Free Press, 1980) 7.

24. Williamson 42.

25. See John G. Mencke, *Mulattoes and Race Mixture* (Ann Arbor, MI: UMI Research Press, 1979).

26. One of the most prominent cases of unacknowledged biracial children emerging out of relations between slave owners and slaves involved Thomas Jefferson, the third president of the United States. Jefferson's household, Monticello, had a number of slaves attached to it. He is widely believed to have sired biracial children with one of them, Sally Hemings, and there are blacks who claim descent from him. Historians, though, are divided as to whether it was Jefferson or some other male in his family who was the actual father of Sally Hemings's biracial children; for accounts, see Fawn M. Brodie, *Thomas Jefferson: An Intimate History* (New York: Norton, 1974); Williamson: and Davis.

27. Calculated from U.S. Bureau of the Census, *Negro Population of the United States, 1790-1915* (Washington, DC: U.S. Government Printing Office, 1918).

28. Davis 36.

29. Mencke 13.

30. Cited in Williamson 18.

31. Williamson, 18.

32. Williamson 81.

33. See Mencke 26.

34. Williamson 3.

35. Davis 21.

Chapter 6

1. Ronald Manzer, *Public Policies and Political Development in Canada* (Toronto: U of Toronto P, 1985) 30.

2. Spurgeon Bell, "Productivity, Wages and National Income," in Richard Edwards, Michael Reich, and Thomas Weisskopf, eds., *The Capitalist System*, 2nd ed. (Englewood Cliffs, NJ: Prentice Hall, 1977) 180; United States, *Statistical Abstract of the United States 2007*, Table 590.

3. James O'Connor, *The Fiscal Crisis of the State* (New York: St. Martin's Press, 1973).

4. John Blair, *Economic Concentration* (New York: Harcourt Brace Jovanovich, 1972).

5. U.S. Bureau of the Census, *Census 2000*, Summary File 3, Tables P50 and P51; Statistics Canada, *2001 Census of Population, Paid Work, Occupation*; and Instituto Nacional de Estadística Geografía e Informática (INEGI), *XII Censo General de Poblacion y Vivienda 2000* (Aguascalientes: INEGI, 2000).

6. Roger Bartra, *Estructura Agraria y Clases Sociales en México* (Mexico City: Ediciones Era, 1974) 131.

7. U.S. Bureau of the Census, *Historical Statistics of the United States*, part 1 (Washington, DC: U.S. Government Printing Office, 1976) 139.

8. Meyer and Sherman.

9. For an account, see Carlos Montemayor, *Las Armas del Alba* (Mexico City: Joaquín Mortiz, 2003).

10. Richard Michel, "An Overview Report on the In-Bond Program: Border Plants and Interior Plants," paper given to "The *Maquiladora* Industry in Mexico: Current Status and Prospects Conference" sponsored by the American Chamber of Commerce in Mexico, 26 April 1978, Club Campestre, Chihuahua. Recording no. 371, 1978. On file at the Institute of Oral History, University of Texas at El Paso.

11. Monica C. Gambril, "The New Role of *Maquiladoras* in the Development of Mexico," paper presented at the 1993 Annual Meeting of the American Sociological Association, Miami, FL.

12. Statistics Canada, http://www40.statcan.ca/l01/cst01/gblec02a.htm.

13. Statistics Canada, *Corporation Returns Act 2005* (Ottawa: Minister of Industry, 2007).

14. See Henry Veltmeyer, "Late Capitalism, Corporate Power, and Imperialism," in J. Paul Grayson, ed., *Introduction to Sociology: An Alternate Approach* (Toronto: Gage, 1983) 125.

15. Gary Teeple, "Introduction," in Gary Teeple, ed. *Capitalism and the National Question in Canada* (Toronto: U of Toronto P, 1972) x.

16. Mel Watkins, "A Staple Theory of Economic Growth," in Hugh Grant and David Wolfe, eds., *Staples and Beyond: Selected Writings of Mel Watkins* (1963; Montreal and Kingston: McGill-Queen's U P, 2006) 7.

Chapter 7

1. For other accounts of how NAFTA developed, see also John R. MacArthur, *The Selling of "Free Trade"* (Berkeley, CA: U of California P, 2001) and Jeff Faux, *The Global Class War* (Hoboken, NJ: John Wiley and Sons, 2006).

2. See Ginger Thompson, "Ex-President in Mexico Casts New Light on Rigged 1988 Election," *New York Times*, 9 March 2004. The ballots, never recounted, were later burned.

3. Interview with Allen L. Sessoms, Deputy Chief of Mission to Ambassador John Negroponte, U.S. Embassy, Mexico City, 12 February 1991. The official posture was non-interference. Unofficially, Mr. Sessoms stated, "we would not have permitted Cárdenas to take office."

4. Thompson.

5. For information on the public relations campaign, see Charles Lewis and Margaret Ebrahim, "Big $$$ Lobbying in Washington: Can Mexico and Big Business USA Buy NAFTA?" *The Nation* 256, (14 June 1993) 23 and MacArthur. In the spring of 1992, Guadalupe Jones, Miss Mexico, was crowned Miss Universe. The standing joke in Mexico was to call her Miss Fast Track and to speculate that she was really a fictional creation of a public relations firm to make Mexico look good. She spoke fluent English as well as Spanish. She supported the United States in the Persian Gulf War, when domestic political considerations obliged the Mexican government to be officially neutral, and went to Los Angeles to welcome U.S. troops home. Her very name symbolized the new relationship, being made up of the quintessential female Mexican first name, Guadalupe, from the Virgin of Guadalupe, and the quintessential U.S. last name, Jones.

6. In 1991, a potential political scandal was averted, which could have undermined the positive image of the Mexican government in the eyes of the United States during the campaign for NAFTA. In September a drug-laden plane landed at a remote, seldom-used army airstrip in Veracruz. Minutes later, a Judicial Police plane in pursuit of the drug traffickers touched down. Army troops at the field then opened fire and killed seven Judicial Police agents in what was initially described in the press as a "tragic night-time confusion." There was considerable speculation within and outside of Mexico that the army may have been abetting the drug traffickers, all of whom escaped. Peasants in the area reported that the army troops had come to the airstrip the day before the drug plane landed, that they had brought with them refueling tanks, and that the gun battle actually took place during daylight hours. It was further reported that a U.S. Drug Enforcement Agency plane had been following both planes and had videotaped the whole incident from the air. President Salinas de Gortari responded to the potential scandal by having the country's official Human Rights Commission carry out an investigation. The commission found that the killings were the result of a "tragic confusion," but one that army officers should have been able to avoid. It made no mention of collaboration between the army and drug trafficking. Several officers were sent to jail, and the issue disappeared from the Mexican press. Though the U.S. press initially reported the incident, it did not follow the story. The potential scandal neither damaged the Mexican government's reputation in the United States nor interfered with the NAFTA negotiations. For more information, see the September and October 1991 issues of *Proceso*, published in Mexico.

7. For an early analysis, see Wayne A. Cornelius, "The Politics and Economics of Reforming the *Ejido* Sector in Mexico," *LASA Forum* 23,3 (Fall 1992): 3-10.

8. Ana de Ita, "Land Concentration in Mexico after PROCEDE," in Peter M. Rosset, Raj Patel, and Michael Courville, eds., *Promised Land: Competing Visions of Agrarian Reform* (Oakland, CA: Food First, 2006) 150.

9. Clyde H. Farnsworth, "Voting in Canada Can Affect NAFTA," *New York Times*, 24 October

1993; Keith Bradsher, "U.S. Says Chretien Will Not Undo NAFTA," *New York Times*, 27 October 1993.

10. For an interview with Prime Minister Chrétien regarding his support for NAFTA, see MacArthur 266-69.

11. Fifteen years later the clash over free trade between elite and base members of the Democratic Party in the United States would re-emerge during the 2008 presidential primaries. Both leading candidates, Senators Barack Obama and Hilary Clinton, ran campaigns very critical of the effects of NAFTA. However, a senior economic advisor to Obama, Austin D. Goolsbee, assured a Canadian government official that the candidate was just engaged in political rhetoric to win votes from workers hard hit by outsourcing of jobs and had no intention of abandoning or substantially altering the agreement. Meanwhile, it was revealed that Senator Clinton's pollster and chief strategist, Mark Penn, was the CEO of Burson-Marsteller, the public relations firm responsible for promoting a free trade agreement with Colombia. After the scandals emerged, the candidates forced both men to resign. There is little doubt, though, of the truth of what was revealed: both candidates essentially supported corporate-backed free trade despite their public pronouncements. See Michael Leo, "Despite NAFTA Attacks, Clinton and Obama Haven't Been Free Trade Foes" and "Memo Gives Canada's Account of Obama Campaign's Meeting on NAFTA," *New York Times*, 2 February and 4 March 2008; and John M. Broder, "Clinton Strategist Lobbied for Trade Pact She Opposes," *New York Times*, 5 April 2008.

12. See Felix M. Padilla, *Puerto Rican Chicago* (Notre Dame, IN: U of Notre Dame P, 1987) 39.

13. C. Wright Mills, Clarence Senior, and Rose Kohn Goldsen, *The Puerto Rican Journey* (New York: Harper and Brothers, 1950).

14. Bonnie Mass, *Population Target: The Political Economy of Population Control in Latin America* (Brampton, ON: Charters, 1976) 95.

15. World Bank, *World Development Report 1990*.

16. National Center for Health Statistics, *Health, United States, 2002* (Hyattsville, MD: Public Health Service, 2002) Tables 26, 27.

17. U.S. Bureau of the Census, *Census 2000* (Washington DC: U.S. Government Printing Office, 2001) Summary File 3, Table 568.

18. U.S. Bureau of the Census, *Statistical Abstract of the United States* (Washington, DC: U.S. Government Printing Office, 2002) Table 1316.

19. The "export goods, not people" formulation was repeated many times by Salinas de Gortari in Mexico and the United States. Frederick W. Mayer in *Interpreting NAFTA: The Science and Art of Political Analysis* (New York: Columbia U P, 1998) 45 traced it to an interview on NBC Nightly News on 11 June 1990. It can also be found in an interview in *Fortune* in 1992 (Marshall Loeb, "Salinas Speaks Out on Free Trade," 28 December).

20. John Negroponte, U.S. Ambassador to Mexico from 1989 to 1993 while NAFTA was being negotiated, is perhaps the most controversial recent figure in the U.S. Foreign Service. His career trajectory has taken him through key policy implementation positions of the most controversial U.S. post-World War II foreign policies. His first diplomatic posting was to the U.S. Embassy in Saigon during the Vietnam War. He was the ambassador to Honduras from 1981 to 1985 during the U.S.-sponsored Contra war against the left-wing Sandinista government of Nicaragua. The Contras

used Honduras as their base of operations for cross-border terrorist attacks. Critics have long cited Negroponte's role in the Contras' terrorist activities and human rights abuses.

Negroponte's role as ambassador to Mexico during the NAFTA negotiations remains under-researched. When he left that post in 1993, Mexican journalist and researcher Adolfo Aguilar Zinser wrote, "with a long-term, historical perspective, we will probably have a lot of nasty things to say about what Mr. Negroponte did here, but we don't know what those things are yet" (quoted in *Financial Times*, "Old Enemies Meet Again at the UN," 19 November 2003).

In 2001, President George W. Bush, appointed Negroponte ambassador to the United Nations. There was a strong likelihood that the Senate would not approve the appointment because of continuing controversy over his activities as ambassador to Honduras; however, he was approved shortly after the September 11, 2001 attacks on New York and Washington, when the Senate was little inclined to oppose the president over an appointment. As ambassador to the United Nations, Negroponte unsuccessfully attempted to obtain Security Council authorization for the 2003 U.S. invasion of Iraq.

Adolfo Aguilar Zinser had since become Mexico's ambassador to the UN and clashed often with Negroponte. After making a speech in Mexico City denouncing the United States for treating Mexico as "its backyard," Aguilar Zinser was removed from his post by President Vincente Fox. There was widespread speculation, officially denied, that Fox had acted after complaints by U.S. Secretary of State Colin Powell and, quite likely, Negroponte. Aguilar Zinser's last act as ambassador was to vote against authorizing the U.S. invasion of Iraq. In 2005 he died in an automobile accident in Mexico.

From 2004 to 2005, Negroponte was the U.S. Ambassador to Iraq. From 2005 to 2007 he was the Director of National Intelligence. In 2007 he was appointed Deputy Secretary of State under Condoleezza Rice in the Bush government.

21. Cited in Faux 37.

22. Cited in David Barkin, "The Reconstruction of a Modern Mexican Peasantry," *The Journal of Peasant Studies* 20,1 (October 2002): 81.

23. Instituto Nacional de Estadística Geografía e Informática (INEGI), *XII Censo General de Población y Vivienda, 2000* (Aguascalientes: INEGI, 2000).

24. José Luís Valdés-Ugalde, *Análisis de los efectos del Tratado de Libre Comercio de América del Norte en la economía mexicana: Una visión sectorial a cinco años de distancia* (Mexico City: Edición del Senado de la República, LVII Legislatura, 2000) 281 and 312.

25. Valdés-Ugalde 272.

26. U.S. Department of Agriculture, Foreign Agricultural Service. "Trade and Agriculture: What's at Stake for Wisconsin?" October 2001; http://www.fas.usda.gov/info/factsheets/TPA/wi.pdf.

27. Jennifer Van Hook and Frank D. Bean, "Estimating Unauthorized Mexican Migration to the United States: Issues and Results," in U.S. Commission on Immigration Reform, *The Binational Study of Migration Between Mexico and the United States*, vol. 2 (Washington, DC: U.S. Commission on Immigration Reform, 1997); Frank D. Bean, Jennifer Van Hook, and Karen Woodrow-Lafield, *Estimates of Numbers of Unauthorized Migrants Residing in the United States: The Total Mexican, and Non-Mexican Central American Unauthorized Populations in Mid-2001* (Washington, DC: Pew Hispanic Center, Pew Charitable Trusts, 2002).

28. Jeffrey S. Passel, "Estimates of the Size and Characteristics of the Undocumented Population" (Washington, DC: Pew Hispanic Center Report, 21 March 2005): 1.

29. The amount of land in *ejidos* and number of *ejidatarios* actually increased modestly between 1991 and 2001, the closest *ejido* census years before and after the initiation of the reform of Article 27 in 1992. See INEGI, *VII Censo Ejital 1991* and *VIII Censo Ejital*. For a more complete analysis of the impact of the reform of Article 27, see de Ita.

30. Barkin 89, n16.

31. Calculated on the basis of information in Bean, et al.; Melissa Therrien and Roberto R. Ramiriz, *The Hispanic Population of the United States* (Washington, DC: U.S. Bureau of the Census Current Population Reports P20-535, March 2001); and Dianne Schmidley, *Profile of the Foreign-Born Population in the United States: 2000* (Washington, DC: U.S. Bureau of the Census Current Population Reports P23-206, February 2001).

32. U.S. Government Accountability Office, *Illegal Immigration: Border-Crossing Deaths Have Doubled Since 1995* (Washington, DC: U.S. Government Accountability Office Report 06-770, August 2006) 16.

33. Cf., "The growing death toll here in recent years follows a Border Patrol clampdown in California and Texas. The goal was to drive migrant traffic away from cities like San Diego and El Paso and into the remote desert on the assumption it would act as a deterrent." Randal C. Archibold, "At the Border the Desert Takes a Rising Toll," *New York Times*, 15 September, 2007.

Chapter 8

1. Researchers and writers have differed over whether it is most valid to conceptualize three upper, middle, and lower social class levels or four levels with an additional working class in between the middle and lower class. For the classic three class model applied to the United States, albeit with upper and lower levels within each, see W. Lloyd Warner, Marcia Meeker, and Kenneth Eeks, *Social Class in America* (Chicago: Research Associates, 1949). Richard Centers (*The Psychology of Social Classes: A Study of Class Consciousness*, Princeton: Princeton U P, 1949) was the first to add the working class as a separate social class.

2. Calculated from U.S. Bureau of the Census, *Census 2000*, Summary File 3, Table P50.

3. INEGI, *XII Censo General de Población y Vivienda 2000*. There is reason to doubt the veracity of these income statistics. Much more income appears to be hidden from census and tax officials in Mexico than in the United States or Canada because of the very large size of the unregulated informal economy.

4. For another estimation of the size of the Mexican capitalist class, see Alejandro Portes and Kelly Hoffman, "Latin American Class Structures: Their Composition and Change during the Neoliberal Era," *Latin American Research Review* 38,1 (February 2003). According to their methodology, "The capitalist class is operationally represented by owners of firms of more than five workers .... [But] if small entrepreneurs [those employing 5 to 20 workers] are excluded, these already low estimates would be cut by 50 per cent or more" (51). Their liberal estimate of owners with more than five workers is 0.9 per cent of the labor force (Table 3). Their more restrictive estimate of owners with more than 20 workers is less than half that, which is close to my estimate.

5. Stephanie N. Mehta, "Carlos Slim, The Richest Man in the World," *Fortune*, 6 August 2007.

6. INEGI, *Encuesta Nacional de Ingresos y Gastos de los Hogares 2004*, Table 2.5.

7. U.S. Census Bureau, Statistics of U.S. Businesses 2004, www.census.gov/csd/susb/usst04.xls. The statistic for Mexico is for principal sources of income of persons; for the United States, it is for businesses that have physical locations. There are many more small businesses in the U.S. without physical locations. Many of these, though, are secondary sources of income for their owners.

8. Cf., "The micro-business sector acts as a full-employment buffer, absorbing and retaining a large share of workers as GDP growth slows and accelerates." Carlos Salas, "Between Unemployment and Insecurity in Mexico: NAFTA Enters Its Second Decade," in *Revisiting NAFTA: Still Not Working for North America's Workers*, Economic Policy Institute Briefing Paper, (28 September 2006) 45.

9. See John C. Cross, *Informal Politics: Street Vendors and the State in Mexico City* (Stanford, CA: Stanford U P, 1998), 105.

10. Organization for Economic Cooperation and Development (OECD), *OECD in Figure, 2006-2007* (Paris: OECD, 2007).

11. OECD, *OECD in Figures, 2006-2007*.

12. INEGI, *Encuesta Nacional de Ingresos*, Table 2.5.

13. INEGI, *XII Censo*.

14. INEGI, *Encuesta Nacional de Ingresos*, Table 3.2.

15. U.S. Bureau of the Census, *Sixteenth Census of the United States: 1940*, vol. II, Characteristics of the Population (Washington, DC: U.S. Government Printing Office, 1940) 14, Table X.

16. Sarah Anderson, John Cavanaugh, Chuck Collins, and Eric Benjamin, *Executive Excess 2006: Defense and Oil Executives Cash in on Conflict*, 13th Annual CEO Survey of the Institute for Policy Studies and United for a Fair Economy, 2006, 30.

17. Anderson, et al.

18. Lipset, *Continental Divide* 207.

19. It is relevant in this context to consider Max Weber's (1905) distinction in *The Protestant Ethic and the Spirit of Capitalism* between booty and "sober bourgeois" capitalists. The former grab wealth through taking advantage of a series of one-time opportunities for spectacular profits. The latter produce wealth through slow but methodical circulations of production, profit, and reinvestment. Political corruption, like the slave trade, the contemporary drug trade, and the pillage of indigenous treasures after the Conquest, belongs in the category of booty capitalism.

20. Transparency International Corruption Index, 2006, http://www.transparency.org/.

21. Internal Revenue Service, "Individual Income Tax, All Returns: Sources of Income, Tax Year 2004," http://www.irs.gov/taxstats/.

22. The Canadian government does not publish an official estimate of the extent of absolute poverty in the country. The 7.2 figure is taken from United Nations Development Programme's estimate of absolute poverty in *Human Development Report 2006*, Table 4.

23. Luxembourg Income Study, cited in Children in North America Project, "Growing Up in North America: Child Well-Being in Canada, the United States, and Mexico," Luxembourg Income Study Working Paper No. 423 (January 2006) 24.

Chapter 9

1. The statistics on racial composition are approximations based on official sources. It is impossible to exactly measure the proportionate sizes of racial groupings for a variety of reasons. First, there are different cultural meanings of race in North America. For some, race is purely a biological category based on the assumption that the human species is made up of qualitatively different racial subspecies. For others, race is a matter purely of appearance, with skin color being the definer. A family could be made up of different races if it contained lighter and darker skinned members. For still others, race is determined by how people identify and present themselves. Indians are Indians if they present themselves as Indians; they are not if they present themselves according to Europeanized customs.

Race itself as a category is present only in the U.S. Census. The Canadian Census employs the category of ethnicity, while the only related category in the Mexican census is that of indigenous language, used to distinguish Indians. Race, ethnicity, and linguistic grouping, while overlapping to some extent, however, are not the same thing. Race as a concept indicates only that one has a physical attribute. There is no necessary implication of common cultural attributes, as implied by the concept of ethnicity. The concept of language assumes neither common physical nor cultural—beyond language itself—attributes.

The U.S. and Canadian Censuses rely on subjective self-identification for categorizing the different racial and ethnic groups, but it cannot be assumed that each person accurately identifies him or herself. The Mexican Census relies on the objective criteria of ability to speak an indigenous language to define persons as Indians. It cannot, though, be assumed that all persons who are able to speak an indigenous language identify themselves as indigenous, much less that all indigenous persons are still able to speak an indigenous language. If the same criterion were employed in the United States, the less than 1 per cent of persons who identify themselves as Indians or Native Americans would shrink even more to barely a trace.

The reality of hundreds of years of race mixture in North America complicates further attempts to exactly measure racial composition. In the end, race in North America as elsewhere is continuous, fluid, and everchanging.

2. Robert W. Gardner, Bryant Robey, and Peter C. Smith, "Asian Americans: Growth, Change, and Diversity," *The Population Bulletin* 40,4 (October 1985); U.S. Bureau of the Census, *Census of Population and Housing 1990*, Summary Tape Files 1C, CD-Rom (Washington, DC: U.S. Government Printing Office, 1992); and U.S. Bureau of the Census, Census 2000 Summary File 1, Table PCT7.

3. Bolaria and Li 133; and Statistics Canada, "Ethno-Cultural Portrait of Canada, 2001," *2001 Census,* http://www12.statcan.ca/.

4. Because Canada and India were both British Commonwealth nations, there was some immigration in the early decades of the twentieth century. The early immigrants took jobs mostly as manual laborers in farming, mining, and lumber. As such, they suffered serious racial discrimination, including being denied the right to vote until 1947 and being a target of the 1907 Vancouver anti-Asian riot.

5. Hispanics or Latinos have surpassed African-Americans as the largest minority per se.

However, the categories "Hispanic" and "Latino" are not racial categories since they contain individuals from different racial groupings within Latin America.

6. Schaefer, *Racial and Ethnic Groups* 226.

7. James Baldwin, "Down at the Cross-Letter from a Region in My Mind," *The Fire Next Time* (New York: Dial, 1963).

8. Frances Fox Piven and Richard A. Cloward, *Regulating the Poor* (New York: Vintage, 1971).

9. For exit poll data on black voters in presidential elections, see Marjorie Connelly, "Portrait of the Electorate," *New York Times*, 10 November 1996; and "How Americans Voted: A Political Portrait," *New York Times*, 7 November 2004.

10. Wilson, *The Declining Significance of Race.*

11. Reported in Luz María Valdés and María Teresa Menéndez, *Dinámica de la Población de Habla Indígena (1900-1980)* (Mexico City: Instituto Nacional de Antropología e Historia, 1987).

12. Mexico is not alone among Latin American countries in not using racial categories in its census. The Cuban government also does not use racial categories on the grounds that all citizens are Cubans regardless of color. The reality that there are racial differences in Mexico, however, is indicated by passport applicants being required to identify their skin color from the following list: *morena oscura* (dark), *morena clara* (light), or *blanca* (white). The first two options generally correspond with Indian and mestizo.

13. Carlos Monsivais argues that there is a clash between the official denial of racial problems and their latent reality: "In Mexico it is believed that the racial problem does not exist because ethnicity, it seems, is not a problem. This, while quantitatively true, is culturally and economically false. Mexico lives today in a boom of psychological Criolloism (moderately racial) that hawks its Anglo-Saxon models on television (the nation prominently blond), and from the very nature of the situation wants to convince those submitted of their natural inferiority. Up until now this Criolloism seems well on top." Carlos Monsivais, "La Raza: Fichas para un Diccionario," paper presented at the conference "Imagenes de la Frontera," Tijuana, Baja California, 4 May 1992, and reported by Arturo García Hernández in "Racismo Latente y Peligroso en México," *La Jornada* (Mexico City), 6 May 1992: 39.

14. Jorge A. Bustamante, "Imagenes Reales y Virtuales de la Frontera," paper presented at the conference "Imagenes de la Frontera," Tijuana, Baja California, 4 May.

15. "In the long process of the transition of racism in Mexican culture since the colonial period until now, there developed a certain disdain toward Mexican migrants in the United States, who the middle and upper classes saw as different than themselves, with whom they felt no identification in racial, ethnic, or social terms." Jorge A. Bustamante, *Migración Internacional y Derechos Humanos* (Mexico City: Editorial Universidad Nacional Autónoma de México, 2002) 73.

16. Cf., "The forms of discrimination are subtle. In large part they are based in the self-discrimination of the mestizos and Indians .... The main people who reinforce the ideas of separation and discrimination are the mestizos who deeply despise their own race." José Agustin Ortriz Pinqueti, "El Festin de los Criollos," *La Jornada*, 29 March 1992. For a sustained critique of the interpretation of Ramos, Paz, and others that an inferiority complex is a deep-seated part of the Mexican national character, see Roger Bartra, *La Jaula de la Melancolía.*

17. Ramos 58.

18. Bennett and Jaenen 201.

19. Calliste.

20. McWilliams, *Prejudice–Japanese Americans* 26.

21. See Max Weber, "Structures of Power," in Hans H. Gerth and C. Wright Mills, trans. and ed., *From Max Weber: Essays in Sociology* (New York: Oxford U P, 1958).

Chapter 10

1. C. Wright Mills, *The Power Elite* (New York: Oxford U P, 1956).

2. See Ralph Miliband, *The State in Capitalist Society* (New York: Basic Books, 1969) and G. William Domhoff, *Who Rules America?* (Englewood Cliffs, NJ: Prentice Hall, 1967) and *Who Rules America Now?* (Englewood Cliffs, NJ: Prentice Hall, 1983).

3. John Porter, *The Vertical Mosaic* (Toronto: U of Toronto P, 1965) 292.

4. Wallace Clement, *The Canadian Corporate Elite: An Analysis of Economic Power* (Toronto: McClelland and Stewart, 1975).

5. See Michael Ornstein, "Three Decades of Elite Research in Canada: John Porter's Unfulfilled Legacy," in Rick Helmes-Hayes and James Curtis, eds., *The Vertical Mosaic Revisited* (Toronto: U of Toronto P, 1998).

6. Paul M. Sweezy, "Power Elite or Ruling Class'" pamphlet (New York: Monthly Review Press, 1956).

7. Nicos Poulantzas, "The Problem of the Capitalist State," *New Left Review* (November-December, 1969).

8. For exit poll data on income and social classes in presidential elections, see Marjorie Connelly, "Portrait of the Electorate" and "How Americans Voted: A Political Portrait." For a specialized study of the relationship between specifically middle-class position and political ideology, see Carolyn Howe, *Political Ideology and Class Formation: A Study of the Middle Class* (Westport, CT: Praeger, 1992).

9. Blanche Petrich, "Entrevista/General José Francisco Gallardo," *La Jornada* (Mexico City), 30 July 2007: 5. See also, José Francisco Gallardo, "Ejército y sociedad en México, reforma de las fuerzas armadas," doctoral dissertation, Faculdad de Ciencias Políticas y Sociales, Universidad Nacional Autónoma de México, 2007.

10. On the other hand, run-off elections do exist for some state and local offices in the United States.

11. In Canada's 1997 federal general election "nearly two-thirds of the members of the House of Commons got less than a majority of the vote, about 15 per cent got less than two-fifths, and almost 2 per cent did not get even a third. Overall, most Canadians voted for someone other than their present MP." J.A.A. Lovink, "Run-off Elections is the Electoral Reform Canada Needs," *Policy Options* (April 1998): 45.

12. Tomás Oropeza Berumen, "Entrevista con Salvador Castañeda," *La Jornada Semanal* (Mexico City) 139, 9 February 1992.

13. Carlos Montemayor, *Guerra en el Paraiso* (Mexico City: Editorial Diana, 1991).

14. The Ejército Popular Revolucionario (EPR) first appeared in June 1996. It was formed by 14 organizations, some with links to Lucio Cabañas's 1960s guerrilla movement, after a peasant

massacre in Aguas Blancas, Guerrero the year before. In August of that year, it carried out 14 armed actions. In June 1998, the Mexican army attacked the EPR as it was holding a community meeting in Ayutla de los Libres, Guerrero. The army killed 11 guerrillas, wounded five, and took 21 prisoners. The EPR resurfaced in July 2007 when it sabotaged the PEMEX oil pipeline in the state of Guanajuato and attacked a jail under construction in the state of Chiapas. The EPR in communiqués said that the attacks were to demand the release of two of its members being held prisoner in Oaxaca. The Mexican government denied that it was holding the EPR members, giving rise to the possibility that it was resuming the practice of "disappearing" political opponents. See Angeles Mariscal, "Se adjudica EPR ataque a cárcel en Chiapa de Corzo," *La Jornada* (Mexico City), 30 July 2007: 3.

15. I have expanded on this point in *Double Standard: Social Policy in Europe and the United States* (Lanham, MD: Rowman and Littlefield, 2006).

16. OECD, *OECD in Figures, 2006-2007.*

17. OECD, Social Expenditure Database http://www.oecd.org.

18. Cf., "Social expenditure is defined as follows for the purposes of the SOCX database:

Social expenditure is the provision by public (and private) institutions of benefits to households and individuals in order to provide support during circumstances which adversely affect their welfare.

Such benefits can be cash transfers, or can be the direct ('in-kind') provisions of goods and services, provided that the provision of the benefits constitutes neither a direct payment for a particular good or service nor an individual contract or transfer.

Social protection usually covers income support or special assistance for elderly people, temporary or permanent departure from the labour market, illness or invalidity, difficult family circumstances, poor housing, or other poverty- or insecurity-related cases .... To conclude, social protection is the share of individual protection that society decides to shoulder collectively, through rules and institutions established for that purpose." OECD, "1980-1998: 20 Years of Social Expenditure," OECD Social Expenditure Database 9.

19. Teresa Munzi and Timothy Smeeding, "Conditions of Social Vulnerability, Work, and Low Income, Evidence for Spain in Comparative Perspective," Luxembourg Income Study Working Paper 448 (June 2006) Table 4.

20. For a discussion of the Canadian welfare state, see Julia S. O'Connor, "Social Justice, Social Citizenship, and the Welfare State, 1965-1995: Canada in Comparative Context," in Rick Helmes-Hayes and James Curtis, eds., *The Vertical Mosaic Revisited* (Toronto: U of Toronto P, 1998).

21. OECD, *OECD in Figures, 2006-2007.*

22. Roberto Gonzalez Amador, "En una generación los ancianos no tendrán protección social," *La Jornada* (Mexico City), 3 August 2007: 24.

23. Raul L. Madrid, "Ideas, Economic Pressures, and Pension Privatization," *Latin American Politics and Society* 47,2 (1 July 2005): 24 and 34.

24. Raúl L. Madrid, *Retiring the State: The Politics of Pension Privatization in Latin America and Beyond* (Stanford, CA: Stanford UP, 2003) 73.

BIBLIOGRAPHY

Adams, James Truslow. *The Founding of New England*. Boston, MA: Atlantic Monthly Press, 1921.

Aguirre Beltrán, Gonzalo. *Cuijla: Esbozo Ethnográfico de Un Pueblo Negro*. Mexico City: Fondo de Cultura Económica, 1958.

———. "The Integration of the Negro into the National Society of Mexico." In Magnus Morner, ed., *Race and Class in Latin America*. New York: Columbia U P, 1970.

———. *La Población Negra de México*. 1946; Mexico City: Fondo de Cultura Económica, 1981.

Allahar, Anton L., and James E. Côté. *Richer and Poorer: The Structure of Inequality in Canada*. Toronto: James Lorimer and Company, 1998.

Allen, James S. *Reconstruction: The Battle for Democracy*. New York: International Publishers, 1937.

Alvarez de Testa, Lilian. Mexico City. *Mexicanidad y Libro de Texto Gratuito*. Mexico City: Universidad Nacional Autónoma de México, 1992.

Anderson, Sarah, John Cavanaugh, Chuck Collins, and Eric Benjamin. *Executive Excess 2006: Defense and Oil Executives Cash in on Conflict*. Washington, DC: Institute for Policy Studies and United for a Fair Economy, 2006.

Archibold, Randal C. "At the Border the Desert Takes a Rising Toll." *New York Times* 15 September 2007.

Baldwin, James. *The Fire Next Time*. New York: Dial, 1963.

Barkin, David. "The Reconstruction of a Modern Mexican Peasantry." *The Journal of Peasant Studies* 20,1 (October 2002): 73-90.

Bartra, Roger, ed. *Anatomía del Mexicano*. Mexico City: Plaza y Janés México, 2002.

Bartra, Roger. "Tributo y Tenencia en la Tierra en la Sociedad Azteca." In Roger Bartra, ed., *El Modo de Producción Asiático*. Mexico City: Ediciones Era, 1969.

———. *Estructura Agraria y Clases Sociales en México*. Mexico City: Ediciones Era, 1974.

———. *La Jaula de la Melancolía*. Mexico City: Grijalbo, 1987.

Basave Benítez, Agustín. *México Mestizo: Análisis del Nacionalismo Mexicano en Torno a la Mestizofilía de Andrés Molina Enríquez*. Mexico City: Fondo de Cultura Económica, 1992.

Bean, Frank D., Jennifer Van Hook, and Karen Woodrow-Lafield. *Estimates of Numbers of Unauthorized Migrants Residing in the United States: The Total Mexican and Non-Mexican Central American Unauthorized Populations in Mid-2001.* Washington, DC: Pew Hispanic Center, Pew Charitable Trusts, 2002.

Bean, Frank D., and Marta Tienda. *The Hispanic Population of the United States.* New York: Russell Sage Foundation, 1987.

Bell, Spurgeon. "Productivity, Wages and National Income." In Richard Edwards, Michael Reich, and Thomas Weisskopf, eds., *The Capitalist System.* 2nd ed. Englewood Cliffs, NJ: Prentice Hall, 1977.

Bennett, Paul W., and Cornelius J. Jaenen. *Emerging Identities: Selected Problems and Interpretations in Canadian History.* Scarborough, ON: Prentice Hall Canada, 1986.

Blair, John. *Economic Concentration.* New York: Harcourt Brace Jovanovich, 1972.

Bloch, Marc. *Feudal Society.* Trans. L.A. Manyon. 1940; Chicago, IL: U of Chicago P, 1961.

———. "Feudalism, European." *Encyclopedia of the Social Sciences.* New York: Macmillan, 1933.

Bolaria, B. Singh, and Peter S. Li. *Racial Oppression in Canada.* 2nd ed. Toronto: Garamond Press, 1988.

Bonacich, Edna, and John Modell. *The Economic Basis of Ethnic Solidarity: Small Business in the Japanese American Community.* Berkeley, CA: U of California P, 1980.

Bonfil Batalla, Guillermo. *México Profundo.* Mexico City: Grijalbo, 1990.

Boyd, Robert. *The Coming of the Spirit of Pestilence: Introduced Infectious Diseases and Population Decline among Northwest Coast Indians, 1774-1874.* Seattle, WA: U of Washington P, 1999.

Bradsher, Keith. "U.S. Says Chretien Will Not Undo NAFTA." *New York Times* 27 October 1993.

Broder, John M. "Clinton Strategist Lobbied for Trade Pact She Opposes." *New York Times* 5 April 2008.

Brodie, Fawn M. *Thomas Jefferson: An Intimate History.* New York: Norton, 1974.

Brown, Dee. *Bury My Heart at Wounded Knee.* New York: Henry Holt and Company, 1970.

Brown, George, and Ron Maguire. "Indian Treaties in Historical Perspective." In James S. Frideres, ed., *Native People in Canada.* Scarborough, ON: Prentice-Hall Canada, 1983.

Bustamante, Jorge A. "Imagenes Reales y Virtuales de la Frontera." Paper presented at the conference "Imagenes de la Frontera," Tijuana, Baja California, 4 May 1992.

———. *Migración Internacional y Derechos Humanos.* Mexico City: Editorial Universidad Nacional Autónoma de México, 2002.

Calliste, Agnes. "Canada's Immigration Policy and Domestics from the Caribbean: The Second Domestic Scheme." In Jesse Vorst, ed., *Race, Class, Gender: Bonds and Barriers.* Toronto: Between the Lines, 1989.

Campbell, Randolph B. *An Empire for Slavery: The Peculiar Institution in Texas, 1821-1965.* Baton Rouge, LA: Louisiana State U P, 1989.

Centers, Richard. *The Psychology of Social Classes: A Study of Class Consciousness*. Princeton: Princeton U P, 1949.

Children in North America Project. "Growing up in North America: Child Well-Being in Canada, the United States, and Mexico." *Luxembourg Income Study* Working Paper No. 423 (January 2006).

Clement, Wallace. *The Canadian Corporate Elite: An Analysis of Economic Power*. Toronto: McClelland and Stewart, 1975.

Connelly, Marjorie. "Portrait of the Electorate." *New York Times* 10 November 1996.

———."How Americans Voted: A Political Portrait." *New York Times* 7 November 2004.

Consejo Nacional de Población (CONAPO). *Población y Desarrollo en México Y el Mundo*. Mexico City: CONAPO, 1988.

Cornelius, Wayne A. "The Politics and Economics of Reforming the Ejido Sector in Mexico." *LASA Forum* (Latin American Studies Association) 23,3 (1992): 3-10.

Crosby, Alfred M. *The Columbian Exchange: Biological and Cultural Consequences of 1492*. Westport, CT: Greenwood Press, 1972.

Cross, John C. *Informal Politics: Street Vendors and the State in Mexico City*. Stanford, CA: Stanford U P, 1998.

Cumberland, Charles C. "The Sonora Chinese and the Mexican Revolution." *Hispanic American Historical Review* 40 (May 1960): 191-223.

Davidson, David M. "El Control de los Esclavos Negros y su Resistencia en el México Colonial." In Richard Price, ed., *Sociedades Cimarronas*. Mexico City: Siglo Veintiuno Editores, 1981.

Davis, F. James. *Who Is Black? One Nation's Definition*. University Park, PA: Pennsylvania State U P, 1991.

de Ita, Ana. "Land Concentration in Mexico after Procede." In Peter M. Rosset, Raj Patel, and Michael Courville, eds., *Promised Land: Competing Visions of Agrarian Reform*. Oakland, CA: Food First, 2006.

DeNavas-Walt, Carmen, Bernadette D. Proctor, and Cheryl Hill Lee. "Income, Poverty, and Health Insurance Coverage in the United States: 2005." *Current Population Reports*, 2006.

Diamond, Jared. *Guns, Germs, and Steel: The Fates of Human Societies*. New York: W.W. Norton, 1999.

Domhoff, G. William. *Who Rules America?* Englewood Cliffs, NJ: Prentice Hall, 1967.

Domhoff, G. William. *Who Rules America Now?* Englewood Cliffs, NJ: Prentice Hall, 1983.

Du Bois, W.E.B. *Black Reconstruction in America*. 1935; New York: Russell and Russell, 1962.

Durkheim, Emile. *The Division of Labor in Society*. Trans. George Simpson. 1893; New York: Free Press, 1964.

El Paso, TX. Chamber of Commerce Twin Plant Publications, 1968-1980.

Ellis, George W., and John E. Morris. *King Philip's War*. New York: Grafton Press, 1906.

Engels, Friedrich. "Letter to Hermann Schláter (March 30, 1892)." *Karl Marx and Friedrich Engels, Letters to Americans.* New York: International Publishers, 1963.

———. "Letter to Sorge (September 12, 1888)." *Karl Marx and Friedrich Engels, Letters to Americans.* New York: International Publishers, 1963.

Erdmans, Mary Patrice. *The Grasinski Girls: The Choices They Had and the Choices They Made.* Athens: Ohio U P, 2005.

Farnsworth, Clyde H. "Voting in Canada Can Affect NAFTA." *New York Times* 24 October 1993.

Fast, Howard. *Freedom Road.* New York: Duell, Sloan and Pierce, 1944.

Faux, Jeff. *The Global Class War.* Hoboken, NJ: John Wiley and Sons, 2006.

Feldstein, Stanley, and Lawrence Costello. "Introduction." In Stanley Feldstein and Lawrence Costello, eds., *The Ordeal of Assimilation: A Documentary History of the White Working Class.* Garden City, NY: Anchor Press, 1974.

Financial Times. "Old Enemies Meet Again at the United Nations." 31 March 2003.

Foner, Eric. *Reconstruction: America's Unfinished Revolution, 1863-1877.* New York: Harper and Row, 1988.

Francis, R. Douglas, Richard Jones, and Donald B. Smith. *Origins: Canadian History to Confederation.* Toronto: Holt, Rinehart and Winston, 1988.

Franco, José L. "Rebeliones Cimarronas Y Esclavas En Los Territorios Españoles." In Richard Price, ed., *Sociedades Cimarronas.* Mexico City: Siglo Veintiuno Editores, 1981.

Gagné, Gilles, and Simon Langlois. *Les Raisons Fortes: Nature et Signification de L'appui a la Souveraineté du Québec.* Montreal: Les Presses de l'Université du Montréal, 2002.

Gallardo, José Francisco. *Ejército y sociedad en México, reforma de las fuerzas armadas.* Doctoral dissertation. Facultad de Ciencias Políticas y Sociales, Universidad Nacional Autónoma de México, 2007.

Gambril, Monica C. "The New Role of Maquiladoras in the Development of Mexico." Paper presented at the Annual Meeting of the American Sociological Association in Miami, FL, 20 August 1993.

García Hernández, Arturo "Racismo Latente Y Peligroso En México." *La Jornada* (Mexico City) 6 May 1992: 39.

Gardner, Robert W., Bryant Robey, and Peter C. Smith. "Asian Americans: Growth, Change, and Diversity." *The Population Bulletin* 40,4 (October 1985).

Gates, Henry Louis Jr. "Forty Acres and a Gap in Wealth." *New York Times* 18 November 2007.

Gibson, Campbell J., and Emily Lennon. "Historical Census Statistics on the Foreign-Born Population of the United States: 1850-1990." Population Division Working Papers No. 29. Washington, DC: U.S. Bureau of the Census, February 1999.

Gómez Izquierdo, José Jorge. "El Movimiento Anti-Chino En México, 1871-1934." Mexico City: Universidad Nacional Autónoma De México Facultad De Ciencias Políticas Y Sociales, 1988.

Gonzalez Amador, Roberto. "Én Una Generacion Los Ancianos No Tendrán Protección Social." *La Jornada* (Mexico City) 3 August 2007: 24.

González Navarro, Moises. *La Colonización en México, 1877-1910.* Mexico City: Talleres de Impresión de Estampillas y Valores 1960.

Greene, Graham. *The Power and the Glory.* New York: Viking, 1940.

Greer, Allan. *Peasant, Lord, and Merchant: Rural Society in Three Quebec Parishes 1740-1840.* Toronto: U of Toronto P, 1985.

Hall, Thomas D. *Social Change in the Southwest, 1350-1880.* Lawrence, KS: U P of Kansas, 1989.

Herrera Casasus, María Luisa. *Presencia y Esclavitud del Negro en la Huasteca.* Mexico City: Porrúa, 1989.

Hook, Jennifer Van, and Frank D. Bean. "Estimating Unauthorized Mexican Migration to the United States: Issues and Results." *The Binational Study of Migration between Mexico and the United States.* Vol. 2. Washington, DC: U.S. Commission on Immigration Reform, 1997.

Howe, Carolyn. *Political Ideology and Class Formation: A Study of the Middle Class.* Westport, CT: Praeger, 1992.

Hu-DeHart, Evelyn. "Immigrants to a Developing Society: The Chinese in Northern Mexico, 1875-1932." *Journal of Arizona History* (Autumn 1980): 275-313.

Huerta Preciado, María Teresa. *Rebeliones Indígenas en el Noreste de México en la Epoca Colonial.* Mexico City: Instituto Nacional de Antropología e Historia, 1966.

Hum, Derek, and Wayne Simpson. "Revisiting Equity and Labour: Immigration, Gender, Minority Status, and Income Differentials in Canada." in Sean P. Hier and B. Singh Bolaria, eds., *Race and Racism in 21st-Century Canada: Continuity, Complexity, and Change.* Peterborough, ON: Broadview Press, 2007.

Instituto Nacional de Estadística Geografía e Informática (INEGI). *Encuesta Nacional de Ingresos y Gastos de los Hogares.* 2002.

———. *Encuesta Nacional de Ingresos y Gastos de los Hogares 2004.* Aguascalientes: INEGI, 2005.

———. *II Conteo de Población y Vivienda 2005.*

———. *La Diversidad Religiosa en México.* 2003.

———. *Estadística de la Industria Maquiladora de Exportación, 1978-1988.* Aguascalientes: INEGI, 1989.

———. *Estadística de la Industria Maquiladora de Exportación, 1991.* Aguascalientes: INEGI, 1992.

———. *Estadística de la Industria Maquiladora de Exportación, Febrero 2007.* Aguascalientes: INEGI, 23 February 2007.

———. *Los Extranjeros en México, 2007,* http://www.inegei.gob.mx.

———. *La Población Indígena en México.* Aguascalientes: INEGI, 2004.

———. *VII Censo Ejital 1991.* Aguascalientes: INEGI, 1994.

———. *VIII Censo Ejital 2001.* Aguascalientes: INEGI, 2003.

———. *XI Censo General de Población y Vivienda 1990*. Aguascalientes: INEGI, 1992.

———. *XII Censo General de Población y Vivienda, 2000*. Aguascalientes: INEGI, 2000.

———. *XII Censo General de Población y Vivienda 2000*. "Lengua Indígena, 2000," http://www.ingegi.gob.mx.

Instituto Nacional Indigena. *Estimación de la población indígena y vivienda*, 2000 INEGI, http://www.cdi.gob.mx/ini/.

Internal Revenue Service. "Individual Income Tax, All Returns: Sources of Income, Tax Year 2004." Internal Revenue Service, 2004, http://www.irs.gov/taxstats/.

Jackson, Jack, ed. *Texas by Terán: The Diary Kept by General Manuel De Mier Y Terán of His 1828 Inspection of Texas*. Austin, TX: U of Texas P, 2000.

Jaffee, A.J., Ruth M. Cullen, and Thomas D. Boswell, *The Changing Demography of Spanish Americans*. New York: Academic Press, 1980.

Johansen, Bruce, and Roberto Maestas. *Wasi'chu: The Continuing Indian Wars*. New York: Monthly Review Press, 1979.

Klein, Herbert S. *African Slavery in Latin America and the Caribbean*. New York: Oxford U P, 1986.

Kroll, Lisa, and Allison Fass. "The World's Billionaires." *Forbes* 8 March 2007.

Lagassé, Jean H. *The People of Indian Ancestry in Manitoba*. Winnipeg, MB: Department of Agriculture and Immigration, 1959.

Langlois, Simon. "Canada and Québec: An Update." *Footnotes*. American Sociological Association. March 2006.

Leo, Michael. "Despite NAFTA Attacks, Clinton and Obama Haven't Been Free Trade Foes." *New York Times* 28 February 2008.

———. "Memo Gives Canada's Account of Obama Campaign's Meeting on NAFTA." *New York Times* 4 March 2008.

Lewis, Charles, and Margaret Ebrahim. "Big $$$ Lobbying in Washington: Can Mexico and Big Business USA Buy Nafta?" *The Nation* 14 June 1993.

Lipset, Seymour Martin. *Continental Divide: The Values and Institutions of the United States and Canada*. London: Routledge, 1990.

Loeb, Marshall. "Salinas Speaks Out on Free Trade." *Fortune*, 28 December 1992.

Lovink, J.A.A. "Run-Off Elections Is the Electoral Reform Canada Needs." *Policy Options* (April 1998): 45-47.

MacArthur, John R. *The Selling of "Free Trade."* Berkeley, CA: U of California P, 2001.

Madrid, Raúl L.*Retiring the State: The Politics of Pension Privatization in Latin America and Beyond*. Stanford, CA: Stanford U P, 2003.

———. "Ideas, Economic Pressures, and Pension Privatization." *Latin American Politics and Society* 47,2 (1 July 2005): 23-50.

Mann, Charles C. *1491: New Revelations of the Americas before Columbus*. New York: Vintage, 2006.

Manzer, Ronald. *Public Policies and Political Development in Canada*. Toronto: U of Toronto P, 1985.

Mariscal, Angeles. "Se adjudica EPR ataque a cárcel en Chiapa de Corzo." *La Jornada* (Mexico City), 30 July 2007.

Marx, Karl. *Capital, Vol. 1.* 1867; Moscow: Progress Publishers, n.d.

Mass, Bonnie. *Population Target: The Political Economy of Population Control in Latin America.* Brampton, ON: Charters, 1976.

Mayer, Frederick W. *Interpreting NAFTA: The Science and Art of Political Analysis.* New York: Columbia U P, 1998.

McWilliams, Carey. *Prejudice—Japanese Americans: Symbol of Racial Intolerance.* Boston, MA: Little, Brown, 1944.

——. *Brothers under the Skin.* Boston. MA: Little, Brown, 1964.

——. *North from Mexico.* 1949; Westport, CT: Greenwood Press, 1968.

——. *Factories in the Field.* 1935; Santa Barbara, CA: Peregrine Smith, 1971.

Mehta, Stephanie N. "Carlos Slim, the Richest Man in the World." *Fortune* 6 August 2007.

Melendy, H. Brett. *Asians in America: Filipinos, Koreans, and East Indians.* Boston, MA: Twayne, 1977.

Mellafe, Rolando. *Negro Slavery in Latin America.* Berkeley, CA: U of California P, 1975.

Mencke, John G. *Mulattoes and Race Mixture.* Ann Arbor, MI: UMI Research Press, 1979.

Meyer, Michael, and William L. Sherman. *The Course of Mexican History.* New York: Oxford U P, 1979.

Michel, Richard. "An Overview Report on the in-Bond Program: Border Plants and Interior Plants." University of Texas at El Paso: Institute of Oral History Recording 371, 26 April 1978.

Miles, Robert. *Racism.* London: Routledge, 1989.

Miliband, Ralph. *The State in Capitalist Society.* New York: Basic Books, 1969.

Miller, Robert Ryal. *Shamrock and Sword: The Saint Patrick's Battalion in the U.S.-Mexican War.* Norman, OK: U of Oklahoma P, 1989.

Mills, C. Wright. *The Power Elite.* New York: Oxford U P, 1956.

Mills, C. Wright, Clarence Senior, and Rose Kohn Goldsen. *The Puerto Rican Journey.* New York: Harper and Brothers, 1950.

Monsivais, Carlos. "La Raza: Fichas Para Un Diccionario." Paper presented at the conference "Imagenes de la Frontera," Tijuana, Baja California, 4 May 1992

Montemayor, Carlos. *Guerra En El Paraiso.* Mexico City: Editorial Diana, 1991.

——. *Las Armas Del Alba.* Mexico City: Joaquin Mortiz, 2003.

Mörner, Magnus. *El Mestizaje en la Historia e Ibero-América.* Mexico City: Instituto Panamericano de Geografía e Historia, 1961.

——. *Race Mixture in the History of Latin America.* Boston, MA: Little, Brown, 1967.

Munzi, Teresa, and Timothy Smeeding. "Conditions of Social Vulnerability, Work and Low Income, Evidence for Spain in Comparative Perspective." Luxembourg Income Study Working Paper 448 (June 2006).

National Center for Health Statistics. *Health, United States, 2002.* Hyattsville, MD: Public Health Service, 2002.

Navarro, Moises González. *La Colonización en México, 1877-1910*. Mexico City: Talleres de Impresión y Estampillas y Valores, 1960.

———. "Mestizaje in Mexico during the National Period." In Magnus Mörner, ed., *Race and Class in Latin America*. New York: Columbia U P, 1970.

Nee, Victor G., and Bret de Barry Nee. *Longtime Californ': A Documentary Study of an American Chinatown*. New York: Pantheon Books, 1973.

O'Connor, James. *The Fiscal Crisis of the State*. New York: St. Martin's Press, 1973.

O'Connor, Julia S. "Social Justice, Social Citizenship, and the Welfare State, 1965-1995: Canada in Comparative Context." In Rick Helmes-Hayes and James Curtis, eds., *The Vertical Mosaic Revisited*. Toronto: U of Toronto P, 1998.

Officer, James E. *Hispanic Arizona, 1536-1856*. Tucson, AZ: U of Arizona P, 1987.

Organization for Economic Cooperation and Development (OECD). "1980-1998: 20 Years of Social Expenditure — the OECD Data Base." 2007, http://www.oecd.org/dataoecd/3/63/2084281.pdf.

———. *OECD in Figures, 2006-2007*. Paris: OECD, 2007.

———. "Social Expenditure Database." 2007, http://www.oecd.org.

———. *OECD Stat Extracts*, http://stats.oecd.org/WBOS/default.aspx?DatasetCode=CSP-2007.

Ornstein, Michael. "Three Decades of Elite Research in Canada: John Porter's Unfulfilled Legacy." In Rick Helmes-Hayes and James Curtis, eds., *The Vertical Mosaic Revisited*. Toronto: U of Toronto P, 1998.

Oropeza Berumen, Tomás. "Entrevista con Salvador Castañeda." *La Jornada Semanal* (Mexico City) 9 February 1992.

Ortriz Pinqueti, José Agustín. "El Festin De Los Criollos." *La Jornada* (Mexico City) 29 March 1992.

Ota Mishima, María Elena. *Siete Migraciones Japonesas en México, 1890-1978*. Mexico City: El Colegio de México, 1982.

Othon de Mendizábal, Miguel et al., eds. *Ensayos sobre las Clases Sociales en México*. Mexico City: Editorial Nuestro Tiempo, 1968.

Padilla, Felix M. *Puerto Rican Chicago*. Notre Dame, IN: U of Notre Dame P, 1987.

Palerm Vich, Angel. "Factores Históricos de la Clase Media en México." In Miguel Othon de Mendizábal et al., eds., *Ensayos sobre las Clases Sociales en México*. Mexico City: Editorial Nuestro Tiempo, 1968.

Palmer, Howard. "Reluctant Hosts: Anglo-Canadian Views of Multiculturalism in the Twentieth Century." In R. Douglas Francis and Donald B. Smith, eds., *Readings in Canadian History: Post-Confederation*. 2nd ed. Toronto: Holt, Rinehart and Winston, 1986.

Passel, Jeffrey S. *Estimates of the Size and Characteristics of the Undocumented Population: PEW Hispanic Center Report*, 21 March 2005.

Paz, Octavio. *El Laberinto de la Soledad*. Mexico City: Fondo de Cultura Popular, 1950.

———. *The Labyrinth of Solitude*. Trans. Lysander Kemp. New York: Grove Press, 1961.

Petrich, Blanche. "Entrevista/General José Francisco Gallardo." *La Jornada* (Mexico City), 30 July 2007.

Pettigrew, Thomas F. *Racial Discrimination in the United States*. New York: Harper and Row, 1975.

Piven, Frances Fox, and Richard A. Cloward. *Regulating the Poor*. New York: Vintage, 1971.

Porter, John. *The Vertical Mosaic*. Toronto: U of Toronto P, 1965.

Portes, Alejandro, and Kelly Hoffman. "Latin American Class Structures: Their Composition and Change During the Neoliberal Era." *Latin American Research Review* 38,1 (February 2003): 41-82.

Poulantzas, Nicos. "The Problem of the Capitalist State." *New Left Review* (November-December 1969).

Price, Richard, ed., *Sociedades Cimarronas*. Mexico City: Siglo Veintiuno Editores, 1981.

Prucha, Frances Paul. *The Great Father: The United States Government and the American Indians*. Lincoln, NB: U of Nebraska P, 1984.

Ramos, Samuel. *El Perfil del Hombre y Y la Cultura en México*. 1934; Mexico City: Colección Austral 1990.

Reina, Leticia. *Las Rebeliones Campesinas en México, 1819-1906*. Mexico City: Siglo Veintinuno Editores, 1980.

Ruiz, Ramon Eduardo. *The People of Sonora and Yankee Capitalists*. Tucson, AZ: U of Arizona P, 1988.

Russell, James W. *Modes of Production in World History*. London: Routledge, 1989.

———. *Double Standard: Social Policy in Europe and the United States*. Lanham, MD: Rowman and Littlefield, 2006.

———. *Societies and Social Life: An Introduction to Sociology*. 3rd ed. Cornwall-on-Hudson, NY: Sloan Publishing, 2006.

Salas, Carlos. "Between Unemployment and Insecurity in Mexico: NAFTA Enters Its Second Decade." *Revisiting NAFTA: Still Not Working for North America's Workers*. Economic Policy Institute Briefing Paper, 28 September 2006.

Schaefer, Richard T. *Racial and Ethnic Groups*. 4th ed. Glenview, IL: Scott, Foresman, 1990.

Schmidley, Dianne. *Profile of the Foreign-Born Population in the United States: 2000*. Washington, DC: U.S. Bureau of the Census Current Population Reports, 2001.

Schwartz, Rosalie. *Across the Rio to Freedom: U.S. Negroes in Mexico*. Southwestern Studies Monograph 44. El Paso, TX: Texas Western Press, 1975.

Shin, Hyon B., and Rosalind Bruno. "Language Use and English-Speaking Ability: 2000 (Census 2000 Brief)." Washington, DC: U.S. Bureau of the Census, October 2003.

Statistics Canada. "Aboriginal Peoples of Canada," 2001 Census, http://www.statcan.ca/.

———. *Corporation Returns Act 2005*. Ottawa: Minister of Industry, 2007.

———. "Ethno-Cultural Portrait of Canada, 2001." *2001 Census*, http://www12.statcan.ca/.

————. "Paid Work, Occupation." *2001 Census*, http://www.statcan.ca.

————. *A Portrait of Children in Canada*. Ottawa: Minister of Industry, Science and Technology, 1990.

————. "Language Composition of Canada: Highlight Tables." *2001 Census*, http://www.statcan.ca/.

————. *Mother Tongue, 2001 Counts*. *2001 Census*, http://www.statcan.ca/.

————. "Income of Individuals, Families, and Households," *2001 Census*, http://www.statcan.ca/.

St-Onge, Nicole. "Race, Class and Marginality in a Manitoba Interlake Settlement, 1850-1950." In Jesse Vorst, ed., *Race, Class, Gender: Bonds and Barriers*. Ed. Toronto: Between the Lines, 1989.

Sullivan, Edward J. "Un Fenómeno Visual de América." *Artes de México* 1990.

Sweezy, Paul M. "Power Elite or Ruling Class?" Pamphlet. New York: Monthly Review Press, 1956.

Székely, Miguel. *Pobreza y Desigualdad en México entre 1950 y el 2004*. Mexico City: Secretaria de Desarrollo Social, 2005.

Taylor, Lawrence Douglas. *El Nuevo Norteamericano: Integración Continental, Cultura e Identidad Nacional*. Mexico City: Universidad Nacional Autónoma de México, 2001.

Teeple, Gary, ed. *Capitalism and the National Question in Canada*. Toronto: U of Toronto P, 1972.

Therrien, Melissa, and Roberto R. Ramiriz. *The Hispanic Population of the United States*. Washington, DC: U.S. Bureau of the Census Current Population Reports P2-535, 2001.

Thomas, W.I., and Florian Znaniecki. *The Polish Peasant in Europe and America*. 1918-20; New York: Dover, 1958.

Thompson, Ginger. "Ex-President in Mexico Casts New Light on Rigged 1988 Election." *New York Times* 9 March 2004.

Torres, Blanca. *Historia de la Revolución Mexicana, 1940-1952*. Mexico City: El Colegio de México, 1979.

Transparency International. "Transparency International Corruption Index," 2006, http://www.transparency.org/.

Trumper, Ricardo, and Lloyd L. Wong. "Canada's Guest Workers: Racialized, Gendered, and Flexible." In Sean P. Hier and B. Singh Bolaria, eds., *Race and Racism in 21st-Century Canada: Continuity, Complexity, and Change*. Peterborough, ON: Broadview Press, 2007.

Tulloch, Headley. *Black Canadians*. Toronto: N.C. Press, 1975.

Ujimoto, K. Victor "Racism, Discrimination and Internment: Japanese in Canada. "Racism, Discrimination and Internment: Japanese in Canada." In B. Singh Bolaria and Peter S. Li., eds., *Racial Oppression in Canada*. 2nd ed. Toronto: Garamond Press, 1988.

United Nations Development Program (UNDP). *Human Development Report 2006*. New York: Palgrave Macmillan, 2006.

————. Population Division. *The World at Six Billion*. New York: United Nations, 1999.

————. Statistical Office, *Demographic Yearbook 2004.* New York: United Nations, 2004.

United States Bureau of the Census, *Census of Population: 1950.* Vol. II, Part 54: *Characteristics of the Population.* Washington, DC: U.S. Government Printing Office, 1953.

————. *2005 American Community Survey.* Washington, DC: U.S. Government Printing Office, 2005.

————. *Census 2000.* Summary File 3 (P157). Washington, DC: U.S. Government Printing Office, 2003.

————. *Census 2000.* Summary. "Social, Economic, and Housing Characteristics, Phc-2-1." Washington, DC: U.S. Government Printing Office, 2003.

————. *Census 2000.* Washington DC: U.S. Government Printing Office, 2001.

————. *Census 2000.* Summary File 1, www.factfinder.census.gov.

————. *Census of Population and Housing 1990, Summary Tape Files 1c.* CD-Rom. Washington, DC: U.S. Government Printing Office, 1992.

————. *Census of Population.* 1950, 1960, 1970, 1980, 1990, 2000. Washington, DC: U.S. Government Printing Office.

————. *Census of the United States: 1940.* Vol. II: *Characteristics of the Population.* Washington, DC: U.S. Government Printing Office, 1940.

————. *Historical Statistics of the United States.* Vol. 1. Washington, DC: U.S. Government Printing Office, 1976.

————. *Migration between the United States and Canada* Washington, DC: U.S. Government Printing Office, 1990.

————. *Negro Population of the United States, 1790-1915.* Washington, DC: U.S. Government Printing Office, 1918.

————. *Sixteenth Census of the United States: 1940.* Vol. II: *Characteristics of the Population.* Washington, DC: U.S. Government Printing Office, 1942.

————. *Statistical Abstract of the United States.* Washington, DC: U.S. Government Printing Office, 1989.

————. *Statistical Abstract of the United States.* Washington, DC: U.S. Government Printing Office, 2002.

————. *Statistical Abstract of the United States 2007.* Washington, DC: U.S. Government Printing Office, 2006.

————. *Statistical Abstract of the United States 2006.* Washington, DC: U.S. Government Printing Office, 2005.

————. *Statistics of U.S. Businesses 2004.*, http://www.census.gov/csd/susb/usst04.xls.

United States Department of Agriculture, Foreign Agricultural Service. "Trade and 2001 Agriculture: What's at Stake for Wisconsin?" (October 2001), http://www.fas.usda.gov/info/factsheets/TPA/wi.pdf.

United States Government Accountability Office. *Illegal Immigration: Border-Crossing Deaths Have Doubled since 1995.* Report 06-770. Washington, DC: U.S. Government Accountability Office, August 2006.

Valdés, Luz María, and María Teresa Menéndez. *Dinámica del La Población de Habla Indígena (1900-1980)*. Mexico City: Instituto Nacional de Antropología e Historia, 1987.

Valdés-Ugalde, José Luis. *Análisis de los Efectos del Tratado de Libre Comercio de América del Norte en la Economía Mexicana: Una Visión Sectorial a Cinco Años de Distancia*. Mexico City: Edición del Senado de la República, LVII Legislatura, 2000.

Vasconcelos, José. *La Raza Cósmica*. 1925; Mexico City: Espasa-Calpe Mexicana, Colección Austra edition, 1993.

Veltmeyer, Henry. "Late Capitalism, Corporate Power, and Imperialism." In J. Paul Grayson, ed., *Introduction to Sociology: An Alternate Approach*. Toronto: Gage, 1983.

Walker, James W. *A History of Blacks in Canada*. Ottawa: Minister of State and Multiculturalism, 1980.

Warner, W. Lloyd, Marcia Meeker, and Kenneth Eeks. *Social Class in America*. Chicago, IL: Research Associates, 1949.

Watkins, Mel. "The Political Economy of Growth." In Wallace Clement and Glen Williams, eds., *The New Canadian Political Economy*. Montreal: McGill-Queen's U P, 1989.

———. "A Staple Theory of Economic Growth." In Hugh Grant and David Wolfe, eds., *Staples and Beyond: Selected Writings of Mel Watkins*. Montreal: McGill-Queens U P, 2006.

Weber, David J. *Myth and the History of the Hispanic Southwest*. Albuquerque, NM: U of New Mexico P, 1988.

Weber, Max. *The Protestant Ethic and the Spirit of Capitalism*. 1905; New York: Scribner's, 1948.

———. "Structures of Power." In Hans H. Gerth and C. Wright Mills, eds. and trans., *From Max Weber: Essays in Sociology*. New York: Oxford U P, 1958.

———. *General Economic History*. Trans. Frank H. Knight. 1923; New York: Collier Books, 1961.

Wilkie, James W., ed., *Statistical Abstract of Latin America*. Los Angeles, CA: UCLA Latin American Center Publications, 1992.

Williamson, Joel. *New People: Miscegenation and Mulattoes in the United States*. New York: Free Press, 1980.

Wilson, William Julius. *The Declining Significance of Race: Blacks and Changing American Institutions*. Chicago, IL: U of Chicago P, 1980.

Winks, Robin W. *The Blacks in Canada*. New Haven, CT: Yale U P, 1971.

World Bank. *World Development Report 1990*. New York: Oxford U P, 1990.

———. *World Development Report 2007*. Washington, DC: World Bank, 2006.

———. *2007 World Development Indicators*. Washington, DC: World Bank, 2007.

INDEX